3/26/99

EU ENLARGEMENT AND ITS MACROECONOMIC EFFECTS IN EASTERN EUROPE

STUDIES IN ECONOMIC TRANSITION

General Editors: Jens Hölscher, Commerzbank Professor for Money and Finance, University of Chemnitz, and Honorary Professor, Institute for German Studies, University of Birmingham; and Horst Tomann, Professor of Economics, Free University Berlin

This new series has been established in response to a growing demand for a greater understanding of the transformation of economic systems. It brings together theoretical and empirical studies on economic transition and economic development. The post-communist transition from planned to market economies is one of the main areas of applied theory because in this field the most dramatic examples of change and economic dynamics can be found. The series aims to contribute to the understanding of specific major economic changes as well as to advance the theory of economic development. The implications of economic policy will be a major point of focus.

Titles include:

Irwin Collier, Herwig Roggemann, Oliver Scholz and Horst Tomann (*editors*)
WELFARE STATES IN TRANSITION: East and West

Hubert Gabrisch and Rüdiger Pohl (*editors*)
EU ENLARGEMENT AND ITS MACROECONOMIC EFFECTS IN EASTERN EUROPE: Currencies, Prices, Investment and Competitiveness

Jens Hölscher and Anja Hochberg (*editors*)
EAST GERMANY'S ECONOMIC DEVELOPMENT SINCE UNIFICATION
Domestic and Global Aspects

Emil Kirchner (*editor*)
DECENTRALIZATION AND TRANSITION IN THE VISEGRAD
Poland, Hungary, the Czech Republic and Slovakia

Johannes Stephan
ECONOMIC TRANSITION IN HUNGARY AND EAST GERMANY
Gradualism and Shock Therapy in Catch-up Development

Studies in Economic Transition
Series Standing Order ISBN 0–333–73353–3
(*outside North America only*)

You can receive future titles in this series as they are published by placing a standing order. Please contact your bookseller or, in case of difficulty, write to us at the address below with your name and address, the title of the series and the ISBN quoted above.

Customer Services Department, Macmillan Distribution Ltd
Houndmills, Basingstoke, Hampshire RG21 6XS, England

EU Enlargement and its Macroeconomic Effects in Eastern Europe

Currencies, Prices, Investment and Competitiveness

Edited by

Hubert Gabrisch
Head of Division
Institute for Economic Research, Halle
Germany

and

Rüdiger Pohl
President
Institute for Economic Research, Halle
Germany

First published in Great Britain 1999 by
MACMILLAN PRESS LTD
Houndmills, Basingstoke, Hampshire RG21 6XS and London
Companies and representatives throughout the world

A catalogue record for this book is available from the British Library.

ISBN 0–333–73549–8

 First published in the United States of America 1999 by
ST. MARTIN'S PRESS, INC.,
Scholarly and Reference Division,
175 Fifth Avenue, New York, N.Y. 10010

ISBN 0–312–22040–5

Library of Congress Cataloging-in-Publication Data
EU enlargement and its macroeconomic effects in Eastern Europe :
currencies, prices, investment and competitiveness / edited by
Hubert Gabrisch, Rüdiger Pohl.
p. cm. — (Studies in economic transition)
Includes bibliographical references and index.
ISBN 0–312–22040–5 (cloth)
1. European Union—Europe, Eastern. 2. Europe, Eastern—Foreign
economic relations—European Union countries. 3. European Union
countries—Foreign economic relations—Europe, Eastern. 4. Europe-
-Economic integration. I. Gabrisch, Hubert. II. Pohl, Rüdiger.
III. Series.
HC240.25.E852E9 1998
337.4047—dc21 98–37121
CIP

Selection and editorial matter © Hubert Gabrisch and Rüdiger Pohl 1999
Chapter 1 © Hubert Gabrisch 1999
Chapters 2–8 © Macmillan Press Ltd 1999

All rights reserved. No reproduction, copy or transmission of this publication may be made without written permission.

No paragraph of this publication may be reproduced, copied or transmitted save with written permission or in accordance with the provisions of the Copyright, Designs and Patents Act 1988, or under the terms of any licence permitting limited copying issued by the Copyright Licensing Agency, 90 Tottenham Court Road, London W1P 9HE.

Any person who does any unauthorised act in relation to this publication may be liable to criminal prosecution and civil claims for damages.

The authors have asserted their rights to be identified as the authors of this work in accordance with the Copyright, Designs and Patents Act 1988.

This book is printed on paper suitable for recycling and made from fully managed and sustained forest sources.

10 9 8 7 6 5 4 3 2 1
08 07 06 05 04 03 02 01 00 99

Printed and bound in Great Britain by
Antony Rowe Ltd, Chippenham, Wiltshire

Contents

List of Tables	vii
List of Figures	ix
Acknowledgements	xi
Notes on the Contributors	xii
Preface	xv
List of Abbreviations	xvi
Introduction	xviii

I PRICE CONVERGENCE, DEMAND AND GROWTH

1 Effects of Accession to the EU on Prices, Wages and Aggregate Demand in CEE Countries
   Hubert Gabrisch — 3

2 Macroeconomic Problems of Trade Liberalisation and EU Eastern Enlargement
   Kazimierz Laski — 26

3 Non-tradable Goods and Deviations Between Purchasing Power Parities and Exchange Rates: Evidence from the 1990 European Comparison Project
   Leon Podkaminer — 62

II EXCHANGE RATE SYSTEMS, CAPITAL AND TRANSFER INFLOWS

4 Real Exchange Rates and Growth/After EU Accession: The Problems of Transfer and Capital Inflow Absorption
   Witold M. Orlowski — 97

5 Capital Inflows and Convertibility in the Transforming Economies of Central Europe
   Lucjan T. Orlowski — 116

vi   *Contents*

6   Exchange Rate Policy, Fiscal Austerity and Integration Prospects: The Hungarian Case
Jens Hölscher and Johannes Stephan   151

III SECTORAL ADJUSTMENT ISSUES   175

7   Adjusting the Common Agricultural Policy for an EU Eastern Enlargement: Alternatives and Impacts on the Central European Associates
Klaus Frohberg and Monika Hartmann   177

8   Changes in Production Structures after Accession: Experiences from the Southern Enlargement of the EU and Prospects for Eastern Enlargement
Claudia Löhnig   198

Name Index   223

Subject Index   225

List of Tables

1.1	Comparative price level indices of final demand (purchasing power parity/exchange rate in 1993	18
1.2	Wage unit costs in four CEE countries	23
2.1	PPP, *Ne* and price levels in selected Western European countries, 1960–90	43
2.2	European exchange rates *vis-à-vis* the German mark and PPPs for tradables in 1990	44
2.3	Price levels for Greece, Portugal and Spain between 1980 and 1993	45
2.4	Real exchange rates in NCU per DEM (PPI deflated)	47
2.5	Real wages (CPI-deflated) and USD money wages in CEECs	49
2.6	Price levels in CEECs, 1990–95	50
2.7	Price levels in CEECs, 1990 and 1993	50
3.1	Exchange rates, PPPs and ERDIs in Europe, 1990	66
3.2	The effects of Austro-Hungarian free trade	70
3.3	Trade effects	80
3.4	Post-trade ERDIs	82
4.1	Changes in import structure of MC-3 after EU accession	107
4.2	Efficiency of growth after joining the EU	112
5.1	Selected economic indicators and capital flows	137
5.2	Growth of broad money and inflation rates	141
6.1	Hungary's foreign position	154
6.2	Hungary's state budget	155
6.3	Changes in the structure of Hungary's domestic demand	156
6.4	Development of consumption and investment	157
6.5	Forint exchange rate devaluations and average market exchange rate changes against the pegged currency basket	160
6.6	Development of central government expenditures	165
6.7	The Maastricht convergence criteria: Hungary in comparison with EU economies	169
7.1	Allocation of commitment appropriations, 1992 and 1999	181
7.2	Agricultural protection in the EU and selected CEAs in 1994	191
8.1	Gross value added by kind of activity	205

8.2	Output of the biggest three and five industries in relation to output of total manufacturing	207
8.3	Output shares of the biggest five industries in total manufacturing (ranking position in brackets)	208
8.4	Correlation coefficients of output shares for Greece, Portugal and Spain, 1975, 1986 and 1993 (ISIC 3-digit)	209
8.5	Specialisation patterns in manufacturing	211
8.6	Output shares of 'sensible' products	214
8.7	Gross value-added by kind of activity, 1993	214
8.8	Coefficients correlation of output shares 1993 (ISIC 3-digit)	215
8.9	Output shares of the biggest three industries in total manufacturing, 1993 (ISIC 3-digit)	216

List of Figures

1.1	The Spanish development	12
1.2	The Portuguese development	13
1.3	The Greek development	14
1.4	Balance of trade of Greece, Portugal and Spain with the EU	14
1.5	The Austrian development	16
1.6	Gross domestic product per inhabitant in US dollars, according to 1995 purchasing power parities	17
2.1	Import surplus and GDP	31
2.2	Two strategies of easing difficulties in foreign trade	34
2.3	ERDIs in CEECs (stylised facts)	46
2.4	Export surplus increase at falling real wage rate	53
2.5	Export surplus at given real wage rate	55
4.1	Cumulated GDP growth differentials against Germany after the accession of the MC-3 countries	99
4.2	Official transfers received before and after accession of the MC-3 countries	101
4.3	Capital inflows and the current account for MC-3 countries before and after accession	102
4.4	Increased inflows of transfers and private investment to the MC-3 countries before and after accession	103
4.5	Real exchange rate development for MC-3 countries before and after accession	104
4.6	Yields on I-bonds for Greece before and after accession	105
4.7	Changes in MC-3 current accounts before and after accession	106
4.8	The ratio of investment to GDP for MC-3 countries before and after accession	108
4.9	The ratio of domestic savings to GDP for MC-3 countries before and after accession	109
4.10	Fiscal deficits of MC-3 countries before and after accession	110
4.11	Real interest rates of MC-3 countries before and after accession	111
5.1	The import of capital inflows a domestic money balances, interest rates and exchange rates	123

List of Figures

6.1	Hungarian inflation	158
6.2	Development of earnings	159
6.3	Development of real GDP	167
8.1	GDP per capita: absolute values in constant prices and constant exchange rates (USD, basis year: 1990)	200
8.2	GDP per capita related to EU12	201
8.3	FDI inflows per capita	202
8.4	Relative distribution of FDI inflows per capita	203
8.5	The Euklid measure of the intensities of structural change	206
8.6	Specialisation patterns compared to the EU (12)	213

Acknowledgements

This volume stems from a workshop on macroeconomic problems of an EU enlargement to the East organised by the Institute for Economic Research Halle (IWH) in Halle on 28 February and 1 March 1997. The analysis of possible problems and policies reflects one of the major research areas of the institute. Some papers presented were written after the workshop. They follow up the discussions of the workshop or deal with issues which were not discussed in detail at the workshop itself. Funding for the meeting was generously provided by the Volkswagen Foundation. The workshop was prepared and coordinated by Hubert Gabrisch, head of the Central and Eastern Europe division of the IWH. Special thanks go to Johannes Stephan for the copy-editing of the volume, to Kimberly Crow for improving the quality of language and to Katrin Renneberg for technical assistance.

RÜDIGER POHL
President of the IWH

Notes on the Contributors

Klaus Frohberg is the Executive Director of the Institute of Agricultural Development in Central and Eastern Europe (IAMO) in Halle/Salle, Germany, and Head of the Division of External Environment for Agriculture and Policy Analysis. Prior to taking on this position he was with the Institute of Agricultural Policy, Marketing and Rural Sociology at the University of Bonn. His research interests are in agricultural policy, institutional and regional economics and in quantitative methods. He has co-authored two books analysing the global agricultural and food system and free trade policies.

Hubert Gabrisch is head of the Central and East European division at the Institute for Economic Research Halle (IWH), after being deputy director of the Vienna Institute for Economic Research (WIIW). He took his doctoral degrees on Poland's integration into the Comecon. His research interests concentrate on economic integration and selected aspects of transition policies, particularly macroeconomics. He records many publications, recently mainly on the relations of the EU with Central and Eastern Europe. He is a member of the scientific advisory board of the Institute of Agricultural Development in Central and Eastern Europe (IAMO) in Halle (Germany).

Monika Hartmann is Head of the Division of Agricultural Markets, Marketing and World Agricultural Trade at the Institute of Agricultural Development in Central and Eastern Europe (IAMO) in Halle/Saale, Germany. Prior to taking on this position she was with the Institute of Agricultural Policy at the University of Frankfurt/Main. Her research interests are in analysis of agricultural policies and markets, theory and analysis of trade and in welfare economics. Recent publications focus on competitiveness of agriculture and the food sector in transition countries and on implications of the EU eastern enlargement.

Jens Hölscher holds the Commerzbank Chair for Money and Finance at Chemnitz University and was coordinator of economic research at the Institute for German Studies of the University of Birmingham, after lecturing at the University of Wales, Swansea, and the Free University, Berlin, where he took his doctoral degree on the post-war

German economic miracle. His research interests concentrate on the economic theories of money and development with special reference to the German economy and the transition processes in the economies of Central East Europe.

Kazimierz Laski is a retired professor of the University of Linz (Austria). He worked over many years with Michal Kalecki at the then High School for Planning and Statistics (SGPiS) in Warsaw. In 1968, he emigrated to Austria. Until 1991 he teached quantitative economics at the University of Linz, and from 1991 to 1996 he was the scientific director of the Vienna Institute for Comparative Economic Studies. He is a member of various national and international associations, and his main fields of research and teaching include quantitative economics, the theory of economic growth and the theory of planning. He has published many books and articles in renowned economics journals.

Claudia Löhnig earned her doctoral degrees in economics from the University of Regensburg. Her doctoral research focused on economic restructuring in the transition economies of Central and Eastern Europe and the former Soviet Union. In 1996 and 1997, she was with the staff of the Institute for Economic Research Halle, department for Central and Eastern Europe. Since autumn 1997 she has been a research associate at the Leipzig Graduate School of Management. Her principal interests are in the field of international trade, especially the eastern enlargement of the European Union.

Lucjan T. Orlowski is a tenured Professor of Economics and International Finance at Sacred Heart University in Fairfield, Connecticut, with scholarship concentrating on stabilisation policies in transforming economies. As a consultant to the Center for Economic and Social Research in Warsaw, the Foreign Trade Research Institute in Warsaw, the European Investment Bank, and the Institute for East–West Studies in New York and Prague he coordinated and completed research projects on monetary policies formulation and the development of financial markets in transforming economies and on the eastern enlargement of the European Union. With Dominick Salvatore he is the editor of *Trade and Payments in Central and Eastern Europe's Transforming Economies*.

Witold M. Orlowski deputing director of the Research Institute of the Central Statistical Office in Warsaw. He previously worked at the University of Lodz, and during negotiations on Poland's association with the European Union he served as an advisor to the Polish government. In 1992–93 he was a director of the economic division at the European Integration Office of the Government of Poland. From 1993 to 1997 he was with the World Bank (Central Europe Department), Washington, DC. His research interests concentrate on the macropolicies during the transition and the EU integration of Central and Eastern European countries. Most recent publications focus on the problems of the EU accession of the Central and East European countries.

Leon Podkaminer took his doctoral degrees in agricultural economics. He was formerly associated with the Polish Academy of Sciences and is currently with the Vienna Institute for Comparative Economic Studies (WIIW). His interests include cross-country comparisons of relative prices and consumption structures, the process of transformation of former centrally planned economies and macroeconomic theory. He has contributed many papers to internationally renowned economics journals.

Johannes Stephan is a graduate of the Free University, Berlin, and obtained his doctorate at the University of Birmingham on the economics of systemic transformation and economic development in post-socialist economies. On completion of that project, he was appointed to a Research Fellowship at the Institute for Economic Research Halle (IWH). His research interest concentrates on the conditions for economic development with particular emphasis on monetary considerations for integration and the pattern of international division of labour amongst 'unequal partners'.

Preface

This volume in the series *Studies in Economic Transition* focuses on the macroeconomic effects of the eastward enlargement of the European Union in Central Europe. The work contributes to the open-minded character of the series by rejection of the commonly shared view that an integration into the western economic sphere would be automatically beneficial for the new eastern member states. In contrary to the widespread accession enthusiasm for the consequences of EU membership, here possible effects on the economies of the new prospective members are analysed very carefully in order to achieve insights for improved preparations in Eastern Europe. The overriding question of the whole book is, whether and under which specific conditions East European members can survive increased competition within a common European market area.

As the eastern enlargement effects on the current members have been investigated in numerous studies the reversal of the question seems to be overdue. In his detailed introduction Hubert Gabrisch modestly describes the aim of the book to contribute to the EU enlargement debate with some new aspects. However, if the theoretical underpinnings of the contributions to this work will turn out as robust enough, the whole enlargement debate might take another direction. Even if the EU enlargement is a case of the primacy of politics with its own dynamics, the economic implications of the integration of East European states have to be recognised.

Birmingham and Chemnitz	JENS HÖLSCHER
Berlin	HORST TOMANN

List of Abbreviations

AIDS	Almost ideal demand system
ATS	Austrian schilling
bn	billion
BOP	Balance-of-payments
CAP	Common Agricultural Policy
CEA(s)	Central European Associate(s)
CEE	Central East Europe
CEEC(s)	Central East European Country(ies)
CPI	Consumer price index
CZK	Czech koruna
DEM	German mark
EAGGF	European Agricultural Guarantee and Guidance Fund
ECB	European Central Bank
ECP	European Comparison Project
ECU	European currency unit
EMS (II)	European Monetary System (II)
EMU	European Monetary Union
ERDF	European Regional Development Fund
ERDI	Exchange rate deviations index
ESF	European Social Fund
EU	European Union
FDI	Foreign direct investment
FIML	Full information maximum likelihood
GDP	Gross domestic product
GNP	Gross national product
HUF	Hungarian forint
ICP	International Comparison Projects
IMF	International Monetary Fund
IPC	Interest Rate Parity Condition
ISIC	International Standard Industrial Classification
LOP	Law of One Price
MC-3	Mediterranean countries (Greece, Portugal and Spain)
mn	million

OECD	Organisation for Economic Co-operation and Development
PPP(s)	Purchasing power parity(ies)
PZL	Polish zloty
REER	Real effective exchange rate
SOE(s)	State-owned enterprise(s)
trn	trillion
UN	United Nations
USA	United States of America
USD	US dollar
VAT	Value added tax
WIIW	Wiener Institut für Internationale Wirtschaftsvergleiche
WTO	World Trade Organisation

Introduction

This volume engages perspectives on the subject of the eastern enlargement of the European Union which are rather unusual in the ongoing debate. Different from most books and articles recently published it studies the ability of new eastern member countries to withstand competition on the EU markets. It therefore can be understood as a contribution to defining one of the most open criteria decided on at the Copenhagen summit of the Union and at the same time delivering answers to a topic greatly neglected in the enlargement literature so far.

The book takes a somewhat one-sided approach: it deals with the adjustment burden for new members. The widespread belief that an eastern enlargement of the Union would be overwhelming to the detriment of the present EU (budgetary costs, locational decisions, trade deficits) is rejected. All authors discuss the lack of competitiveness of potential new members and their need for structural adjustment (for example in the financial sector, agriculture or manufacturing) and for appropriate policies. The main issues considered critically are the problem of price convergence in integrated markets, the positive approach to foreign capital inflow (including transfers and foreign direct investment), and the simplifying view on current account deficit.

In most contributions a comparative approach plays an important role. Many authors try to include in their analysis experiences drawn from the southern enlargement of the EU. This volume, therefore, also contributes to an explanation as to why the southern members of the Union have not shown an impressive catching-up (in GDP per capita terms) with the core EU since their admission.

The book comprises of three parts: Part I studies the impact of membership on prices, demand and growth. The subjects of Part II are monetary and financial impacts: the exchange rate, capital and transfer inflows. Part III is devoted to adjustment problems in the two paramount sectors of agriculture and manufacturing.

The problem of price convergence is covered in Part I: its evidence, causes and its impact on growth. Statistical observation – recently provided by an OECD study – suggests remarkable price differences between western and eastern countries. Prices not only differ on an aggregate basis but also on a disaggregate level: East European prices of tradable goods are closer to their western counterparts than prices of nontradables. Prices of tradable goods that experience market entry barriers are lower than the western ones. There are two main problems discussed in this section: (1) will a complete opening of eastern markets entail an increase of prices on their domestic markets? (2) what consequences may be expected for exports, growth and employment?

All three authors concerned with that matter depart more or less from the Law of One Price, which suggests that price arbitrage will close the gap between domestic and foreign prices of tradables. However, while Podkaminer sees some factors which might hold the overall domestic price level constant, Gabrisch and Laski expect an increase of the overall price level. The main difference between Podkaminer on the one side and Gabrisch and Laski on the other concerns the role of nontradables. Podkaminer believes that under strict neo-classical assumptions on international trade and consumer behaviour, trade may increase differences between the prices of tradables and nontradables. Prices of tradables may increase (according to the law of one price) and the prices of nontradables may decrease. In this case, the existing differences between purchasing power parities and exchange rates must not erode but might even increase which would be tantamount to a real depreciation of East European currencies. He presents the results of an empirical estimate of an almost ideal demand system with two tradable and one nontradable commodity that underline this point. Gabrisch and Laski reject this argumentation because of its too unrealistic assumptions. Gabrisch's main argument for an increase of the prices of nontradables is based on the application of EU subsidy standards which will increase the tariffs of services. A second argument is provided by 'wage infection': if wages in the tradable sector would converge to foreign wages, there could be a spillover on wages in the nontradable sector. Both, Gabrisch and Laski consider the case of a labour market reaction on increasing prices. If wages in the tradable sector would follow prices, real wages would remain constant and a real currency appreciation would result with a more or less fixed exchange rate.

The second aspect discussed concerns the effects of a price increase of tradables on income growth and employment. The neo-classical model of tradables and nontradables denies any negative impact of a price increase. If domestic prices for tradables increase a shift from domestic consumption to exports would follow; employment and output remained at the given production possibility frontier of the country in consideration. Gabrisch and Laski, however, provide two arguments: Gabrisch, again, stresses the wage argument: if profits increase (due to price arbitrage) nominal wages would respond. With a more or less given exchange rate a steady inflation would emerge and the trade balance would deteriorate instead of improving. Laski, on the other hand, fears that even with constant nominal wages, income and employment would be affected. He argues with redistributing effects: households or workers in Central and East European countries dispose primarily over wage incomes and spend them mainly on consumption goods. Their propensity to save is regularly lower than that of capital owners. An increase of prices and a fall of real wages might raise the savings ratio and curb domestic consumption. GDP may still increase, but may also remain constant or even decrease. The latter possibility cannot be excluded because the export surplus is rather small in relation to GDP, while consumption out of wages represents a rather large proportion of GDP.

Some issues that were mentioned only briefly in the Part I are the main subjects of the second part: foreign exchange flows such as transfers and capital and exchange rate policies. There is the widespread view that Central and East European countries would receive significant transfer inflows under various EU policies (regional, agricultural) and might attract more capital investment. Transfers and capital would help to modernise and restructure the outdated capital stocks. The three authors of this part, however, share a rather sceptical view on this proposition. Witold Orlowski discusses the possible transfer problems of Central and East European countries on the background of experiences from the southern enlargement of the Union. He concludes that increased official transfers enhanced by private capital inflow may lead to a real appreciation of currencies of new member countries and lower their competitiveness. Emerging big deficits in trade may lead to negative long-term growth effects. In his opinion, both Iberian members of the Union suffered from this 'generalised Dutch disease effect', as he calls it, since their and Greece's accession to the Union during the first two years of their membership.

Lucjan Orlowski concentrates on capital flows which soared during recent years due to the quick implementation of capital account convertibility. The problem he marks is the high vulnerability of emerging financial markets in Central and East European countries against shock-like changes in international capital markets. Against the background of international experience he concludes that Poland, Hungary and the Czech Republic are not yet able to neutralise considerable capital inflows or cushion sudden reversed outflows. He holds that the banking sectors' and the central banks' instruments are not yet efficient to absorb international capital market shocks. Accession programmes should, therefore, not demand full capital account convertibility until the banking sector has been strengthened. He, as well as Witold Orlowski stresses that the best method for the neutralisation of large capital inflows is a sound fiscal policy, accomplished primarily by cuts in government consumption.

The third contribution of this part is a case study delivered by Jens Hölscher and Johannes Stephan. In their opinion, Hungary (in particular the austerity programme of 1995) is an example in which a huge current account deficit and weak fiscal discipline placed an increasing adjustment burden on underdeveloped domestic capital markets. The early Hungarian transformation strategy of 'over-spending' domestically by use of foreign markets proved to be unsustainable in the long run and forced a reorientation in late 1994. Hungary's growing stock of national and foreign debts inhibited the emergence of a stable monetary constitution: aggravating deficits in the current account and the state's budget undermined the credibility of the forint and led to capital flight, accelerating inflation and a renewed increase in interest rates. Whilst the subsequently necessary austerity programme of 1995, which was additionally coupled with several steps of devaluation of the forint, focused on the Hungarian 'twin deficit', it curbed the investment boom of 1993 and 1994. It remains to be seen what effect it will have on the long-run growth prospects. In their view, the Hungarian monetary constitution will have to exhibit sufficient stability to warrant a fixed, or pegged exchange rate without resulting in unsustainable real exchange rate revaluation.

Two sectors, agriculture and industry, are exposed more than other sectors to the EU membership. The interplay of market forces and Union policy (reforms) determine the adjustment needs in both and the spillover effects on the other sectors. These problems are the subject of the volume's third part. Klaus Frohberg and Monika Hartmann discuss the effects of the Union's Common Agricultural Policy (CAP) on new member states. The transmission of the present CAP to eastern members would cause the protective level for their agricultural sectors to increase. Farmers' output prices for almost all agricultural products would increase as well as production. EU-wide subsidised surpluses would also increase. For Eastern European countries, two negative consequences would emerge: (1) the structural problems of their agricultural sector – low quality, low efficiency of food industries and low rural infrastructure – would remain; (2) consumer prices would go up and private households would suffer (here, the spillover effects on industry might be significant: a prospering farming sector and price/wage convergence might entail a Dutch disease problem for industry). The two authors, however, do not consider this scenario to be very realistic. The budgetary burden for the Union calls for CAP reform. In addition, transition countries cannot raise their level of agricultural protection without conflicts with GATT.

Frohberg and Hartmann, then, discuss the case of a more market-oriented reform of the CAP that would be desirable also from the point of view of the transition countries. One could conclude from their analysis that output ('farm gate') prices would not increase that dramatically and that the possible spillover effects to industry are of minor relevance. What seems to be important is that the burden of adjustment would remain in the agricultural sector. Farmers might not be competitive in the new eastern member states within the framework of a market-oriented CAP because of the above mentioned structural problems. Then, an extension of EU structural policies to the eastern members would be a reasonable solution.

The last chapter of the book deals with adjustment needs in industry, mainly manufacturing. The new theories of trade and development relate the income catching-up (measured as GDP per capita convergence) to the assimilation of industrial production structures. Intra-industry trade and industrial cores are the keywords. Claudia Löhnig studies the changes in composition of manufacturing industries in the three countries Greece, Portugal and Spain after their accession to the European Union. Spain was only relatively successful, Portugal and Greece, however, specialised on 'sensitive' and labour-intensive industries which are under more competitive pressure. Empirical results for eight Central and East European countries give evidence of an already high degree of assimilation, higher than for the three southern members in the year of their accession. However, Löhnig concludes that the access to a wider market is not a guarantee for an assimilation of structures and for catching-up. This could be seen as an argument for sound industrial policies which, however, should be covered and supported by other policies. Some of them were discussed in earlier contributions of the volume, as for example income policies, exchange rate policies, fiscal policies and, of course, the strengthening of the monetary constitution.

The chapters in this book point to new aspects related to a (possibly premature) integration of emerging market economies in the East with severe structural problems. Obviously, the list of problems is not complete and many questions cannot be answered yet. The editor, however, hopes that he and his co-authors have brought some issues into the ongoing debate on an eastern enlargement of the Union that have not been considered earlier.

HUBERT GABRISCH

I
Price Convergence, Demand and Growth

1 Effects of Accession to the EU on Prices, Wages and Aggregate Demand in CEE Countries

Hubert Gabrisch

INTRODUCTION

The great debate about the European Union's eastward enlargement has so far been marked by a prejudiced view that is probably rooted in pressure for early accession exerted by the transition countries on the one hand, and in the EU's procrastination policy on the other. This prejudice holds that under present general conditions – that is, different factor endowments in the East and the West, hence, relatively low wages in the East, and current EU policies – the countries joining the EU would be the potential winners of accession, while the current members would be the losers. In reality the distribution of macro-economic costs and burdens is considerably more complicated.

A look at the available literature on the subject shows that quite a lot of research exists on the effect that accession would have on the EU, but that hardly any studies have been conducted in the EU or in Central and Eastern Europe dealing with its effect on the new member countries themselves.[1] This means that the identification of pressure for EU reform due to the accession of Central and East European (CEE) countries will remain uncertain.

This study deals with some of the consequences the EU eastward enlargement will have for the new member countries. There are various approaches that could help to understand possible adjustment processes in the potential new member states. One approach could study the structural and inter-sectoral consequences or relative price changes along with the traditional theory of international trade. This approach underlies various studies on the integration of CEE countries into the world or EU economy since 1990 (CEPR, 1992; Baldwin, 1992). Most of these studies conclude positive structural effects for new members from CEE. All these rather traditional general equilibrium approaches presuppose neutrality of a change of relative prices concerning the aggregate price level, the trade balance and employment. A more critical view is provided by W. Orlowski (1996) mentioning among other aspects a possible Dutch disease problem. Landesmann and Pöschl (1995) only offer a macroeconomic approach by trying to measure the positive growth effects resulting from a likely lessening of balance-of-payments constraints for CEE countries.

The following contribution to the debate elaborates on impacts of open CEE markets on their aggregate prices and wages and on multiplier effects on aggregate income. The aim is to describe dilemmas for economic policies in these countries which stem from adjustments of absolute prices on the firms' and on the macro level. My considerations are based on the experience that prices on two markets in international currency start to converge when trade becomes free. Behind this process is something like the action of the *law of one price* on integrated markets of tradable goods. There is a second observation: higher forms of integration are coupled with some pressure to streamline subsidy standards which in turn include the non-tradable sector (utility industries, for example). Diverging subsidy standards may distort cost relations of tradables. The third observation is that usually the nominal exchange rate loses its classical role to maintain price differences between countries. Free trade agreements seem to have an influence on exchange rate policies, too. Governments try to exert some influence on the governments of partner countries to stabilise the nominal exchange rate. On the other hand, free trade benefits must be calculable for firms, and firms do not like volatile exchange rates very much. Hence, firms try to exert some pressure on their own governments to stabilise the nominal exchange rate. What is more, a stable nominal exchange rate is extremely important for international capital flows including foreign direct investment. If the law of one price holds, an appreciation of the real exchange rate of CEE currencies affecting competitiveness of their firms would be inevitable with a stiff nominal exchange rate system.

How to deal with the exchange rate is an important problem to be discussed when we talk about the policy implications of an eastern enlargement of the European Union. The suspicion behind the considerations presented is rather simple: If a country does not dispose of a flexible foreign exchange market for buffering external price shocks it needs a flexible labour market. If neither of both are accessible, the country would be confronted with inflation or trade deficits affecting GDP growth.

The study is organised as follows: the first section tries to guess into what kind of EU will eastern countries be admitted. The aim here is to describe the most important features of the framework for the argumentation which follows. A theoretical framework is then developed for understanding the effects of integration on prices, wages and income, followed by some statistical evidence of macroeconomic price convergence from various countries that have already been admitted to the EU. The final two sections present some statistical figures on price differences between CEE and EU countries from a recent OECD study, and some conclusions for policy dilemmas and their possible solution.

INTO WHAT KIND OF EU WILL CENTRAL AND EAST EUROPEAN COUNTRIES BE ADMITTED?

At its September 1995 meeting in Madrid, the EU Council decided that half a year after the end of the Maastricht II conference series, that is, probably in early 1998, negotiations on accession should begin with CEE countries that wish to join. It is impossible to predict when and under which transition arrangements they will actually be admitted. However, up to a certain degree it is possible to foresee the likely future economic policy framework to which they will accede.

The European monetary union (EMU) will, no doubt, be the most important element, but it is also impossible at present to predict whether this union will already exist when the CEECs are admitted. However, some deferment is not the crucial problem. The crux rather is that the Maastricht conference will not revise the convergence criteria. It is more likely to expect that the degree of commitment demanded of all EU member countries will not only be reconfirmed but even raised. While the degree of commitment (particularly regarding fiscal criteria) was formulated quite loosely in the Maastricht treaty, which at first triggered off discussions about the treaty's imperativeness or even about possible revisions (Kees, 1994; and Hasse, 1994), its interpretation has successively become more restrictive regarding compliance with the criteria, not least due to the attitude taken by the German government.

The most important consequence of monetary union for non-members will be the limitation of their autonomy in exchange rate policy. This sounds paradoxical, since monetary union in the first instance implies that it will be the EMU members who lose their independence in exchange rate and monetary policy. However, Article 109, Paragraph 2, of the Maastricht treaty obliges all countries not participating in EMU to treat their exchange rate policies as a matter of common interest. The institutional framework that will most probably be adopted to carry out this obligation will be a new European Monetary System (EMS II). Whatever its form, it will result in non-members of EMU not being allowed to devalue their currencies unilaterally. This will be a completely logical consequence of the EMU, because non-participants will have to aspire to later EMU membership and will therefore have to follow the convergence criteria even more closely than before. The exchange rates of nonparticipants, among them many new EU members from Central and Eastern Europe, would thus lose much of their force as instruments of economic adaptation, so that monetary policy and, ultimately, fiscal policy would be paralysed by a one-sided exchange rate orientation. Among all present EU members, this painful loss will be most strongly felt by Greece which never joined the EMS intervention mechanism and tried to compensate the rate of inflation higher than in other countries by strong devaluation. Part of this higher inflation was likely due to a lack of fiscal, monetary and income discipline. Thus, no doubt, the limitation of freedom regarding exchange rate policy may exert a beneficial disciplinary effect. To what extent this also applies to the CEECs, where rising price levels are not mainly the result of insufficiently restrictive monetary and fiscal policy[2] but may be caused by integration into the Single European Market, will be discussed in the following sections.

THE LAW OF ONE PRICE AND THE INCOME MULTIPLIER

The law of one price (LOP) states that each tradable good has a single price throughout the world, and that arbitrage ensures price convergence. If this holds for all tradable goods, the LOP extends also to aggregate price level. Assume the nominal exchange rate being an exogenous variable for firms, the LOP then is defined by:

$$Pv = P^*e_0 \tag{1}$$

with P being the aggregate level of prices in domestic currency terms and P^* as the appropriate level of prices on the foreign market expressed in foreign currency units; e_0 is the exchange rate expressed as domestic currency units per unit of foreign currency, and v is a variable which reflects arbitrage and information costs and explicit and implicit impediments to trade which are all – seen from the micro-level – outside of the single firm's disposal. However, on the macro-level, a change of v can be interpreted as the familiar expression for a change of the real exchange rate; it then becomes an indicator of the LOP.

Price differences between markets go hand in hand with cost differences. Assuming wage costs and mark-up pricing of firms, the domestic price level for tradables is defined as:

$$P = w + \pi \qquad (2)$$

with w as unit labour costs and π as unit profits.[3] Neglecting productivity changes the domestic price level will then increase if money wages increase. The same applies to an increase of profit margins. After substituting equation (2) into equation (1) and rearranging terms, total differentiation of equation (1) yields:

$$\frac{dv}{d\pi} = \frac{P^* \frac{de_0}{d\pi}}{w+\pi} - \frac{P^* e_0}{(w+\pi)^2}\left(\frac{dw}{d\pi}+1\right) \text{ with } P^* \text{ held constant } (dp^* = 0) \qquad (3)$$

Equation (3) displays how the price arbitrage term $d\pi$ may affect the real exchange rate via the domestic price level. The LOP acts through dealers who use the existing price differences for extra profits. The term '1' in the second element of the right side of the equation describes this aspect. Workers may but must not react. However, 'wage infection' $\left(\frac{dw}{d\pi}\right)$ becomes very realistic if workers are able to compare the domestic and the foreign price in the common currency. A good example was provided by Polish workers after Fiat took over a car plant in the town of Tychy in order to assemble cars for export. The workers demanded the same wages as their Italian fellow-workers and went on strike. If both markets are even part of a currency union a price and wage comparison may occur rather instantaneously and wage infection caused by price arbitrage would strengthen price convergence. Examples can be found around the world.[4]

If we assume the LOP to hold[5] price convergence may affect aggregate demand and, thus, income and employment. We start the analysis with some assumptions:

- Firms of small CEE countries act as price takers on the world markets.
- The model consists of two tradable goods: consumer goods and investment goods.
- All wages are consumed and all profits are saved.

For exports of the economy we write:

$$E = E(v) \quad (4)$$

with v being the term which reflects the firms sector's ability to compete. (Ability includes of course market entry chances, hence, the existence of explicit and implicit market barriers.) We add an independent aggregate saving and investment function:

$$S = S(P, Y) \quad (5)$$
$$I = I(P, Y) \quad (6)$$

Both functions reflect the direct effects of price arbitrage on savings and investments through price changes, and indirect effects through a change in the national income. Finally, the condition for macro-equilibrium reads:

$$S = (P, Y) = I(P, Y) + E(v) \quad (7)$$

After total differentiation of equation (7), rearranging terms and replacing the terms dv and dP by the appropriate terms obtained from equations (1) and (2), we obtain the basic income multiplier:

$$\frac{dY}{d\pi} = \frac{\left(I_p - S_p - E_v \dfrac{v}{p}\right)\left(\dfrac{dw}{d\pi} + 1\right) + E_v \dfrac{v}{e_0} \dfrac{de_0}{d\pi}}{S_Y - I_Y} \quad (8)$$

S_Y, I_Y, E_v are the partial derivatives and describe the reaction of savings, investments and exports to income changes. I_p and S_p, and being also partial derivatives, describe the reaction of investment and savings when the price level is changing. The denominator of this expanded multiplier formula represents the condition of stability which is always positive $[1 > S_Y > I_Y \geqslant 0]$. The first term of the nominator presents the direct and the indirect arbitrage effect on I, S and E. The second term in the nominator describes how the exchange rate may react when profit margins were raised.

We study first the EMU case: the nominal exchange rate is fixed ($de_0 = 0$), or, more extremely formulated, there is no domestic currency. The second term will take the value zero. Two elements enter the multiplier with a negative sign: (a) savings which increase due to higher profits and less consumption; (b) E_v and $\dfrac{v}{P}$ are preceded by a positive sign. A real appreciation leads to a deterioration in the trade balance (and vice versa) and E_v becomes positive. With this, the product of both values is also preceded by a positive sign, but it has a negative calculation sign in the multiplier. The only positive element are investments. The reaction of investment seems not to be determined, although we have implied a positive reaction so far. We may, however, assume a rather weak reaction in one or the other direction. If investment remains constant two negative terms provided by savings export competitiveness reduce income. If there is no wage infection the multiplier displays the remaining arbitrage effect:

$$\frac{dY}{d\pi} = \frac{\left(I_P - S_P - E_v \dfrac{v}{P}\right)}{S_Y - I_Y} \tag{8a}$$

The price level in domestic currency units increased and the real wage rate went down as nominal wages stayed constant. The redistribution of income in favour of profits presses private consumption down. With a given nominal exchange rate the real exchange rate will appreciate and the economy's competitiveness will shrink. The result is a decline of aggregate income.

If we include wage infection we obtain:

$$\frac{dY}{d\pi} = \underbrace{\frac{\left(I_P - S_P - E_v \dfrac{v}{P}\right)}{S_Y - I_Y}}_{\text{direct arbitrage effect}} + \underbrace{\frac{\left(I_P - S_P - E_v \dfrac{v}{P}\right)\left(\dfrac{dw}{d\pi}\right)}{S_Y - I_Y}}_{\text{wage infection effect}} \tag{8b}$$

Compared with the previous situation, aggregate incomes will further contract for any dw between 0 and dπ. The deterioration results mainly from the trade balance. Consumption may instead remain constant due to constant real wages in domestic currency units, and aggregate savings will not fall. As inflation is higher than without wage infection, v shrinks more; foreign goods become cheaper and the trade balance will deteriorate. Could the government avoid the negative income effect by a devaluation? For studying this case equation (8) needs to be reformulated a little as:

$$\frac{dY}{d\pi} = \underbrace{\frac{(I_P - S_P)\left(\frac{dw}{d\pi}+1\right)}{S_Y - I_Y}}_{\text{price arbitrage and wage}} + \underbrace{\frac{E_v \frac{v}{d\pi}\left(\frac{d_e}{e_0} - \frac{dP}{P}\right)}{S_Y - I_Y}}_{\text{exchange rate effect}} \text{ with } dP = dw + d\pi \quad (8c)$$
$$\text{infection effect}$$

If the rate of devaluation equals the inflation rate the second term takes on value 0; there will be no negative influence on the trade balance; firms' ability to compete remains constant. In common currency units, the domestic price level has not changed. However, the devaluation required needs to be stronger in the case of wage infection than without. The exchange rate effect must be positive to compensate for the negative first term. The additional devaluation holds the nominal wage rate in the common currency at its previous level. The devaluation has been absorbed by both higher profits *and* wages in domestic currency. The price in domestic currency has increased. The obvious conclusion is that the price to be paid for holding aggregate income and employment constant is domestic inflation. The inflation is the outcome of struggles over income distribution between wages and profits.

STATISTICAL EVIDENCE OF RECENT PRICE ADJUSTMENT AND REAL EXCHANGE RATE APPRECIATION OF EU MEMBERS

In view of the theoretical framework developed above we may formulate a few expectations when considering concrete countries:

1. If the LOP holds, countries at a lower level of economic development, with lower wages and productivity, should show a positive inflation differential to the EU average; countries at a higher level should show a negative inflation differential.

2. If wage infection holds, real wages for the poorer countries concerned should show a downward rigidity.
3. If the nominal exchange rate shows only weak flexibility, a real devaluation should be an indicator for LOP.
4. Poor countries should suffer from a sudden and heavy deterioration of their balances in trade with the EU.

To begin with the experience of recent enlargements of the EC/EU, we consider two sets of countries: the southern enlargement comprising Greece (1981) Spain and Portugal (both 1986), and the 1995 enlargement comprising Austria, Sweden and Finland. All countries (with the exception of Spain) were rather small compared with the then EC or EU, measured in population size. Hence, their determining role on the prices in European markets was rather small. When a small and a large market integrate one can expect that prices of the larger market will rise or fall only little, but price movements on the smaller market will turn out stronger. Both sets differ in one important aspect: the southern set comprised countries on a significantly lower level of income in comparison with the average EU level measured in purchasing power parities. Hence, the aggregate level of prices, wages and, of course, productivity was lower than in the richer EU countries. Integration should then entail a positive inflation differential. The northern set comprised countries on a higher or at least (Finland) similar level as the EU average; integration should then entail a negative inflation differential.

With regard to exchange rate policies, Greece never joined the European intervention mechanism; Spain joined it in June 1989, Portugal in April 1992. Austria joined the EMS in January 1991; however, it was a shadow member before because of the pegging of the Austrian schilling to the DM. In August 1993, the bands for obligatory interventions of the central banks of these member countries of the EMS were widened to ±15 per cent. This change was provoked by the EMS crisis that began in the summer of 1992, during which the nominal exchange rates of some currencies – among others the peseta and the escudo – were adjusted upwards (nominal devaluation).

Spain

Since 1983, the immediate pre-accession period, the real value of the peseta against the ECU appreciated. The nominal exchange rate was rather stable, but domestic consumer prices continued to increase.

Effects of Accession to the EU on Prices

Figure 1.1   The Spanish development

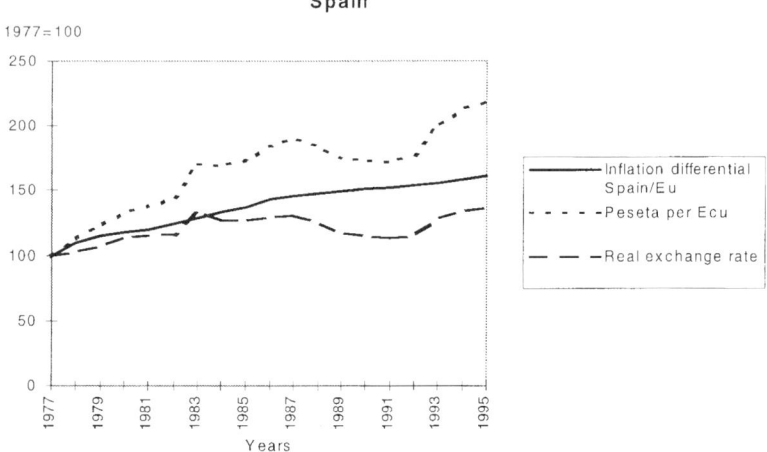

Note: The inflation differential is the domestic consumer price index in relation to the consumer price index of the EU (both: 1977 = 100).
Source: Deutsche Bundesbank, Devisenkursstatistik, 1995. IMF, May 1996; own calculations.

Since 1987, the nominal exchange rate appreciated. This might have been due to productivity gains in the tradable sector and/or to foreign exchange inflows of the economy that forced the nominal exchange rate to revalue. While the real wage level increased by 8.3 per cent over the period 1986–90, productivity measured as real GDP growth per employed person increased by only 5 per cent. On the other side, however, the inflation differential (measured in consumer prices) to the ECU area was positive.[7] The increase of domestic costs and/or profit margins exceeded the productivity gains, and the real exchange rate appreciated. In 1989, Spain joined the EMS, the nominal exchange rate stabilised, but inflation continued; the real exchange rate continued to appreciate till 1993 (see Figure 1.1).

Portugal

As in Spain, the inflation differential to the EU was positive during the pre-accession period. The period of nominal depreciation was by far stronger than in Spain indicating lower productivity gains or foreign exchange inflow. On the other side, real wages increased over

Figure 1.2   The Portuguese development

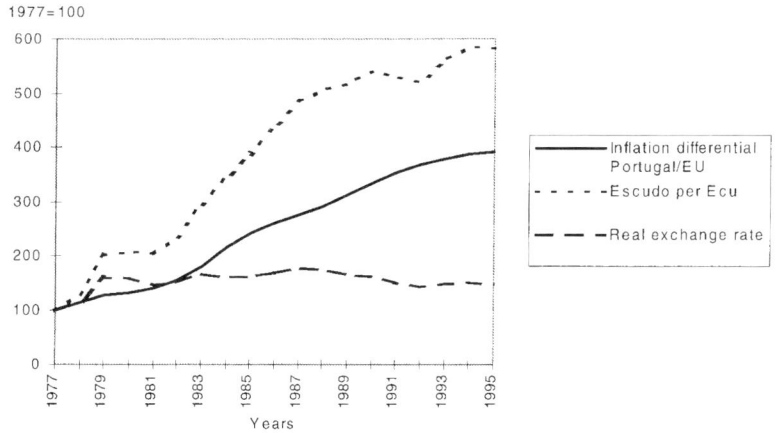

Note and sources: see Figure 1.1.

the period 1990/1985 by 8 per cent as in Spain. The nominal exchange rate answered and appreciated. In total, the real appreciation against the ECU was weaker; the price difference between the EU and Portugal did not erode that drastically as in the case of Spain (Figure 1.2).

Greece

Greece never joined the EMS. Figure 1.3 shows that the nominal exchange rate always followed inflation, and the real exchange rate remained more or less constant. Hence, the macroeconomic price differential between Greece and the EC/EU countries did not erode. Inflation had various sources in Greece: fiscal and monetary policies accommodating wage increases, but also the integration into EC/EU markets, and weak productivity progress. Greece is an example of a country with a weak income policy that could only resort to devaluation in order to avoid an erosion of the price difference and the emergence of huge trade deficits after inclusion into the EC markets. Between 1980 and 1985 real wages increased dynamically, but fell by 5.5 per cent by 1990. The picture shows how the exchange rate protected the economy against the negative impacts of various sources of inflation, among others the LOP. However, as it is well-known, real economic growth was weak, as well as productivity growth.

Figure 1.3 The Greek development

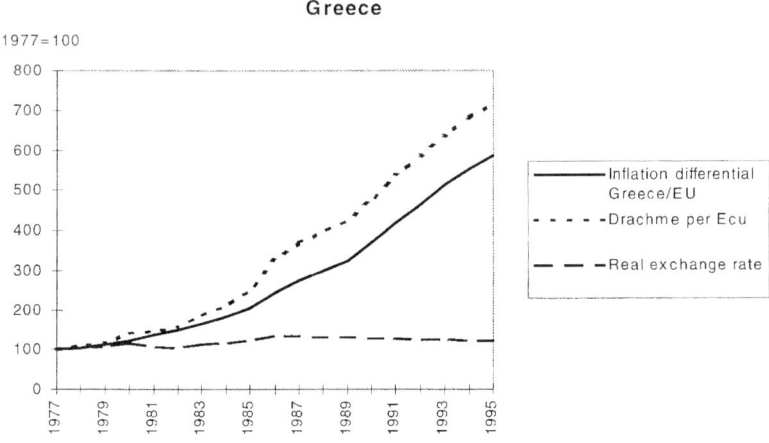

Note and sources: see Figure 1.1.

As expected, all three countries' trade balances deteriorated, particularly that of Spain the country with the strongest real appreciation of its currency (Figure 1.4). While Greece's deficit increased relatively moderately, trade deficits were balanced by large transfers from the

Figure 1.4 Balance of trade of Greece, Portugal and Spain with the EU

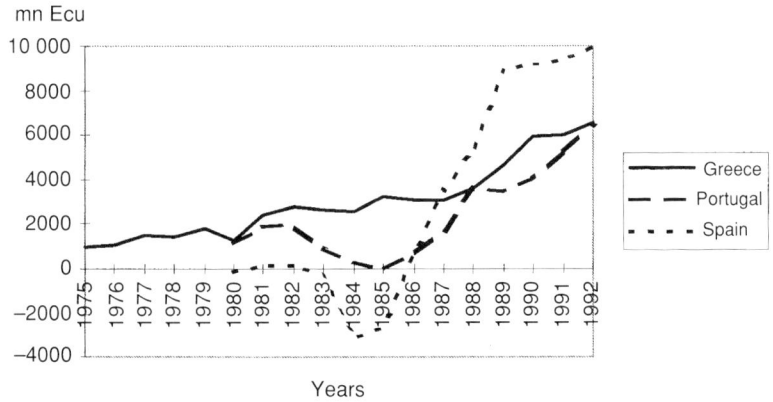

Note: minus sign indicate a trade surplus.
Source: Eurostat.

EU but with only small inflows of direct investments, Spain registered sizeable foreign direct investments (FDI) besides high transfers from the EU. Comparing the real economy development, foreign direct investment in Spain triggered off more productivity growth than transfers from the EU in Greece. A remarkable feature of Spain is the reduction of its unemployment rate from 21 to 16 per cent during 1986–1990, combined with a simultaneous rise in real wages. The strong inflow of foreign direct investment apparently helped to offset the negative effects of price and wage increases. Foreign investors placed their capital in an economy that had opened up almost completely during the 1960s and 1970s, that had stable market-economy-type institutions and that, moreover, joined the EMS in 1989, which presupposed at least a reasonably stable currency situation. But it should be noted that productivity gains did not help to stabilise the real exchange rate. Hence, Spain was a candidate for speculation against the peseta and for realignment. The continuous stream of FDI broke after 1992, and the value of the peseta was realigned in 1993. Without nominal devaluation Spain would have been forced to leave the European intervention mechanism.

Austria

Austria may also serve as an example of the effects of EU accession on a country with a relatively high income and price level. A negative inflation differential should be the distinguishing sign as compared with Spain, Greece and Portugal. Austria was especially known for the high prices of its food sector, as its agriculture was protected more strongly than that of the EU, and its producer price level also was higher. After adoption of the Common Agricultural Policy one therefore expected a lowering of producer prices and consequently of consumer prices in the food sector, although considering the small difference between the Austrian income and price level and that of the EU the drop should have been a minor one. According to a study by Pollan (1996), farmers' producer prices did in fact drop by an average of 23 per cent at the beginning of 1995; in some segments they even dropped as early as the autumn of 1994, in anticipation of the EU accession. The price drop showed up in the February and March 1995 producer price index. If one takes the West German price development during 1995 as a guideline, the price-lowering effect of EU accession can be estimated at nearly half a percentage point in the first half of 1995, and nearly three-quarters of a percentage point in

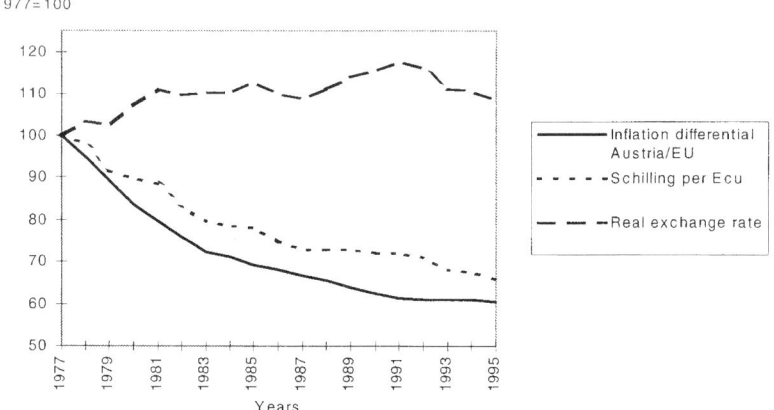

Figure 1.5 The Austrian development

Note and sources: see Figure 1.1.

the second half of that year, with the major share of the price reduction attributable to food (see Figure 1.5).

For many years Austria pegged its currency to the DM and was therefore practically a member of the EMS before EU accession. The nominal appreciation of the ATS against the ECU followed more or less the declining inflation differential, the latter indicating strong productivity growth and capital inflows. The real exchange rate remained rather constant.

PRICE DIFFERENCES BETWEEN CEE AND EU COUNTRIES AND THEIR SOURCES

It is well-known that the Central and East European countries will enter an EU consisting of economies characterised by greater economic power and thus a higher per capita income (Figure 1.6), and furthermore by different structures in the production and distribution of goods and income.

Purchasing power parities (PPP) reveal the real economic reasons for price differences. The relation between the nominal exchange rate and the PPP is called the exchange rate deviation index (ERDI),

Figure 1.6 Gross domestic product per inhabitant in US dollars, according to 1995 purchasing power parities

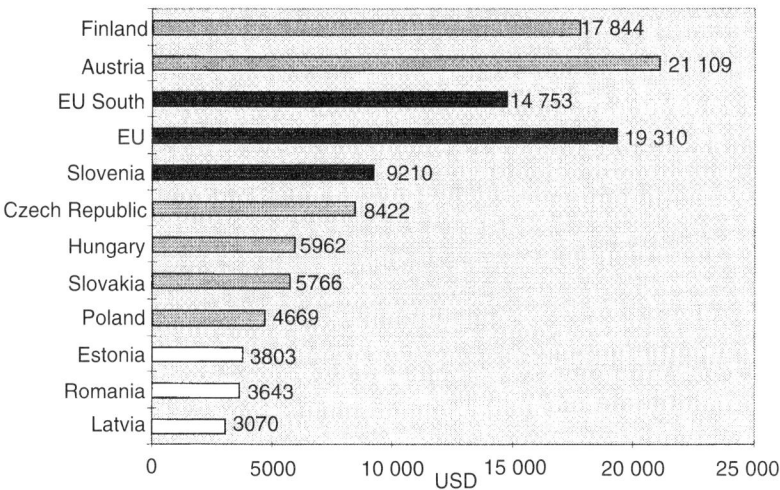

Note: EU South includes Greece, Spain and Portugal.
Source: OECD (1996a and b).

and its reciprocal is called the comparative price level index. A deviation of the nominal exchange rate to the PPP indicates the effects of explicit and implicit trade barriers and exchange rate policies on price differences. An OECD study on comparative price indices of Central and East European countries that was conducted for the first time in 1993 reveals the price differences of aggregate demand (Table 1.1). This OECD study also calculated the comparative indices for single demand aggregates (private consumption, investment and so on).

The price difference was the largest in the case of non-tradable services (rents, medical treatment or energy supply to households), as was to be expected. The aggregate price difference in the case of tradable goods, difference between domestic and world market level depends on the degree of market openness. The price differences between CEE countries and OECD countries were smallest in the case of machinery and transport equipment – this is no surprise owing to the deregulation already obtained in bilateral trade. The price difference in the case of food and textiles were rather large – again no surprise since CEE countries still have restricted access to EU markets in the field of agricultural goods, food and textiles.

Table 1.1 Comparative price level indices of final demand (purchasing power parity/exchange rate) in 1993 (Austria = 100)

Use of GDP	Bulgaria	Poland	Romania	Slovakia	Slovenia	Czech Rep.	Hungary
Private domestic consumption	**21.5**	**36.9**	**20.4**	**28.2**	**54.9**	**26.0**	**43.6**
Food	34.0	44.3	34.6	33.2	65.1	33.4	52.4
Bread and cereal products	29.2	37.7	18.6	19.4	52.8	21.0	46.7
Meat and meat products	32.0	41.4	40.4	37.1	62.7	35.1	48.5
Milk, cheese, eggs	35.1	42.6	40.3	31.6	61.4	32.1	47.5
Clothing and shoes	22.5	47.1	22.9	36.6	83.4	36.3	51.8
Clothing including repairs	21.6	44.2	21.4	33.1	84.8	35.4	49.3
Shoes including repairs	26.5	60.2	31.0	54.5	77.7	40.4	63.7
Rent, energy	25.9	19.2	9.0	12.1	43.6	13.7	30.2
Rent for housing	27.9	14.2	6.0	7.3	42.0	9.9	28.2
Energy	20.2	37.7	18.0	26.6	49.1	25.3	36.7
Furniture, household effects	38.3	49.7	30.1	47.0	74.4	40.4	60.6
Household furnishings	44.1	33.5	24.6	53.5	79.4	41.3	71.5
Household textiles	25.5	46.8	28.6	39.1	79.6	32.8	76.0
Electrical household appliances	49.9	61.8	41.0	44.8	69.7	43.7	54.1
Other household effects domestic services	27.9	58.9	28.7	40.6	68.3	36.1	51.8
Medical treatment	15.6	22.8	17.3	20.6	46.5	20.0	40.9

Table 1.1 (Cont'd)

Use of GDP	Bulgaria	Poland	Romania	Slovakia	Slovenia	Czech Rep.	Hungary
Transport and telecommunications	*36.1*	*55.5*	*28.0*	*40.4*	*58.5*	*43.6*	*69.1*
Vehicles, purchase	76.1	111.0	71.1	82.9	93.8	82.0	92.1
Vehicles, maintenance	32.1	49.6	25.7	34.6	46.6	39.4	69.9
Transport services	35.8	42.9	28.1	35.3	48.5	29.5	50.3
Telecommunications services	18.4	39.0	9.3	27.3	46.0	31.9	58.6
Recreation, entertainment, education	*12.5*	*27.7*	*14.7*	*20.4*	*52.6*	*22.2*	*32.1*
Services	10.6	23.4	7.3	12.7	53.2	15.9	27.8
Books and periodicals	15.1	37.3	9.3	22.6	88.1	21.9	38.5
Education and training	8.0	18.0	8.3	14.0	41.9	16.3	24.4
Other goods and services	*16.9*	*51.5*	*18.6*	*49.5*	*56.7*	*27.7*	*47.9*
Hotels, restaurants, cafés	15.5	58.9	15.9	26.9	47.0	28.4	49.0
Public consumption	**21.4**	**36.4**	**23.8**	**31.3**	**52.0**	**32.5**	**72.7**
Gross fixed investment	**42.2**	**54.1**	**46.9**	**42.9**	**68.3**	**42.6**	**81.0**

Table 1.1 (Cont'd)

Use of GDP	Bulgaria	Poland	Romania	Slovakia	Slovenia	Czech Rep.	Hungary
Construction	25.0	39.5	33.2	22.6	49.4	23.5	57.5
Housing construction	19.7	22.1	27.7	16.0	39.9	17.9	39.5
Other above-ground construction	32.0	55.1	37.6	25.3	63.1	26.7	81.9
Underground construction	24.8	58.4	33.6	26.1	48.9	26.6	61.8
Change in stock	**39.8**	**57.1**	**53.5**	**48.3**	**76.3**	**48.3**	**67.0**
Foreign trade balance	**100.0**	**100.0**	**100.0**	**100.0**	**100.0**	**100.0**	**100.0**
Gross domestic product	**24.7**	**39.8**	**25.8**	**30.9**	**57.7**	**30.1**	**51.8**

Source: Rittenau (1995a, 1995b).

What may CEE countries expect concerning these price differences after admission to the European Union?

- *Agricultural products*: producer prices in CEE countries' agriculture are relatively low because the share of wage incomes is low, and also the wage rates. The adoption of the Common Agricultural Policy of the EU might trigger off *price arbitrage* with the consequence that input prices for CEE food industries and domestic food prices will increase.
- *Textiles*: higher input prices (services, labour) might lead to higher costs of textile production. But even if input prices remained constant producers might increase their domestic *mark-up* rate when they feel they can sell their goods on EU markets at a higher price.
- *Non-tradable services (I)*: a part of non-tradable services is subsidised – rents, transport tariffs, energy. The application of EU subsidy standards will surely increase tariffs. Part of services is input to the production of tradable goods, for example, transport fees, and hence the cost of this production would increase. However, high subsidies would have to be financed by taxes which in turn put a burden on firms in the tradable sector. Cutting subsidies might entail higher competitiveness of this sector. On the other hand, high subsidies act as a substitute for higher wages, and curbing subsidies might provoke wage hikes in the entire economy. But this is not the whole story:
- *Non-tradable services (II)*: there is a certain 'wage infection' between tradables and non-tradables. As productivity in the tradable sector usually tends to increase faster than in the non-tradable sector, wages tend to follow (if we assume that wages reflect more or less the marginal product of labour). If, however, wages in the tradable sector increase, wages in the service sector will surely follow exerting some price pressure.

Price arbitrage and higher production costs, especially wage costs, would lead to a higher aggregate price level. The governments of potential new members will then be confronted with a dilemma:

- If, on the one side, the nominal exchange rate would not be flexible enough to maintain the price difference, the labour market must be flexible enough. If employment remained unchanged, the real wage rate must decline to ensure exports. This implies a reduction of private consumption. With less consumption and higher exports

the GDP might fall, remain constant or increase. In the latter case, the increase of the GDP after the opening of the economy will turn out to be by far smaller than hoped for.
- If, on the other side, the labour market is not flexible enough to yield a real wage decline, the exchange rate must bring down the money rate in international currencies, say the Euro. A flexible exchange rate system could help to compensate a domestic price increase by an appropriate devaluation. This kind of devaluation would only protect the export level. There remains, however, the negative impact of higher prices on private consumption as can be seen from the expanded multiplier formula noted earlier in this chapter. An additional devaluation is needed to compensate for losses in consumption, hence a real depreciation. But two other problems appear: first, a strong devaluation would implant a continuous competition between exports and private consumption, or wages and profits, and the outcome could be inflation. Second, inflation would also be induced through the import side (import prices going up). This scenario seems to be the true story that the Greek case is telling us.

SOME POLICY CONCLUSIONS

The method to solve the dilemma would be to allow the exchange value of the CEE currencies to fall by the amount required to give the necessary bounty to exports and then to resist any agitation to raise money-wages.

The first issue is the flexibility of the CEE countries' labour markets that determine the success or failure of income policies. All countries recently experienced strong increases of labour unit costs as shown in Table 1.2. A recent study on the Czech Republic and Slovakia (Frensch, 1997, p. 25) revealed that in both countries there exists a long-term equilibrium relation between consumer prices and wages. A disturbance of this relation is quickly corrected and the real wage balance is maintained. Exchange rate flexibility was and is needed to compensate for wage cost increases. On the other hand, it is well-known that exchange rate policies in the four countries mentioned above (and particularly in the Czech Republic and Slovakia) to date aim at stabilising the nominal exchange rate (nominal anchor concept). If we extrapolate the wage unit cost increases of 1995 over 1994, a yearly devaluation in the range of 5 to 23 per cent would be necessary.

Table 1.2 Wage unit costs in four CEE countries

Country	1994	1995	1995 over 1994 in per cent
Poland	2470	3046	23.3
Slovakia	181	195	7.7
Czech Republic	255	273	7.1
Hungary	284	299	5.3

Notes: Nominal wage index deflated with the consumer price index; labour productivity in industry; 1989 = 100.
Sources: National statistics via WIIW databank (Wiener Institut für Internationale Witschaftsvergleiche).

If we assume an EMS II with intervention bands of ±15 per cent for the so-called 'outs' of a monetary union, all countries would have severe problems to avoid a deterioration of their competitiveness.

The second issue is that of exchange rate flexibility. A period of devaluations seems indispensable until nominal wages are sufficiently flexible or, what seems to be more realistic, until labour productivity starts to catch up with wage increases. But it is precisely this kind of devaluation which the Maastricht scheme's device of EMU and EMS II forbids. The EU would have to accept steady devaluation or, alternatively, a strong initial undervaluation and then hold the nominal *and* real exchange rate constant (in order to attract foreign direct investment). The EU would have to accept something like what in EU countries to date has been called 'exchange rate dumping' because it implies a decline of wages in international currency below the level of productivity. The same result would emerge if income policies were to press real wages down. This is called 'social or wage dumping'. The proposition is to reject this kind of argumentation. The EU should accept that the German economic miracle in the 1950s was based on a strong undervaluation of the DM accepted by the United States, completed by import and capital controls; this would help to dampen wage growth.

Notes

1. Here we hold especially in mind studies on agricultural policies ordered by the European Commission in 1994. Among these we refer especially to Tangermann and Josling (1994). A more recent overview on various estimates of budget costs of an EU enlargement including structural policies is provided by Breuss and Schebeck, 1996.

2. If fiscal and monetary discipline is reflected by high real interest rates and low budget deficits, most CEE countries need not fear critics from the EU!
3. The equation is derived from the macroeconomic equation $PY = w^*L + \pi^*K$ where Y is aggregate income (for simplicity: of the tradable sector), w^* are money wages, π^* is the firms' profit margin, and L and K are the stocks of labour and capital respectively. Division by Y yields $P = \dfrac{w^*}{q} + \dfrac{\pi^*}{r}$ with $q = \dfrac{Y}{L}$ labour productivity and $r = Y/K$ as capital productivity. Then, w^*/q is the term for unit labour costs.
4. In Germany, wage demands of workers in the most northern part are more influenced by wage rises in the southern part than by wage rises in nearby Denmark. Another example was the franc-zone between France and its past west and central African colonies in the 1960s. Last, but not least, see the example of the German-German unification (Sachverständigenrat, 1990).
5. The author is quite aware of the fact that this assumption is one of the most debated in empirical economics (among recent empirical literature see Ardeni, 1989, Goodwin, 1992, Parsley und Wei, 1996 and Nessen, 1996). However, the author is convinced that the empirical debate is unresolved.
6. *Independent* means that aggregate savings do not determine aggregate investment.
7. The reader should note that the inflation rate of the ECU area includes the weighted inflation of Spain. Thus, the inflation differential was actually higher.

Bibliography

ARDENI, P. G. 'Does the Law of One Price Really Hold for Commodity Prices?', *American Journal of Agricultural Economics*, vol. 71(3), August 1989, pp. 661–9.
BALDWIN, R. *An Eastern Enlargement of EFTA*, Geneva, 1992.
BREUSS, F. and SCHEBECK, F. 'Ostöffnung und Osterweiterung der EU', *Wifo-Monatsberichte*, 2/1996, Vienna, 1996, pp. 139–52.
CEPR, *Is Bigger Better? The Economics of EC Enlargement, Monitoring European Integration*, 3, London, 1992.
FRANZMEYER, F. (ed.) *Das Konvergenzproblem – Wirtschaftspolitik im Europa von Maastricht*, DIW Sonderheft no. 151, Berlin, 1994.
FRENSCH, R. *Wechselnde Ursachen persistenter Inflation im tschechischen und slowakischen Transformationsprozeß*, working paper no. 199, Osteuropa-Institut München, München, 1997.
GOODWIN, B. K. 'Multivariate Cointegration Tests and the Law of One Price in International Wheat Markets', *Review of Agricultural Economics*, vol. 14(1), 1992, pp. 117–24.

HASSE, R. H. 'Konvergenzkriterien des Maastricht-Vertrages: Können sie Glaubwürdigkeit erzeugen?', in FRANZMEYER, F. (ed.), *Das Konvergenzproblem – Wirtschaftspolitik im Europa von Maastricht*, DIW Sonderheft no. 151, Berlin, 1994, pp. 73–93.
KEES, A. 'Die Konvergenzkriterien als wirtschaftspolitische Imperative des Maastricht-Vertrages', in FRANSMEYER, F. (ed.), *Das Konvergenzproblem – Wirtschaftspolitik im Europa von Maastricht*, DIW Sonderheft no. 151, Berlin, 1994, pp. 52–73.
LANDESMANN, M. and PÖSCHL, J. *Balance-of-Payments Constrained Growth in Central and Eastern Europe and Scenarios of East–West Integration*, WIIW-Forschungsberichte no. 222, Vienna, 1995.
NESSEN, M. 'Common Trends in Prices and Exchange Rates. Test of Long-Run Purchasing Power Parity', *Emperical Economics*, vol. 21(3), 1996, pp. 381–400.
ORLOWSKI, W. M. *Droga do Europy. Makroekonomia wstepowania do Unii Europejskiej*, GUS and PAN papers, Zeszyt 234, Warsaw, May 1996.
PARSLEY, D. C. and WEI, S.-J. 'Convergence to the Law of One Price Without Trade Barriers or Currency Fluctuations', *Quarterly Journal of Economics*, November 1996, pp. 1211–36.
POLLAN, W. 'Die Auswirkungen des EU-Beitritts auf die Verbraucherpreise', *Wifo-Monatsberichte*, 1/1996, Vienna, 1996, pp. 45–60.
RITTENAU, R. 'Wirtschaftsvergleiche mit Österreichs Nachbarländern 1993', *Statistische Nachrichten*, 9/1995, Wien, 1995a, pp. 703–11.
RITTENAU, R. 'Wirtschaftsvergleich Osteuropa 1993', *Statistische Nachrichten*, 10/1995, Wien, 1995b, pp. 797–808.
SACHVERSTÄNDIGENRAT, *Jahresgutachten des Sachverständigenrats 1990/91*, Stuttgart, 1990.
TANGERMANN, S. and JOSLING, T. E. *Pre-accession Agricultural Policies for Central Europe and the European Union*, Gutachten im Auftrag der Europäischen Kommission, Brussels, December 1994.

Statistics

DEUTSCHE BUNDESBANK: *Devisenkursstatistik*, Frankfurt a.M., May 1996.
EUROSTAT: *Aussen- und Intrahandel der Europäischen Union, Reihe 6B*, monthly statistics, Luxemburg, various issues.
IMF: *International Financial Statistics, Yearbook 1995*, Washington D.C., 1995.
OECD: *Purchasing Power Parities and Real Expenditures*, Volume II, Paris 1996a.
OECD: *Purchasing Power Parities for Eastern Europe, Press Release*, 14 February 1996b.
Wiener Institut für Internationale Witschaftsvergleiche (WIIW) WIIW DATABANK, Vienna.

2 Macroeconomic Problems of Trade Liberalisation and EU Eastern Enlargement
Kazimierz Laski

We concentrate our interest in this chapter upon the four Central and East European countries (CEECs): the Czech Republic, Hungary, Poland and the Slovak Republic, which have already concluded association agreements with the European Union, and we shall investigate only two new moments which are generally expected to happen after the CEECs have joined the Union. These are: a much stronger inflow of foreign capital, especially foreign direct investment (FDI), and price changes related to the opening of the common market to sensitive goods, especially food and textiles and footwear. We analyse the macroeconomic consequences of these two developments in a rather general manner. First, a model of GDP determined by aggregate demand is presented which takes special account of the consequences of the abrupt foreign trade liberalisation at the start of the transformation. In subsequent sections the model is then used for the question of the macroeconomic consequences of foreign capital inflows, and of the expected price changes in sensitive goods.

THE EXPORT SURPLUS AS A FACTOR CO-DETERMINING SAVINGS AND GDP IN A MARKET ECONOMY

I

Our basic assumption is that investment decisions (made in real, not only nominal terms) by firms precede in time the investment undertaken in a given period. Since – in a closed economy – investment and savings of a given period are *ex post* identical, it follows that investment of a given period, being determined by previous investment decisions, cannot be determined by savings of the same period. Consequently investment must causally determine savings and not vice versa.

The mechanism by which investment governs savings can be explained relatively simply by dividing the economy into two vertically integrated sectors, sector C, producing consumer goods, and sector I, producing investment goods. Let us assume for the sake of simplicity that workers do not save and capitalists do not consume. Hence, workers in sector C buy that part of consumer goods output which equals their wage bill, but the other part, corresponding to profit, that is, savings, in the same sector (to be called consumer goods surplus) can be sold only outside sector C. It is sector I, namely, workers of this sector, who buy the surplus of consumer goods. Without investment, this market would not come into existence, and without a market for the surplus of consumer goods, the very production in sector C would be impossible. On the other hand, when investment takes place it creates through the wage bill of sector I a market for the above-mentioned surplus. Hence the wage bill of sector I matches savings in sector C. Keeping in mind that the value of investment consists of the wage bill and savings, and taking into account the proposition that the 'wage bill in sector C equals savings in sector I', we come to the conclusion that investment equals the sum of savings in both sectors. This conclusion does not depend on the assumption of the so-called classical savings function made above.

The fact that savings are governed by investment does not mean that they do not in turn influence investment. Savings, particularly in the form of retained profits, are of the utmost importance as a factor co-determining investment decisions and hence future investment. Indeed, retained profits increase the capital owned by firms. And the higher the capital owned by a firm, the higher the degree of risk acceptable to the firm, and the larger the finance at the firm's disposition, directly, because of self-financing, and indirectly, because of easier access to the capital market.

II

Extending the equality between investment and savings to an open economy with a government budget, we get the general equation,

$$SP = IP + D + E \qquad (1)$$

where IP is the private (gross) investment of the business sector; $D = G - T$ is the budget deficit, being the difference between G, government expenditure for goods and services, and T, government revenue from all kinds of taxes including social security payments; $E = X - M$ is the trade surplus, being the difference between exports X and imports M of goods and non-factor services (nfs); and SP is private (gross) savings of individual households plus undistributed profits.

A shortened version of equation (1) can be obtained when we take into account that government expenditure G can be split into government consumption CG and government investment IG. Hence, we get for the budget deficit:

$$D = G - T = CG + IG - T = IG - (T - CG)$$
$$D = IG - SG \qquad (2)$$

because the term in brackets, being the difference between government revenue T and consumption expenditure of the government, denotes government savings SG. Accordingly, the budget deficit can also be defined as the difference between government investment and government savings. Substituting equation (2) into equation (1) we get:

$$SP = IP + IG - SG + E$$
$$SP + SG = IP + IG + E$$

or

$$SD = ID + E \qquad (3)$$

where $SD = SP + SG$ denotes domestic savings, and $ID = IP + IG$ denotes domestic investment (gross capital formation).

According to equation (3) it is the sum of domestic investment and export surplus which determines domestic savings SD and not vice versa.

III

We now investigate the role of the export surplus E as an element of aggregate demand in a more detailed way. From the import function:

$$M = Ma + mY \qquad (4)$$

we get the export surplus function as:

$$E = X - Ma - mY \tag{5}$$

where *Ma* and *m* denote autonomous imports and marginal propensity to import, respectively. At the very beginning of the transformation process, foreign trade was abruptly liberalised. As the command economies had previously been to a high degree isolated from the influence of the world market, the rapid liberalisation exhibited their weak competitiveness caused basically by the maladjustment of the structure of aggregate supply (including in this notion the quality of goods as well) to that of aggregate demand. We can formalise the reduced level of competitiveness by increasing in the import function the term *Ma* by ΔMa, where ΔMa has to comprise the effect of the trade liberalisation upon imports, independent of the level of GDP. We thus get from equation (5) a new export surplus function:

$$E' = X - Ma - \Delta Ma - mY, \Delta Ma > 0 \tag{6}$$

What is – in an abstract model – the direct consequence of increasing *Ma* by ΔMa, given *ID* and *X*? For the GDP we have equations:

$$Y = Ca + (cd)Y + ID + X - Ma - mY$$

$$Y = \left[\frac{1}{sd+m}\right](Ca + ID + X - Ma) \tag{7}$$

and

$$\Delta Y = -\left[\frac{1}{sd+m}\right]\Delta Ma \tag{8}$$

where $CD = Ca + (cd)Y$, *sd* and $[1/(sd + m)]$ denote domestic consumption *CD* (consisting of *Ca*, the autonomous part, and *(cd)Y*, the variable part, of domestic consumption), the marginal domestic propensity to save ($sd = 1 - cd$) and the multiplier in an open economy, respectively.[1] The direct consequence of *Ma* increasing by ΔMa is the fall of GDP by ΔY, with $|\Delta Y|$ greater than ΔMa because $0 < (sd + m) < 1$. The related change in imports is

$$\Delta M = \Delta Ma + m\Delta Y$$

which, using equation (8) becomes

$$\Delta M = \Delta Ma - \left[\frac{m}{sd+m}\right]\Delta Ma = \left[\frac{sd}{sd+m}\right]\Delta Ma$$

Hence $\Delta M < \Delta Ma$, that is, the increase in imports is smaller than ΔMa, because the term $[sd/(sd + m)]$ is smaller than 1. Assuming, as we did, that exports remain constant, the change in the export surplus $|\Delta E| = -\Delta E$ is also smaller than ΔMa.

To present graphically in Figure 2.1 the change in GDP provoked by ΔMa, we come back to the equilibrium condition equation (3), which requires

$$SD = ID + E$$

We have for domestic savings SD

$$SD = Y - CD$$
$$SD = -Ca + (sd)Y \qquad (9)$$

with SD as an increasing function of Y. On the other hand, we have for the sum $ID + E$ two expressions, namely, according to equation (6):

$$ID + E = (ID + X - Ma) - mY$$

and, according to equation (7):

$$ID + E' = (ID + X - Ma - \Delta Ma) - mY$$

Both functions are decreasing functions of Y and are drawn in Figure 2.1.

In Figure 2.1 at point A, the $ID + E$ line cuts the SD line and determines the level of GDP equal to Y_0 which finds a market, because at this level $SD = ID + E$. We have drawn, for the sake of simplicity, both functions in such a way that point A lies also on the investment line ID. This means that at Y_0 we have $E_0 = 0$ and domestic savings SD_0 are equal to domestic investment. In other words, absorption corresponding to Y_0 is equal to GDP.

If now the E line is shifted downwards by a distance $-\Delta Ma$, $\Delta Ma > 0$, we get a new line E' which is used in Figure 2.1 to get the line $ID + E'$. The latter cuts the savings function at point D. The new GDP which

Figure 2.1 Import surplus and GDP

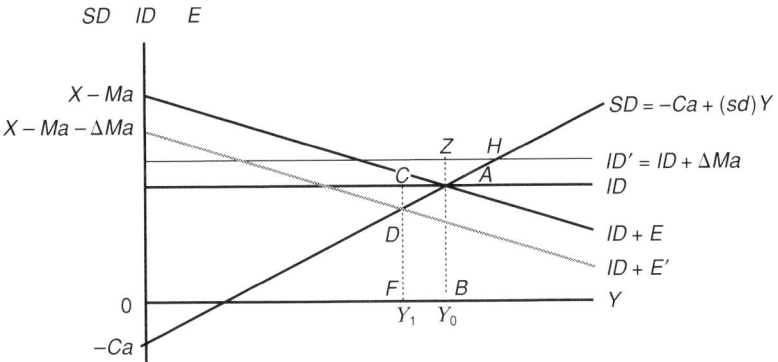

finds a market is Y_1, equal to the abscissa of point D. Thus GDP declines by $\Delta Y = FB$ because of markets lost to foreign competitors.[2] At Y_1 we have $SD_1 = FD$ and at investment $ID = FC$ we get $E'_1 = DC$, $E'_1 < 0$, resulting in $SD_1 = ID + E'_1, E'_1 < 0$. Domestic savings decreased from $SD_0 = BA$ to $SD_1 = FD$ because autonomous imports increased, leading to an import surplus $-E$.

The trade liberalisation in CEECs has been as a rule linked with a strong devaluation of national currencies. This devaluation coupled with a very restrictive wage policy helped to expand exports and prevented an increase of imports for quite a while. Hence, the consequences of the rapid trade liberalisation for the external balances of CEECs were hidden for some time. However, with real appreciation following the initial devaluation, with a less restrictive wage policy and foremost with growth restarting, the weakness of the CEECs' external position has come to the forefront with full force.

IV

At GDP equal to Y_0, absorption (being the sum of domestic consumption and domestic investment) is equal to GDP. Under these conditions, real wealth increases (gross) by ID, while the financial wealth with $E_0 = 0$ remains constant. Hence total wealth at Y_0 increases (gross) by ID. On the other hand, absorption at Y_1 is greater than GDP; indeed investment $ID = FC$ is greater than domestic savings $SD_1 = FD$ corresponding to Y_1, because the export surplus is negative, $E_1 < 0$. We shall investigate the question of financing the import surplus amounting to $-E$ in another place. For the sake

32   Macroeconomic Problems of Trade Liberalisation

of simplicity, we assume here that it can be financed only by drawing on forex reserves. This means, however, that at Y_1 the change of national wealth differs from that at Y_0. Indeed, while at Y_1 real wealth continues to increase (gross) by ID, financial wealth declines by $|E| = -E, E < 0$, resulting in an increase of total wealth by $ID - |\Delta E| < ID$, that is, by a term smaller than domestic investment.

We can see Y_1 as one extreme consequence of $\Delta Ma > 0$ (lower GDP and loss of forex reserves at the same level of domestic investment). As another extreme consequence of $\Delta Ma > 0$ we can treat an increase in domestic investment which would allow for an unchanged GDP at Y_0. In Figure 2.1 we achieve this result by increasing domestic investment from ID to ID', $ID' = ID + \Delta(ID)$, where $\Delta(ID) = \Delta Ma$. In other words, we assume that domestic investment increases by exactly the same amount by which autonomous imports increase, resulting in $ID' + E' = ID + E$. In Figure 2.1 we assume $\Delta(ID) = AZ$. Hence, with an unchanged Y_0, we get $\Delta E = -\Delta Ma$ or $|\Delta E| = \Delta Ma$, which means that $\Delta(ID) = |\Delta E|$, the condition we specified before.[3] It is worth noting that with Y_0 and investment ID' real wealth increases (gross) by $ID + \Delta(ID)$, while financial wealth decreases by $|\Delta E| = -\Delta E$. Total national wealth thus increases by $I + \Delta I - \Delta E = ID$, exactly as was the case at Y_0 and initial domestic investment ID.

If investment happens to be higher than ID but lower than ID' (that is, in terms of Figure 2.1 the savings function is cut at points lying between points H and A), then not only is GDP smaller than Y_0, but the (gross) increase in total wealth is also smaller than initial domestic investment, because it does not compensate the decrease in financial wealth; indeed, $ID + \Delta(ID) - |\Delta E| < ID$, $\Delta ID < |\Delta E|$. On the other hand, if investment happens to reach a level above ID' (that is, in terms of Figure 2.1 the savings line is cut to the right of point H), then the increase in real wealth is larger than the initial domestic investment, because $ID + \Delta(ID) - |\Delta E| > ID$, $\Delta(ID) > |\Delta E|$.[3]

V

Under present conditions in CEECs, the import surplus is the greater, the higher the level of GDP. If we assume that the only method of financing ΔE, $\Delta E < 0$, is the outflow of forex reserves, such a strategy is not sustainable beyond a rather short period. The basic solution to this problem is an upward shift of line $ID' + E'$, which can hardly be achieved as long as the forex reserves are not yet exhausted. Nevertheless, it is useful to analyse the measures necessary to achieve this goal. The term responsible for the required shift of line $ID' + E'$ is the term $X - Ma - \Delta Ma$. It is obvious that a reduction of ΔMa would well serve this purpose, as the whole process has started with an increase in ΔMa provoked by deteriorating competitiveness. Hence an improved competitiveness is the best and only way to alleviate or remove altogether the growth bottleneck constituted by difficulties in foreign trade. Increased competitiveness broadly speaking is also the best and only way to increase exports X, which until now have been assumed to remain constant. Two factors seem to be especially important in this respect: first, investment, and second, a competitive real exchange rate. Investment improves competitiveness indirectly by expanding and modernising infrastructure, including here the development of education and science, and directly by creating new capacity able to increase exports and slow down the increase in imports. A competitive real exchange rate serves the same purpose even more quickly because, given the domestic wage and price level, it facilitates exports and make imports more difficult even at a given production capacity. A competitive real exchange rate is – in the short and also in the medium term – of utmost importance in preventing the import surplus from getting out of control. It should, however, be stressed that the exchange rate can play this role only if the foreign demand for exports and domestic demand for imports are characterised by sufficient price elasticities as stipulated in the Marshall–Lerner condition.[4]

Very often, in the presence of an unsustainable import surplus, a different strategy is suggested; countries are required to increase their domestic savings, mostly through lower budget deficits. This goal should be achieved by cutting government expenditures and/or by higher budget revenues, that is, by increasing government savings. We can formalise the increase in domestic savings by changing the term Ca by $\Delta Ca < 0$ in (7). The direct consequence of this change in terms of GDP is

$$\Delta Y = \left[\frac{1}{sd + m} \right] \Delta Ca, \Delta Ca < 0 \qquad (10)$$

where the fall of GDP, $|\Delta Y| = -\Delta Y, \Delta Y < 0$, is $[1/(sd + m)]$ times higher than the fall of autonomous consumption. The indirect effect of the change in the term Ca is according to equation (6), given X and Ma:

$$\Delta E = -m\Delta Y = -\left[\frac{m}{sd + m} \right] \Delta Ca \qquad (11)$$

Figure 2.2 Two strategies of easing difficulties in foreign trade

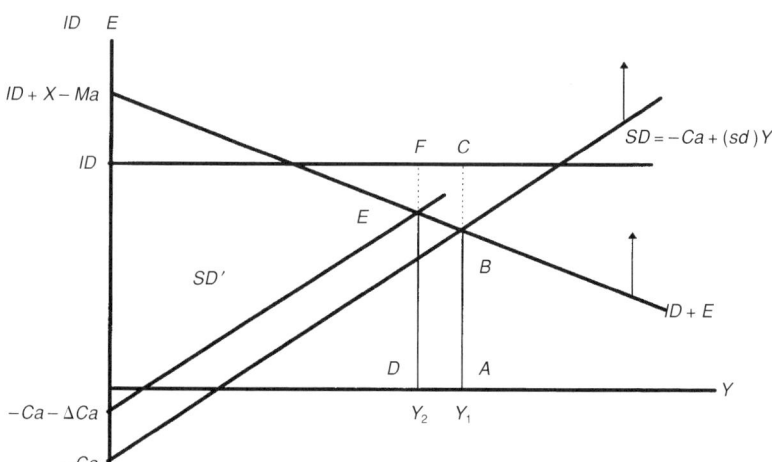

where $\Delta E > 0$. To put it differently, the direct consequence of increased domestic savings is the decline of the GDP, and the indirect one, the improvement in the foreign trade balance, due to reduced imports caused by the fall of GDP.

In Figure 2.2 the savings function SD is shifted upwards (by a distance $-\Delta Ca > 0$) and denoted SD'. The result consists in the decline of GDP from Y_1 to Y_2. At the same time – given domestic investment ID – the import surplus declines from $-E_1 = BC$ to $-E_2 = EF$ and domestic savings increase from $SD_1 = AB$ to $SD_2 = DE$. The improvement in the foreign trade balance is due exclusively to the contraction of GDP and the variable part of imports. A reduction of the trade deficit brought about by the contraction of aggregate demand and income is unlikely to be a sustainable strategy in the longer run – because it means sacrificing the growth potential of the economy indefinitely for a stronger international payment position.

The defensive strategy based on increasing domestic savings in Figure 2.2 is symbolised by an arrow above the line SD. It is confronted with an alternative offensive strategy, aiming at an increase of the term $(X - Ma)$, discussed earlier in this paper. It is symbolised by an arrow above the line $ID + E$. The shift of the line $ID + E$ implies here that E is shifted upwards stronger than ID. In terms of the growth process, an offensive strategy aims at on acceleration of export growth relative to import growth in order to narrow and then altogether abolish the existing deficit in the trade balance and current account. This strategy is often called 'export-led growth'; it should replace the current strategy in CEECs which can be nicknamed 'internal-absorption-led growth'.

CAPITAL INFLOWS

I

The financing of the import surplus is in reality not limited to the reduction of forex reserves. In the past few years the CEECs have experienced, together with rising import surpluses, an increase instead of a decrease of forex reserves. The explanation of this development can be found in the capital part of the balance of payments (BOP). If the capital account overcompensates the current account (of which the balance of trade and nfs is the most important part) then – *pari passu* with a current account deficit – a country would register an increase in forex reserves.

Every capital inflow (here and further we mean net capital inflows) can serve the goal of compensating (or even overcompensating) the current account deficit, but it is useful to differentiate between long- and short-term capital inflows. Indeed, if the capital inflows belong to the first group, we can calculate the 'basic balance' of the BOP in the form 'current account plus long-term capital account' and treat the international payment position of a country as satisfactory when the basic balance is non-negative. The reasoning behind this conclusion is based on the assumption that in the long run, capital inflows may result in balancing the current account itself by promoting export growth and (or) slowing down the import growth. On the other hand, if capital inflows belong to the second group, the 'basic balance' is negative and demonstrates the vulnerability of the payment position of a country because short-term capital inflows have to be repaid very quickly without any effect on increased export capacity.

It seems useful to add two comments to the concept of a non-negative 'basic balance'. First, the international financial community observes rather carefully the balance of trade and the current account of each country. Hence, even if the 'basic balance' is non-negative, the size of the deficit of the current account, especially in relation to exports and GDP, does matter. A current account deficit above 5 per cent of GDP would probably be judged as dangerous in most cases and might slow down or even withhold further capital inflows into the country. Second, the assumption that long-term capital inflows would result in balancing the foreign trade in the future depends on different factors, first of all on an increase in investment in the presence of a lasting import surplus. This goal can be best achieved by an increase in domestic investment $\Delta(ID)$ equal to the increase in the import surplus $|\Delta E| > 0$, $\Delta E < 0$, so that the resulting GDP growth would not be negatively affected by the deterioration of the balance of trade. A slowing down of growth would materialise, however, if the increase in domestic investment were to stay behind the increase in the import surplus. It should also be repeated that the policy of supporting domestic savings does not present a viable alternative to an increase in domestic investment, because it would, given the level of domestic investment, only slow down the GDP growth.

The fact that an increasing import surplus is used mostly for additional investment growth does not guarantee that the strategy would be successful – because the efficiency of investment might be low, especially in terms of overcoming difficulties in balancing foreign trade flows. Hence the described policy may be interpreted as a necessary but not a sufficient condition.

II

Foreign direct investment (FDI) is one of the items of capital inflows, but it differs from other items because it is related to real investment in a special way. This link is direct in the case of 'green-field investment', it is indirect in the case of privatisation of domestic assets by foreign firms if the new owners, as happens in most cases, commit themselves to some additional investment. FDI, both in the form of 'green-field investment' and privatisation of existing assets, also assures as a rule a high technological level of new capacity or modernisation of old capacity, better organisation of production, better management and marketing, and so on. These are the very reasons why FDI is treated as the most important item of capital inflows in the period of transformation. Experience shows that in CEECs it is the privatisation of existing real assets that is the most important form of FDI. However, this type of FDI will sooner or later come to a halt when the privatisation of assets, especially of the economically attractive ones, has been concluded. This circumstance should be taken into account when long-run estimates about future FDI are made.

FDI already plays an important role in modernizing the transformation countries' economies. The CEECs hope that after the eastern enlargement of the EU the inflow of FDI would greatly intensify and help to fill the technological gap existing now between them and even the poorest EU members. Very often, however, FDI is treated as a magic device opening all doors. This applies also to difficulties in foreign trade which, according to expectations, FDI should help to overcome. In reality it is not so clear whether foreign firms act in this direction and whether they themselves do not constitute a part of the problem. Big international corporations are first of all interested in the CEECs' local markets. Of course they export a lot, but they import a lot as well. Being international by their very nature, they import components from outside, and in this sense are import-intensive. An additional factor also plays a role, namely the tendency to charge higher (internal – from the point of view of the corporation) prices if the corporation for some reason intends to show profits rather in another country. This so-called 'overpricing' is almost impossible to check and results in increased import intensity. There exists some evidence that foreign firms as a whole not only do not improve the balance of trade, but may even be responsible for a large part of its deficit.[5] This may also be related to the fact that FDI, as it happens, is frequently engaged in activities with low export intensity (telecommunications, energy, banking and insurance, retail trade).[6] Of course these activities improve the general conditions for business firms, also for those which are directly involved in foreign trade. It seems, however, that the government should actively support these firms by measures which may accelerate export growth and decelerate import growth and not limit itself to a 'wait-and-see' policy. Since measures of this kind will be much more difficult after the CEECs have become members of the EU, they will be well-advised to use the time they still have at their disposal.

One should not expect that a massive inflow of FDI must result in accelerating growth or – at least – in preventing serious breakdowns of production. The example of Spain is quite interesting from this point of view. Spain became a member of the EU in 1986. In the years 1986–95 Spain registered an inflow of FDI amounting to about USD 120 billion, that is an average of about USD 10 billion per year (UNCTAD, 1996, p. 239). If we compare, however, the last three decades in Spain, we note that the highest rate of GDP growth per year, 6 per cent, was registered in 1965–75, while in the years 1976–85 it amounted to only 2 per cent and in 1986–95 it reached a level of 3 per cent. Immediately after joining the EU, in 1986–90, the rate of GDP growth per year was quite impressive, at 4 per cent, but in the period 1991–95 it was only –1 per cent. Hence, Spain approached the average EU level of GDP per capita not after, but before 1986, especially in the years 1965–75. Of course these data do not prove that the inflow of FDI was the cause of this development; it cannot be excluded that without this injection of foreign capital the situation would be even worse. What we wanted to show is only the fact that FDI alone, even at a formidable level, cannot prevent a slowing-down of growth or even a deep economic crisis.

III

A special case of capital inflows in the transformation countries is represented by speculative capital, sometimes called 'hot money'. Foreign financial speculators are interested in two parameters only: the rate of interest and the expected change in the exchange rate. Taking into account these two parameters, speculators estimate the profitability of their investment, first of all in government bonds. In the CEECs the rate of interest is relatively high, because the rate of inflation is high as well. Indeed, the rate of interest must be higher than the rate of growth of consumer prices if the real rate of interest for private households has to be positive. On the other hand, there is a tendency in the CEECs to keep the rate of depreciation of local currencies below the growth rate of producer prices in order to prevent an inflationary pressure arising from costs of imported materials and components. The resulting real appreciation of local currencies is very often treated also as an external brake on nominal wage pressure not justified by an increase of labour productivity in export-oriented sectors of the economy. The appreciation of local currencies in terms of CPI is even stronger because as a rule consumer prices in CEECs actually grow faster than producer prices. All these factors result in a mostly high profitability of foreign financial investment in bonds, which attracts short-term speculative capital looking for quick gains.[7]

The movement of speculative capital is prone to becoming cumulative. The more that speculative capital flows into the country, the greater the demand for the local currency, the stronger the tendency to slow down its depreciation in relation to the rate of inflation, and the greater the incentive to speculate. Also, the more that speculative capital flows into the country, the larger the forex reserves, the greater foreign speculators' confidence in the local currency, and the greater the incentive to speculate. Hence successful speculation leads to even more intensive speculation. There is no simple way to prevent this kind of speculation once the capital market has been liberalised under the conditions of rather high inflation, with growth of consumer prices exceeding that of producer prices. Perhaps the liberalisation of the capital markets in the CEECs was premature. The majority of western countries (for example Austria, France, Italy and the United Kingdom) needed decades after World War II before liberalising their capital markets.

The real danger of speculation lies in the fact that the above-described cumulative movement may develop in the opposite direction, too. When, for whatever reason, the confidence in the local currency is weakening (for example because the deficit of the current account explodes), the inflow of 'hot money' may slow down and be replaced by its outflow when 'hot money' starts to flee the country. The forex reserves diminish and the confidence in the local currency weakens further. In this situation a drastic devaluation of the local currency becomes unavoidable, which in turn may fuel fears regarding further depreciation, resulting in a still stronger outflow of 'hot money'. The panic may infect residents who lose confidence in their own currency and may move their savings into foreign deposits. This can only further destabilise the local money market. The stronger the speculation, the more the confidence in the local currency has been based on a speculative bubble rather than on real economic development, the greater the danger of this scenario.

Excessive foreign capital inflows that are not directly related to the real economy may destabilise the economy. Two reasons are frequently mentioned in this respect: rising inflationary pressures and otherwise not justified increases in the real exchange rates (Ul Haque et al., 1997, pp. 3–6). The first argument – acceleration of inflation – is usually linked to the quantity theory of money, as increased foreign capital inflows compel the central banks to an additional creation of local currencies. The link between the quantity of money and the price level is far from obvious, especially for the short and medium term. However, additional supply of domestic currencies would induce a decline in the rate of interest. If the central bank wanted to counteract this tendency it would have to sterilise the additional supply of money through open market operation. This would restore the previous level of the rate of interest, but at additional costs for the central bank, and – what is more important – it would attract even more foreign capital to the country and the resulting inflow might overwhelm the efforts to reduce the domestic money supply (Rosati, 1997, p. 498). Also the second argument, the increase in the real exchange rate (real appreciation), deserves serious attention. Normally, an increasing real exchange rate is related to surpluses in foreign trade which result from improved productivity and competitiveness. An appreciation of currencies not supported by real factors becomes sooner or later dangerous because it slows down exports and accelerates import growth. Excessive foreign capital inflows are not only exerting a negative influence on the foreign trade performance (through an increased real exchange rate), but at the same time create conditions for the government to tolerate unsustainable disequilibria in foreign trade and the current account and to postpone unpopular measures necessary to adjust related deficits to the real possibilities of the economy.

EXCHANGE RATES, PRICES OF SENSITIVE GOODS AND GDP

I

The (nominal) exchange rate Ne will be defined as the price of a unit of foreign exchange (for example 1 USD, 1 DEM or 1 ATS), expressed in domestic currency units. If domestic and foreign prices were constant (or grew at the same rate), changes in the nominal exchange rate would also mean a real change. But as prices are not constant, a counterpart of the nominal exchange rate is needed in the form of the real exchange rate Re defined as:

$$Re = \frac{(NePf)}{Pd} \qquad (12)$$

where Pf and Pd denote the foreign and the domestic price of a basket of the same goods, respectively. In equation (12) the real exchange rate Re compares the foreign price of a basket of goods, converted into domestic currency $NePf$, with Pd the domestic price of the same basket of goods. It is, in effect, a measure of overall competitiveness (Claassen, 1996, pp. 2 and 9–10). The problem with this measure of competitiveness is the fact that this relation is not easy to obtain (for reasons which are explained further in the text), and Re is therefore not easy to calculate. Nevertheless, we can use equation (12) for measuring changes of competitiveness in time even if we cannot precisely assess the initial level of Re. Indeed, from equation (12) through logarithmic derivation after time we get

$$g(Re) = g(Ne) - [g(Pd) - g(Pf)] \qquad (12a)$$

where $g(i)$ represents the operator for proportional change of the variable i, $i = Re, Ne, Pd, Pf$. Hence the rate of growth of the real exchange rate Re depends on two factors: positively on the rate of growth of the nominal exchange rate Ne, and negatively on the difference between domestic and foreign inflation. More formally:

$$g(Re) \gtreqless 0 \quad \text{if} \quad g(Ne) \gtreqless g(Pd) - g(Pf)$$

That is, the real exchange rate Re remains constant when the rate of growth of the exchange rate Ne equals the difference between domestic and foreign inflation. It is an open question how to measure domestic or foreign inflation. Sometimes the consumer price and sometimes the producer price indices are used, depending on questions for which an answer is being sought. Re increases (decreases) when Ne increases faster (more slowly) than the difference $g(Pd) - g(Pf)$. When the real exchange rate increases, the domestic currency is depreciating (competitiveness increases) and when the real exchange rate decreases, the domestic currency is appreciating (competitiveness decreases). Note, that we can thus find out whether the currency is depreciating or appreciating, even if we cannot say whether the currency is under- or overvalued because without the value of the relation Pd/Pf we have no reference point for Ne.

Although it is not easy to calculate the relation Pd/Pf, it is not an impossible task. We have in two countries two baskets of goods with different qualities and these qualities must be made somehow comparable. But this is not all. The structure of the goods in the basket and the structure of their prices also differ in the two countries. Although a precise answer to the question of the relation Pd/Pf is not possible in these circumstances, an approximate solution can be found and is being found in special research programmes. The results of these research programmes are published periodically, and the relation

Pd/Pf calculated for GDP (or parts of GDP) is called purchasing power parity (PPP). When PPP is available, it is usual to write equation (12) in a slightly different form, interpreting *Re* as a factor by which the nominal exchange rate *Ne* differs from the relation *Pd/Pf* called PPP. This factor is called exchange rate deviation index (ERDI); hence we get:

$$\text{ERDI} = \frac{Ne}{\text{PPP}} \qquad (13)$$

and

$$\frac{1}{\text{ERDI}} = \frac{\text{PPP}}{Ne} \qquad (13a)$$

If ERDI in equation (13) equals 1, then the nominal exchange rate equals PPP. If ERDI is greater (smaller) than 1, we can call the currency undervalued (overvalued) but only if we accept the PPP as a valid reference value for the nominal exchange rate. This implies also the acceptance of the foreign currency in which *Pf* is measured as an appropriate reference value for the domestic currency (for example USD, DEM and so on). It is now generally accepted that ERDIs are rather large in countries with low GDP per capita, and that they decrease along with economic development. On the other hand, empirical data do not support the thesis that nominal exchange rates in developed countries are exactly determined by the PPPs. The term 1/ERDI in equation (13a) tells us by how much the domestic price level is lower (or higher) than the foreign price level when the nominal exchange rate is taken account of. The expression 100 (1/ERDI) shows the domestic price level as a percentage of the price level in the reference country (if for example *Ne* = 3, while PPP = 2, then ERDI is 1.5 and 100 (1/ERDI) = 66.66 means that the domestic price level is 33.33 per cent lower than the price level in the reference country (for example Austria = 100).

II

It is worth taking a look at the development of PPP and *Ne* in Western European countries, especially those being members of the EU. In Table 2.1, panel A we find data about PPP and *Ne* in some Western

Table 2.1 PPP, *Ne* and price levels in selected Western European countries, 1960–90 (national currency units per USD, GDP-based)

	1960			1980			1990		
	(1)	*(2)*	*(3)*	*(1)*	*(2)*	*(3)*	*(1)*	*(2)*	*(3)*
Panel A									
Germany	3.00	4.17	72	2.37	1.82	130	1.84	1.62	114
France	3.50	4.90	71	5.24	4.23	124	5.82	5.45	105
UK	0.23	0.36	64	0.49	0.43	114	0.53	0.56	95
Italy	4.48	6.21	72	7.49	8.56	87	12.51	11.98	104
Belgium	37.1	50.0	74	36.6	29.2	125	34.7	33.4	104
Netherlands	2.38	3.77	63	2.53	1.99	127	1.91	1.82	105
Spain	31.0	60.0	52	63.6	71.7	89	96.4	101.9	95
Panel B									
Germany			100			100			100
France			99			95			94
UK			89			88			83
Italy			100			67			91
Belgium			103			96			91
Netherlands			87			98			92
Spain			72			68			84

Note:

(1) PPP; (2) *Ne*; (3) = $100\left[\dfrac{(1)}{(2)}\right]$.

Source: Turner and Van't dach (1993), p. 75.

European countries based on USD. Because the relation between the USD and the main European currencies changed quite dramatically several times between 1960 and 1990, we have recalculated in panel B the relation between several Western European countries, taking the price level in Germany as 100. Disregarding Spain, we see that over 30 years the differences between these countries were rather limited and did not – with only one exception (Italy in 1980) – go beyond the margin of 17 per cent. As far as Spain is concerned, it started, in 1960, with a price level about 30 per cent lower than that in Germany, and this relation still prevailed after 20 years; only in the 1980s the relative price level in Spain increased, and in 1990 reached 84 per cent of the German level. The appreciation of the Spanish peseta against the

DEM implied by these data (and similarly that of the Italian lira) should be stressed, because in all other countries domestic currencies depreciated against the DEM in this period. On the other hand, we should not forget that both these countries (Spain and Italy) had to depreciate their currencies rather strongly against the DEM after 1990. The case of Spain is interesting for our topic because, first, it concerns a country with a lower GDP per head than the EU average, and second, because the appreciation of the peseta may have been related to the admission of Spain to the EU in the mid-1980s.

III

It seems that, in general, goods markets in Europe are well-integrated. An indication in this direction is the closeness of the exchange rate to the PPPs for tradables in that area. Turner and Van't dach (1993, pp. 78–80) have compared European exchange rates *vis-à-vis* the German mark in 1990 with the ratio *vis-à-vis* the German PPP for 'tradables'[8] and arrived at quite interesting results (see Table 2.2).

Table 2.2 European exchange rates *vis-à-vis* the German mark and PPPs for tradables in 1990

Country	Average exchange rate vis-à-vis the German mark	Ratio vis-à-vis the German PPP for tradables	$100[(3)/(2)]$
Belgium	20.7	19.9	96
Denmark	3.83	4.15	108
France	3.37	3.52	104
Germany	1.00	1.00	100
Greece	98.0	99.0	101
Ireland	0.373	0.356	95
Italy	742	806	109
Netherlands	1.13	1.07	95
Portugal	88.2	85.0	96
Spain	63.1	64.3	102
United Kingdom	0.347	0.331	95
Austria	7.04	6.35	90
Finland	2.37	2.62	111
Norway	3.87	4.83	125
Sweden	3.66	3.47	95
Switzerland	0.86	0.89	103

Source: Turner and Van't dach (1993, p. 81).

We realise that in all EU countries the gap between the exchange rates *vis-à-vis* Germany and their ratios of PPP to Germany was below 10 per cent. This proves that the closeness of the exchange rate to the PPP is much stronger in the case of tradables than in the case of a basket of goods comprising both tradables and non-tradables and that the EU markets are highly-integrated.

IV

The case of the southern EU members (Greece, Portugal and Spain) is of special interest for the present investigation. Their experience seems to support the hypothesis that their price levels tend to approach the average price level inside the EU (EU-10 for 1980 and EU-12 for 1993).

Within 13 years, between 1980 and 1993, the differences in relative price levels between the above three countries and the EU average diminished, and more strongly so in the categories 'food' and 'clothing and footwear' than for the whole GDP (see Table 2.3). This was probably provoked by a slower increase in the relative prices of non-tradables. The relative prices of food increased in Portugal and Spain by about one-quarter to about one-third, but only by about 5 per cent in Greece. The rise in relative prices of clothing and footwear was the strongest: in all three countries they were cheaper than on the EU average by 42 per cent to 16 per cent in 1980, but only by 9 per cent to 1 per cent in 1993. These numbers seem to support the hypothesis that after admission to the EU relative prices of these goods will increase

Table 2.3 Price levels for Greece, Portugal and Spain between 1980 and 1993

	Greece			Portugal			Spain		
	1980	1993	1993–1980[1]	1980	1993	1993–1980[1]	1980	1993	1993–1980[1]
All GDP-based	71	74.1	3.1	54	67.0	13.0	76	84.6	8.6
Food-based	75	80.2	5.2	63	86.1	23.1	74	91	17
Clothing and footwear-based	84	98.8	14.8	58	91.0	33	76	93.4	17.4

Notes:
[1] In percentage points. EU-10 = 100 for 1980 and EU-12 = 100 for 1993.
Sources: Eurostat (1984, p. 72); Eurostat (1995, p. 58).

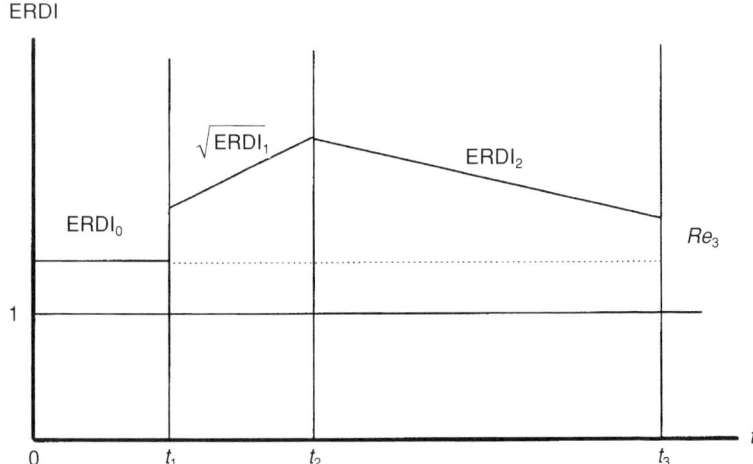

Figure 2.3 ERDIs in CEECs (stylised facts)

in the new member countries as well. This increase would occur additionally to that caused by inflation and the appreciation of the national currencies.

V

It seems that in the CEECs a certain type of development of nominal and real exchange rates can already be discerned. What we have in mind are not facts themselves but stylised facts; these stylised facts do not fully correspond to either country, but at the same time they seem to signal some common pattern of development in most countries.

In Figure 2.3 we denote the exchange rate deviation index corresponding to the nominal exchange rate (used by domestic firms in foreign transactions) before transformation by $ERDI_0$. At time t_1, denoting the start of the transformation, the initial nominal exchange rate Ne_1 was set at a relatively high level, very often above the black market one, and kept constant for quite a while as a nominal anchor for the domestic currency. If we take the time between t_1 and t_2, thought to represent the first phase of the transformation as a whole, the nominal exchange rate Ne increased faster than the domestic price level, resulting in an increase of the exchange rate deviation index represented in Figure 2.3 by $ERDI_1$ (that is, in a depreciation of the domestic currencies). In the second phase of the transformation (the time between t_2 and t_3), the nominal exchange rate increased more slowly than the domestic price level, resulting in an appreciation of the domestic currencies. The development of the exchange rate deviation index in this period is represented by $ERDI_2$. Presently, at time t_3, most countries have an ERDI more or less equal to the initial $ERDI_0$.

As already mentioned, the stylised facts do not correspond exactly to either country.[9] However, in the last years a tendency of appreciation of domestic currencies could be observed in all CEECs. Table 2.4 presents data about the real exchange rates in CEECs. We see that at the beginning of the transformation, real exchange rates increased everywhere, meaning a depreciation of the national currencies. Poland depreciated quite strongly already in 1989, and Hungary practised a policy of competitive real exchange rates even before the transformation process had started. In the last years real exchange rates decreased everywhere, meaning an appreciation of the domestic currencies. Only in Hungary was this trend interrupted in 1994, but already in 1996 it manifested itself anew. In all countries with the exception of Poland the real exchange rate in 1996 was very close to that of the year 1989 irrespective of their exchange rate regime. The Polish case can be explained by the fact that already in 1989 the real exchange rate in Poland was relatively high.

VI

As inflation is much higher in the CEECs than in reference foreign countries (USA, Germany), we make only a small mistake when for

Table 2.4   Real exchange rates in NCU per DEM (PPI deflated)

	Change in per cent against preceding year							Index 1996,
	1990	1991	1992	1993	1994	1995	1996	(1989 = 100)
Czech Republic	38.4	–4.4	–6.0	–10.7	–3.9	–1.3	–7.3	97.6
Hungary	3.8	10.9	1.9	0.6	5.7	6.6	–5.6	99.6
Poland	8.3	–21.2	3.4	–4.9	2.9	–2.2	–5.9	79.4
Slovak Republic	35.3	–3.7	–1.9	–12.2	–2.9	–1.9	–6.0	100.4

Notes: NCU denotes national currency units; minus signs indicate real appreciation.
Source: WIIW database.

the sake of simplicity we assume in equation (12a) constant foreign prices. We then get a simplified formula:

$$g(Re) \cong g(Ne) - g(Pd) \tag{14}$$

and

$$g(Re) \cong 0 \text{ if } g(Ne) \cong g(Pd)$$

Assuming the constancy of foreign prices Pf, the rate of growth of the real exchange rate can also be approximated by the rate of growth of the relation of real wages to nominal wages measured in foreign currency (for example in USD). Indeed, from the real wage rate denoted by $wr = \dfrac{w}{Pd}$, where wr and w denote the real and nominal wage rates respectively, and from the nominal wage rate measured in USD denoted by $w\$ = \dfrac{w}{Ne}$, we get the relation of both:

$$\left(\frac{wr}{w\$}\right) = \left(\frac{w}{Pd}\right)\left(\frac{Ne}{w}\right) = \left(\frac{Ne}{Pd}\right) \tag{15}$$

The logarithmic derivation of equation (15) after time gives:

$$g\left(\frac{wr}{w\$}\right) = g(Ne) - g(Pd) \tag{16}$$

which corresponds to equation (14).

During the transformation, real wages (wr) declined strongly and – except for the Czech Republic – in 1996 were still below their initial level of 1989. At the same time money wages estimated in USD ($w\$$) according to the current nominal rate of exchange showed a very quick rise. This is due to the declining purchasing power of the USD in CEECs because of the appreciation of domestic currencies. In Table 2.5 we find data illustrating this development. Indeed, average monthly wages measured according to the nominal exchange rate in CEECs increased from about 150–200 USD in 1989 to about 250–350 USD in 1996. Over the whole period they increased between 30 per cent and even over 100 per cent. Consequently, the relation $wr/w\$$ declined quite strongly, by an average of about 6 to 14 per cent per year.

Table 2.5 Real wages (CPI-deflated) and USD money wages in CEECs

CEEC	1989	1996
Czech Republic		
wr, 1989 = 100	100	101
$w\$$, in USD	211	356
$w\$$, 1989 = 100	100	169
$wr/w\$$ 1989 = 100	100	60
$g\left(\dfrac{wr}{w\$}\right)$, average per year, in per cent		−7.0
Hungary		
wr, 1989 = 100	100	76
$w\$$, in USD	179	307
$w\$$, 1989 = 100	100	172
$wr/w\$$, 1989 = 100	100	44
$g\left(\dfrac{wr}{w\$}\right)$, average per year, in per cent		−11.1
Poland		
wr, 1989 = 100	100	78
$w\$$, in USD	143	326
$w\$$, 1989 = 100	100	228
$wr/w\$$	100	34
$g\left(\dfrac{wr}{w\$}\right)$, average per year, in per cent		−14.3
Slovak Republic		
wr, 1989 = 100	100	85
$w\$$, in USD	205	266
$w\$$, 1989 = 100	100	130
$wr/w\$$	100	65
$g\left(\dfrac{wr}{w\$}\right)$ average per year in per cent		−6.0

Source: WIIW.

VII

The changes in price levels in CEECs allow for additional information about past developments (see Table 2.6 for the appropriate data). We see that the general price level in CEECs, except for Hungary, amounted to about 25 to 30 per cent of the Austrian level in 1990,

Table 2.6 Price levels (all GDP and ATS based) in CEECs, 1990–95

	1990	1991	1992	1993	1994	1995	1995 (1990 = 100)
Czech Republic	26.6	23.5	26.1	30.1	32.2	33.5	126
Hungary	41.8	47.2	49.2	52.6	52.2	46.6	111
Poland	29.9	41.1	39.9	40.1	39.0	39.4	132
Slovak Republic	28.6	23.1	27.6	30.1	31.2	31.7	111

Note: Austrian price level = 100.
Source: 'Kaufkraft in Ost und West. Österreich im europäischen Wirtschaftsvergleich 1993 (bis 1995)', p. 91.

and decreased in some cases even further at the beginning of the transformation. In the period 1990–95 the general price level increased, reaching 32 to 47 per cent of the Austrian level by 1995. This means that prices in CEECs were still lower by two-thirds to one-half in relation to Austria. It seems that a further development, namely an appreciation of domestic currencies, will continue, but the speed of this development is difficult to predict. Following the case of the southern EU members, access to the EU would greatly accelerate this process in the CEECs as well.

For the years 1990 and 1993 we can calculate price levels also for GDP components. The results are presented in Table 2.7. The prices

Table 2.7 Price levels (all GDP and partial, ATS based) in CEECs, 1990 and 1993

	1990	1993	1990	1993	1990	1993	1990	1993
	Czech Republic[1]		Hungary		Poland		Slovak Republic	
all GDP-based	28.2	30.1	38.1	51.8	26.9	39.8	.	30.9
'machinery & equipment'-based	50.2	85.1	112.5	132.9	50.1	88.3	.	90.9
food-based clothing &	31.0	33.4	46.4	52.4	33.4	44.3	.	33.2
footwear-based	39.4	36.3	57.8	51.8	29.3	47.1	.	36.6

Note: [1]For 1990 CSFR. Austrian price level = 100.
Sources: 'ECP 90, Bilaterale Wirtschaftsvergleiche mit Polen, Ungarn, CSFR, Jugoslawien, Rumänien und Sowjetunion'; 'Wirtschaftsvergleiche mit Österreichs Nachbarländern 1993'; 'Wirtschaftsvergleich Osteuropa 1993'.

for machinery and equipment (used previously as representative of 'tradables'), relatively high already in 1990, increased further and were, except for Hungary, only 15 per cent to 10 per cent below the Austrian level in 1993. In Hungary, prices for machinery and equipment were already higher than in Austria in 1990, and increased further in 1993. But machinery and equipment are much more import-intensive than other 'tradables', hence their price cannot serve as representative for tradables in CEECs.

Also, relative prices of food and clothing and footwear rose, but were lower in 1993 than in Austria by two-thirds to one-half. It is understandable that in this situation tourists from EU countries bordering on a CEEC buy – apart from liquor, cigarettes and services – quite important quantities of so-called sensitive goods (especially food and clothing and footwear) because these are much cheaper than inside the Union. After joining the EU, this unofficial and restricted foreign trade would be substituted by official and liberalised foreign trade and a price arbitrage process would start, leading after some time to more or less similar prices for similar goods as was the case with the southern members of the EU in the past.

VIII

Before we start a macroeconomic analysis of the consequences of the price arbitrage of sensitive goods, we shall make two artificial assumptions to be relaxed at a later stage. First, we assume that price relations between CEECs and EU countries will, at the moment of EU eastern enlargement, be the same as they are now. We assume, further, that outside the sensitive sectors nominal wages do not change spontaneously in the face of an increase in prices of sensitive goods.

The price arbitrage of sensitive goods implies an increase in exports (and in net exports) of food as well as clothing and footwear. In fact, prices would increase if and only if free access to the large EU market were to become a reality. Agricultural goods and food prices would increase because their supply is inelastic (at least in the short run), and increased demand from this market would directly push prices upwards. The immediate impact of this would be an increase in farmers' incomes in the CEECs (and some decline of farmers' incomes in the 'old' EU member countries, because their agricultural price level would somewhat decrease). For clothing and footwear the situation is a bit more complicated, because we assume these prices to be mark-up prices. Given the unit variable costs, these prices should not increase before the capacity level is reached. However, the average price of a commodity group is an important factor for determining the level of the mark-up. Because average prices of clothing and footwear are much higher in the EU than in the CEECs, the mark-up in the latter group of countries would increase and lead to higher prices even at given unit variable costs. The increased profits in these industries would, however, provoke a pressure upon nominal wages because labour would rightly require a share in the increased profitability. If labour were successful in this respect, unit labour costs would increase – we assume, however, that the competitiveness of the discussed industries, though lowered, would still persist.

The implied reduction of the gap between *Pd* and *Pf* means additional inflation and – in comparison with a situation in which this reduction would not take place – an additional appreciation of local currency. But as the discussed increase of the domestic price level applies to sensitive goods only, which previously were relatively cheap in the CEECs, the appreciation of the currency would not impede the competitiveness of all other goods (and nfs) as long as the nominal wages outside the sector producing sensitive goods remain constant. The commodity groups 'food' and 'clothing and footwear' play, however, an important role in total individual expenditure in the CEECs. A share ranging from 28 per cent (Hungary) to 38 per cent (Poland) of total individual expenditure is devoted to these two groups ('Kaufkraft in Ost und West', 1997, p. 80). Hence, an increase in prices in both groups would heavily influence the costs of living for private households getting incomes from sectors other than the sensitive one. It seems reasonable to expect that extra price changes in the CEECs after their admission to the EU will not be limited to sensitive goods. Service prices, as far as they are subsidised beyond margins allowed for by the Union, would have to increase as well. The general cost-of-living increase caused by these factors would require a political choice between two extreme scenarios: either an increase in nominal wages (outside the sensitive sectors) in order to defend the existing real wage level, or a decline of real wages by keeping these nominal wages intact. In the first case the international competitiveness would, *ceteris paribus*, suffer, in the second one the international competitiveness would not suffer, but real wages and consumption out of wages would have to decline. Of course any combination lying between these two extreme scenarios is also feasible.

IX

An investigation of the influence of the increase in the export surplus E is quite simple. From equations (7) and (6), at a given domestic investment ID[10] we get:

$$\Delta Y = \left[\frac{1}{sd+m}\right]\Delta X$$

and

$$\Delta E = \Delta X - m\Delta Y$$

$$\Delta E = -\left[\frac{1-m}{sd+m}\right]\Delta X$$

Hence, the export rise leads to an increase in GDP larger than ΔX, because of the multiplier, and to an increase in the export surplus ΔE smaller than ΔX, because of the endogenous import rise.

The investigation of the consequences of the cost of living increase is more complicated. Let us first assume that the nominal wage rate (outside the sensitive sectors) does not move, hence the real wage rate declines. Under these conditions we do not know what exactly would happen to consumption out of wages and to GDP.[11] In Figure 2.4 the initial situation is represented by point A, in which

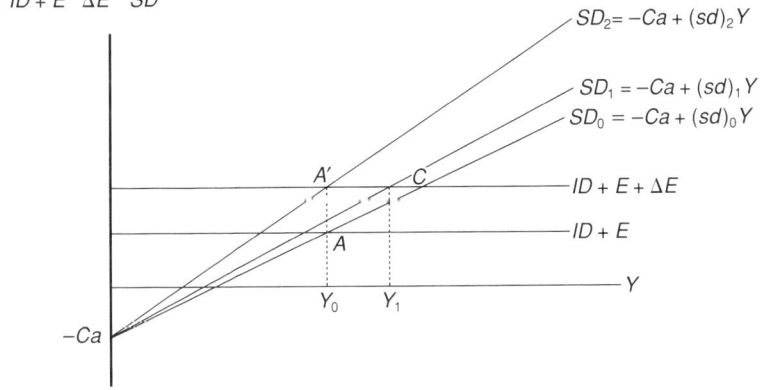

Figure 2.4   Export surplus increase at falling real wage rate

$ID + E$ crosses the savings function SD_0 with the slope $(sd)_0$. Given ΔE, $\Delta E > 0$, point C cannot be reached because the real wage rate falls and the price-wage relation changes. Indeed, as the propensity to save out of profits is higher than out of wages (and that out of undistributed profits is equal to 1), the redistribution of income towards profits would increase the initial (domestic) marginal propensity to save $(sd)_0$. If the new slope of the savings function is represented by $(sd)_1$, the new crossing point between $(ID + E + \Delta E)$ and the savings function SD_1 is A' with consumption *assumed* to be unchanged ($CD_0 = CD_1$ by assumption) and $Y_1 > Y_0$, because savings corresponding to Y_1 are larger than those corresponding to Y_0 ($SD_1 = Y_1'A'$ and $SD_0 = Y_0 A$). If the new marginal propensity to save is represented by $(sd)_2$, the decline in consumption compensates exactly the increase in private savings and GDP remains unchanged. If the new marginal propensity to save is larger than $(sd)_2$, GDP would even have to decline. Hence the volume of GDP cannot under these conditions be unequivocally determined: GDP may still increase, but may also remain constant or even decrease. The latter possibility cannot be excluded because in relation to GDP the export surplus (and its change) is practically small, while consumption out of wages is a rather large part of GDP.

In other words, even small changes in the real wage rate can have large effects upon consumption out of wages and GDP.[12]

So far we have discussed the short-run results. What happens in the longer run depends, however, very much on these short-run results. In particular, if GDP increases, an increase in investment decisions and investment itself in the future should be expected because private savings increase and capacity utilisation improves. If, however, GDP decreases, investment decisions may not increase because higher private savings would be accompanied by lower capacity utilisation. In order to go beyond these general considerations, we would have to run more detailed simulations taking into account empirical data of a given country.

X

The case of the nominal wage rate (outside the sensitive sectors) increasing *pari passu* with the general price level constitutes the second possible scenario. The analysis of the macroeconomic consequences of this policy choice is in general terms rather easy. In

Figure 2.5 Export surplus at given real wage rate

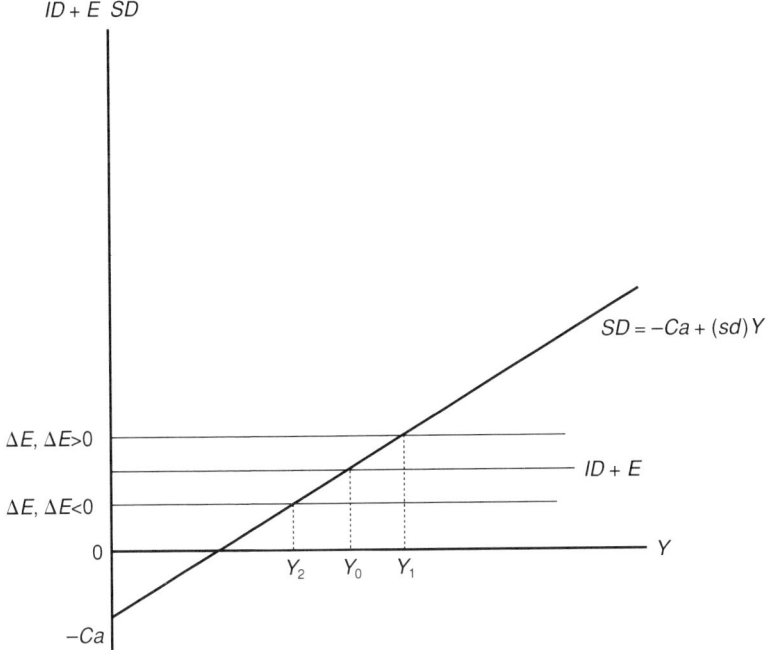

Figure 2.5 the slope of the savings function (sd) is constant, because the price–wage relation has been assumed to remain constant. But an increase of the nominal wage rate and consequently of all prices would have the same result as an additional real appreciation of the domestic currency and would lead to a decrease of the export surplus. Hence, the final result regarding the shift of line $ID + E$ is unknown. If the increase in the export surplus related to price arbitrage is greater than the decrease in the export surplus caused by nominal wage corrections, then the line mentioned above would move upwards and GDP would increase to the level Y_1. In the opposite case, GDP would decline to the level Y_2. These short-term changes would also influence investment decisions and investment in the longer run because changes in savings would go *pari passu* with changes in the utilisation of capacity. Also, here, simulation based on empirical data concerning first of all the price elasticity of foreign demand for exportables of a given country would be required in order to go beyond these general remarks.

XII

Let us come back to the assumptions we made earlier (see section VIII). It seems that sensitive goods prices in CEECs increase faster than in EU countries and, in addition, real appreciation occurs. Hence, the price difference – with respect to sensitive goods – between CEECs and EU countries, as we have analysed before, declines with time. The later the CEECs join the EU, the smaller this difference, and the easier the solution of problems related to the expected price arbitrage. Also the length of the transition period after the EU eastern enlargement would play a similar role.

As far as the nominal wage level outside sensitive sectors is concerned, spontaneous economic forces are also at work limiting the freedom of action of wage policy that we have analysed earlier in the two scenarios. We have already allowed nominal wages in sensitive sectors to increase in the face of price hikes in these sectors. But wage earners also react to changes in the branch structure of wages. Hence, if wages in sensitive sectors increase, employees in other sectors would try to defend their relative position in the sectoral wage structure and require a similar advancement of their wages. The more successful this pressure would be, the more likely the scenario providing for nominal wage increases compensating the price hikes of sensitive goods and leading to losses in competitiveness, and the less likely the other scenario.

Last but not least, the longer the time in which the adaptation to the new price structure takes place, the greater the role of other factors we have so far disregarded. The most important of them is the rise of labour productivity, which creates additional room for nominal wage increases which do not negatively affect unit labour costs and competitiveness. This is another argument against a very quick price adjustment in CEECs in relation to the EU.

XIII

It may seem strange that, when discussing the consequences of an increase in the cost of living upon nominal wages and competitiveness, we did not even mention the exchange rate policy which is quite a natural instrument to be used under similar circumstances. Indeed, let us assume that a compromise solution between the two extreme scenarios has been reached, namely to raise the nominal wage rate by a (for example by 5 per cent) while the increase in the cost of living which would occur at an unchanged nominal wage rate would amount to b (for example 10 per cent). Let us further assume that the increase in the nominal wage rate by a would raise the domestic price level additionally by $0.8a$ (that is by 4 per cent = 0.8×5 per cent); hence the total growth rate of the domestic price level would be $g(Pd) = b + 0.8a$ (for example 10 per cent + 4 per cent = 14 per cent). The real wage rate would change by $g(wr) = g(w) - g(Pd) = a - (b + 0.8a) = 0.2a - b$ (for example by 9 per cent because nominal wages increase by 5 per cent while the costs of living by 14 per cent). The real exchange rate, given Ne and Pf, would change according to equation (13) by $g(Re) = -g(Pd)$ (for example it would decrease – meaning real appreciation – by 14 per cent *pari passu* with the increase of the domestic price level). This appreciation can be traced back partly to price increases of sensitive goods (for example 10 per cent) and partly to price increases following nominal wage rises outside sensitive sectors (for example 4 per cent).

Let us now assume that the nominal exchange rate Ne does not remain constant but increases by $g(Ne) = a$ (that is by 5 per cent) and that the domestic price level would additionally increase by $0.2a$ (for example additionally by 1 per cent resulting in a total price increase by 14 per cent + 1 per cent = 15 per cent). Then the real wage rate would change by $g(wr) = g(w) - g(Pd) = a - (b + a) = -b$ (for example it will decrease by 10 per cent) and the real exchange rate would change by $g(Re) = g(Ne) - g(Pd) = a - (b + a) = -b$ (for example it will decrease also by 10 per cent). We see that with almost the same change of the real wage rate (–10 per cent instead of –9 per cent), the real appreciation of the domestic currency is much smaller (10 per cent against 14 per cent) than in the case of an unchanged Ne.

The increase in the nominal exchange rate *pari passu* with the increase in prices caused by raising the nominal wage rate has two important consequences. First, the competitiveness measured by the real appreciation, at almost the same rate of decline of the real wage rate, suffers much less or even not at all. Second, the probability that the increase in the cost of living caused by the price arbitrage of sensitive goods and the related reduction of the real wage rate would result in a decrease of GDP (because the fall in consumption would more than counterbalance the expansive effect of the increase in the export surplus in sensitive goods) is much lower with a nominal depreciation of the domestic currency than without such depreciation. It should, however, be stressed that the CEECs when joining the EU will most likely be expected to take on the obligation not to depreciate their currencies as a condition of joining Monetary Union at a later date. This is why we disregarded in the main part of our argument the possibility of depreciating the domestic currency when the process of price arbitrage of sensitive goods takes place. Another important conclusion would be to advise the CEECs to try to get, during the negotiations preceding EU eastern enlargement, the Union's approval for pursuing a free nominal exchange rate policy for some time if the consequences of the price arbitrage in sensitive goods would make it necessary – that is, to ask for temporary derogations from obligations implied by European Monetary Union.

XIV

All problems discussed in this chapter have been analysed from a special point of view, namely that of the export surplus (or rather import surplus) and its influence upon aggregate demand and the level of economic activity. In the first part the consequences of rapid trade liberalisation were investigated and basic ways to overcome difficulties in foreign trade were suggested. The necessity of an offensive approach was underlined. In the second part the problem of capital inflows was discussed. Its role in financing the balance of trade and the current account deficit is obvious. However, capital inflows, especially of a speculative nature, may also be a factor destabilising the economy. In the last part of the chapter we have dealt with problems that might arise with respect to prices of sensitive goods and the general price level. The main question here is the increase in the price level and the possible reaction of nominal wages to this change, which in turn may influence the level of aggregate demand and production. Maintaining an autonomous exchange rate policy seems to be one of the CEECs' options to avoid problems related to real appreciation and potential loss of competitiveness at the time of their accession to the EU.

Notes

1. In order to simplify the model we include government consumption CG in the term CD and assume T to be a lump sum tax.
2. It should be stressed that part of the lost output (but only the part corresponding to ΔMa) is no longer saleable under the conditions of a liberalised market economy. We do not discuss (and even disregard) this problem here because it would divert our attention from questions we are really interested in. The author presented his views on this topic in another publication (Laski and Bhaduri, 1997).

3. We have assumed $E_0 = 0$; hence $E'_0 = E_0 + \Delta E = \Delta E$.
4. This condition specifies that the sum of 'price elasticity of foreign demand for exports' and 'price elasticity of domestic demand for imports' (the latter weighted with the initial relation of imports to exports) is larger than 1.
5. According to a report of the Polish Research Institute (IKCHZ), in 1995 foreign firms and firms with foreign capital participation exported USD 7.9 bn, while their imports amounted to USD 12.2 bn. Their import surplus was then about USD 4.3 bn and represented an important part (about 70 per cent) of the total Polish import surplus in 1995 (*Rzeczpospolita*, 29–30 June 1996, p. 8).
6. For a detailed discussion of problems related to FDI see Hunya (1996, pp. 19–21) and Hunya (1997, pp. 275 and 295).
7. Podkaminer (1997, p. 7) estimated quarterly minimum yields on speculative financial investment (US cents per 1 US dollar) taking the interest rate on central bank refinancing credit (or other leading central bank rates) at the beginning of the quarter and correcting them for changes in the exchange rate during the quarter. For the four CEECs and for eight quarters in 1995 and 1996, that is for 32 quarters, he found negative yields (all below 1 cent) for 5 quarters only, and positive yields (sometimes in the range of 10 cents) for 27 quarters. The average for all 32 quarters was 2.8 cents per quarter, that is about 11.2 cents per year.
8. It should be mentioned that the PPP for tradables underlying this calculation is that of 'machinery and equipment' only. This choice has some merits and disadvantages, which cannot be discussed here.
9. A more precise estimation of ERDIs in transformation countries between 1989 and 1995 can be found in Havlik (1996, p. 7, graph 4). These estimates support the presentation of stylised facts in Figure 2.3.
10. Investment in food processing as well as clothing and footwear can increase because of higher profits and better utilisation of resources in these branches, but we disregard this problem here. As far as investment in agriculture is concerned, we assume that EU eastern enlargement would also imply artificial limits on the quantitative expansion of agriculture in CEECs similar to those existing already inside the Union.
11. Here we disregard consumption out of profits and out of income of peasants. Consumption of private households out of profits is determined mostly by their wealth and anyway constitute a small part of total consumption. However, consumption out of peasants' income does play an important role. In simulation, referred to further in the main text, both factors, neglected here, should be taken account of.
12. We would like to illustrate this problem with a numerical example. Let us assume that Y, ID and E are equal to 100, 30 and -5, respectively. Let the marginal propensity to save domestically and the marginal propensity to import be $(sd) = 0.25$ and $m = 0.15$, leading to a multiplier $\left[\dfrac{1}{sd+m}\right] = \left[\dfrac{1}{0.25+0.15}\right] = 2.5$. If now the import surplus declines from

5 to 4, that is by 20 per cent, then $\Delta E = 1$ and $\Delta Y = 2.5(1) = 2.5$. If, on the other hand, consumption amounting at the start to 75 declines as a result of a declining real wage rate only by 5 per cent, the loss of GDP would be $0.05(75) = 3.75$ and would more than compensate the increase of GDP due to the reduction of the import surplus. The result would be a drop in GDP amounting to $\Delta Y = 2.5 - 3.75 = -1.25$.

Bibliography

CLAASSEN, E.-M. *Global Monetary Economy*, Oxford, 1996.
COLLIN, S. M. and PARK, W.-A. 'External Debt and Macroeconomic Performance in South Korea', in J. D. Sachs (ed.), *Developing Country Debt and Economic Performance*, vol. 3, Chicago, 1989.
'ECP 90, Bilaterale Wirtschaftsvergleiche mit Polen, Ungarn, CSFR, Jugoslawien, Rumänien und Sowjetunion', *Statistische Nachrichten*, no. 8, 1990.
EUROSTAT, *Comparison of National Accounts Aggregates Between Austria and the European Community*, Luxembourg, 1984.
EUROSTAT, *Comparison in Real Terms of the Aggregates of ESA. Results for 1992 and 1993*, Luxembourg, 1995.
FALLOWS, J. 'How the World Works', *The Atlantic Monthly*, December 1993, pp. 61–82.
HAVLIK, P. 'Exchange Rates, Competitiveness and Labour Costs in Central and Eastern Europe', *WIIW Research Report*, no. 231, Vienna, October 1996.
HUNYA, G. 'Foreign Direct Investment in Hungary: A Key Element of Economic Modernisation', *WIIW Research Report*, no. 226, Vienna, February 1996.
HUNYA, G. 'Large Privatisation, Restructuring and Foreign Direct Investment', in S. Zecchini (ed.), *Lessons From The Economic Transition. Central and Eastern Europe in the 1990s*, Dordrecht/Boston/London, 1997, pp. 275–300.
AUSTRIAN CENTRAL STATISTICAL OFFICE, 'Kaufkraft in Ost und West. Österreich im europäischen Wirtschaftsvergleich 1993 (bis 1995)', *Beiträge zur Österreichischen Statistik*, no. 1.219, Vienna, 1997.
LASKI, K. and BHADURI, A. 'Lessons to be Drawn from Main Mistakes in the Transition Strategy', in S. Zecchini (ed.), *Lessons From The Economic Transition. Central and Eastern Europe in the 1990s*, Dordrecht/Boston/London, 1997, pp. 103–21.
PODKAMINER, L. *Transition Economies: Overview and Outlook*, The Vienna Institute for Comparative Economic Studies, Vienna, 1997, mimeo.
ROSATI, D. 'Exchange Rate Policies in Post-communist Economies', in S. Zecchini (ed.), *Lessons From The Economic Transition. Central and Eastern Europe in the 1990s*, Dordrecht/Boston/London, 1997, pp. 481–502.
RZECZPOSPOLITA, 29–30 June 1996, p. 8.
SACHS, J. D. (ed.) *Developing Country Debt and the World Economy*, vol. 3, Chicago and London, 1989.

TURNER, P. and VAN'T DACH, J. 'Measuring International Price and Cost Competitiveness', *BIS Economic Paper*, no. 39, Basel, November 1993.
UL HAQUE, N. MATHIESON, D. and S. SHARMA, 'Die Ursachen von Kapitalzuflüssen und politische Reaktionen', in *Finanzierung und Entwicklung, Quarterly Journal of the IMF and The World Bank in cooperation with HWWA – Institute for Economic Research*, Hamburg, March 1997.
UNCTAD, *World Investment Report*, New York, 1996.
'Wirtschaftsvergleiche mit Österreichs Nachbarländern 1993', *Statistische Nachrichten*, no. 9, Wien, 1995.
'Wirtschaftsvergleich Osteuropa 1993', *Statistische Nachrichten*, no. 10, Wien, 1995.
EUROSTAT, 'Vergleich der Aggregate der Volkswirtschaftlichen Gesamtrechnung zwischen Österreich und der Europäischen Gemeinschaft', Bruxelles–Luxembourg, 1984.

3 Non-tradable Goods and Deviations Between Purchasing Power Parities and Exchange Rates: Evidence from the 1990 European Comparison Project

Leon Podkaminer

INTRODUCTION

There is a rich theoretical and empirical literature on the discrepancies between purchasing power parities (PPPs) and exchange rates (see Dornbusch, 1991) for a comprehensive survey. The hypothesis linking persistent discrepancies between PPPs and exchange rates to the presence of relatively cheap non-tradable goods (for example, services) in relatively poorer countries is the oldest (dating back to David Ricardo) and simplest one. Why are services relatively cheaper in poor countries? Contemporary theory tends to attribute this fact to production-side differences. Balassa (1964) and Samuelson (1964) started the tradition of analysis focusing on international labour productivity differentials (tradables vs non-tradables.) Kravis and Lipsey (1983) and Bhagwati (1984) initiated a version of the productivity differential model assuming differential factor endowments and factor rewards. The gist of the argument is that in a poor, labour-abundant country, the relative costs of producing labour-intensive services (non-tradables) are lower than elsewhere.

One problem with the supply-side models explaining the gap is that they do not allow for possible demand-side factors; the demand side tends to be unspecified in these models. There is no way in which the patterns of demand in various countries can affect domestic and international relative prices. Also, the composition of output remains in fact unexplained, although it must have an impact on PPPs (if only because in order to calculate PPPs, it is necessary to average prices with quantities). The key question cannot be answered, to wit: 'if it is true that prices in the service sector are relatively low because of relatively low costs, then why are output and consumption of services disproportionately lower in poor countries'.

Recent studies by De Gregorio, Giovannini and Wolf (1994) and Bergstrand (1991) attempt to explain the PPP–exchange rate gaps by models explicitly incorporating the demand side. Bergstrand assumes non-homothetic tastes, constant-returns-to-scale technologies for both sectors (tradables and non-tradables), full employment and perfect competition. His conclusion (p. 333) is that '... even when differences across countries in capital: labour endowment ratios and levels of productivity in commodities relative to services are accounted for, real per capita income still has a significant positive correlation with relative price levels and outputs'.

The second difficulty with models addressing the PPP–exchange rate deviations is about the treatment of international trade. Trade is assumed to equalise prices of tradable goods (the law of one price). But trade itself is not modelled: actual flows of trade are not considered. Moreover, trade flows *cannot* be meaningfully considered in two-good models with one tradable good. If there is a single tradable good, apparently the same in each country, then Portugal can trade with England (or the rest of the world) 'wine' for ...'wine'. That trade would make sense only if one implicitly assumed that trade is *not* balanced and that there exists yet another commodity, namely internationally accepted fiat money, whose flows counterbalance trade deficits.

The purpose of this chapter is to examine possible behaviour of the PPP–exchange rate gaps when *actual* flows of tradables among countries secure equalisation of relative prices of tradables. To make trade meaningful, the model introduces *three* goods: one non-tradable and two tradables. (Extensions with more tradables and non-tradables are of course possible and welcome.) Trade payments for each country are assumed to be balanced: the value of each country's exports of the first tradable equals the value of imports of the second tradable (both valued with international-market prices). There is no place, explicit or implicit, for fiat monies, whether national or international. Exports and imports are assumed to reflect the forces behind the consumer demand formation in particular countries. Production conditions do not play any role, at least explicitly. It is assumed that domestic endowments (production, or supply) of the three goods are fixed for each country. Countries exchange their fixed endowments of tradables as in neoclassical *general exchange equilibrium* theory. The exchange equilibria stipulate not only the definite reallocation of endowments and equalised relative price of tradables. They also determine the relative *domestic* price of the non-tradable good in any country participating in trade.

Within the proposed framework, one cannot define exchange rates – as there are no monies. It is possible however to approximate the ratios of PPPs and exchange rates, the so-called exchange rate deviation indices, or ERDIs. Indicators approximating the ERDIs are defined in the following section, where data provided by the recent European Comparison Project (for 1990) are used for the calculation of ERDIs proper and their proxies. Following this, a 'didactic' model of free trade between Austria and Hungary indicates that under Cobb–Douglas utility functions for both countries ('calibrated' to fit the actual ECP-1990 data), trade would narrow the PPP/exchange rate gap. However, with an ELES utility function for Hungary, trade would *widen* the gap. Finally, the general exchange equilibrium model for various free trade areas in Europe is specified and analysed on the assumption that consumer behaviour across Europe is governed by almost ideal demand system (AIDS) preferences. The AIDS parameters estimated from the 1990 ECP data are used to specify the model together with the ECP data on actual endowments of European countries. Model solutions indicate that free trade would, as a rule, somewhat narrow the PPP/exchange rate gaps; but in some cases it would *widen* them. Postscript 1 examines the consequences of uniform production growth throughout Europe. It turns out that, in the absence of trade, the gaps would narrow in most cases. Postscript 2 introduces an explicit description of the production side. It turns out that under constant rates of production transformation growth of potential aggregate output must be associated with the demand for non-tradables rising faster than the demand for tradables.

EXCHANGE RATE DEVIATION INDEX: A CONCEPT AND ITS MAGNITUDE

Purchasing power parities (PPPs) are determined within the international comparison projects. The recent European Comparison

Project (ECP) for 1990 provides PPPs for quite detailed categories – and also for some aggregates. Table 3.1 reproduces the ECP's PPPs for almost all of Europe (only Albania and Bulgaria were not covered) for total GDP (column 3) and also for private consumption (column 5). All PPPs are relative to Austria (and so are official exchange rates, reported in column 1). Column 4 contains ERDI (or the exchange rate deviation index) defined as PPP (for all GDP) divided by the exchange rate.

As can be seen, ERDIs are particularly low in former socialist countries – but also in Turkey, Portugal and Greece – all relatively poor. In these countries, the official exchange rates severely underestimate the real value of domestic currencies, and hence real GDP. The opposite happens with all Scandinavian countries and Switzerland. ERDIs are reasonably close to 1 in the remaining West European countries – though in Spain and the UK less so.

ECP does not distinguish between internationally tradable and non-tradable goods. Within private consumption more specific items can still be classified as somewhat tradable, or somewhat non-tradable. The ECP aggregate 'food, drink, tobacco' seems to be a tradable good, and this aggregate will be our first tradable good ('food' in short.) The 'non-tradables' aggregate will consist of the following ECP categories: 'rent and household energy', 'other household goods and services', 'medical care', 'transport and communication, excluding purchases of vehicles', 'recreation, entertainment, education', 'remaining goods and services'. Of course the chosen coverage for 'non-tradables' is necessarily flawed. For instance, some household energy such as electricity is (in Europe) surely exportable. But if we excluded all energy here, we would imply that 'central heating supply' is also exportable. Similarly, within 'medical care' there are both non-exportable services of domestic doctors and hospitals but also consumption of exportable medicines or medical services. The third aggregate of consumer goods consists of all remaining private consumption items (less 'net consumption abroad'). This aggregate is called 'non-food tradables'.

Having calculated, through suitable aggregations, the budget shares of expenditures of our three categories of private consumption for each country, and having calculated relative prices for these categories (against Austria), PPPs for whole private consumption were recomputed. The results are in column 7 of Table 3.1.[1] It is worth noting that on the whole our PPPs for private consumption are almost identical with the ECP's PPPs for private consumption (column 5).[2] Next,

Table 3.1 Exchange rates, PPPs and ERDIs in Europe, 1990

	Per capita income (Austria = 1)	Exchange rate 1AS = …	PPP (all GDP)	ERDI (all GDP)	PPP, all consumption (ECP)	PPP, tradables	PPP, all consumption	ERDI*
Germany	1.115	0.142	0.149	1.046	0.146	0.135	0.146	1.087
France	1.123	0.479	0.471	0.984	0.468	0.476	0.468	0.985
Italy	1.081	105.400	101.184	0.960	97.500	103.838	97.699	0.941
Netherlands	0.949	0.160	0.154	0.963	0.150	0.142	0.150	1.056
Belgium	1.046	2.940	2.811	0.956	2.749	2.838	2.795	0.985
Luxembourg	1.234	2.938	2.826	0.962	2.653	2.654	2.626	0.989
Great Britain	1.112	0.049	0.043	0.868	0.041	0.042	0.041	0.990
Ireland	0.636	0.053	0.049	0.925	0.049	0.052	0.049	0.927
Denmark	1.071	0.544	0.669	1.230	0.689	0.691	0.689	0.997
Greece	0.533	13.950	10.030	0.719	9.650	10.939	9.578	0.876
Spain	0.739	8.955	7.800	0.871	7.730	8.399	7.740	0.922
Portugal	0.607	12.542	7.387	0.589	7.170	9.276	7.226	0.779
Austria	1.000	1.000	1.000	1.000	1.000	1.000	1.000	1.000
Switzerland	1.218	0.122	0.156	1.279	0.158	0.148	0.157	1.062
Finnland	0.962	0.338	0.454	1.344	0.479	0.488	0.479	0.982
Iceland	1.067	5.139	5.894	1.147	6.227	6.686	6.249	0.935
Norway	0.885	0.552	0.683	1.237	0.731	0.755	0.732	0.968
Sweden	1.090	0.522	0.662	1.269	0.671	0.658	0.674	1.024
Turkey	0.282	230.400	107.366	0.466	107.300	134.658	108.134	0.803
Yugoslavia	0.390	0.995	0.646	0.649	0.581	0.823	0.591	0.718

Table 3.1 (Cont'd)

	Per capita income (Austria = 1)	Exchange rate 1AS = ...	PPP (all GDP)	ERDI (all GDP)	PPP, all consumption (ECP)	PPP, tradables	PPP, all consumption	ERDI*
Poland	0.278	835.500	226.421	0.271	202.800	294.839	208.300	0.706
Czechoslovakia	0.504	1.587	0.443	0.279	0.413	0.576	0.424	0.737
Hungary	0.428	5.563	2.125	0.382	1.835	2.644	1.904	0.720
Soviet Union	0.343	0.069	0.038	0.545	0.040	0.061	0.041	0.677
Romania	0.286	1.966	0.773	0.393	0.608	0.796	0.602	0.757

Source: Columns 1–5, 'Europa im Wirtschaftsvergleich', 1993; Columns 6–8, author's calculations.

we computed the PPPs for the consumption of tradables (that is, for consumption consisting of 'food' and 'non-food tradables'. The results are in column 6.

The tradable consumption goods are, by (our) definition, exposed to international trade. PPPs for all tradable consumption may be viewed as proxies for the exchange rate at which trade in consumption goods would, on the margin, be transacted between Austria and any other country.[3]

Of course it would be incorrect to compare our partial PPPs for the consumption of tradables with the official exchange rates directly. The official exchange rate applies to all trade of a country – not only to its trade in private consumption items, but also to trade in investment goods and raw materials. It goes without saying that the exchange rate is also strongly influenced by non-trade factors, such as differences in interest rates, foreign direct investment and other capital flows. What does make some sense is to compare *our* PPPs for all consumption with *our* partial PPPs for tradable consumption. On dividing our PPPs for all consumption by our partial PPPs for consumption of tradables, we arrive at a version of the ERDI – the exchange rate deviation index (column 8). We shall denote our ERDI by ERDI*.

Remarkably, the patterns of divergence from 1 are quite similar for both ERDI and ERDI*. ERDIs and ERDI*s for West European countries deviate in the same direction, the order of the magnitudes is similar. Different patterns of divergence appear in the case of the Scandinavian countries. ERDIs suggest these countries are hugely different from the rest of Western Europe, but ERDI*s suggest they are not different at all. With ERDI*, the UK and Spanish irregularities suggested by the ERDIs vanish. At the same time ERDI*s for the poor countries continue to be quite low – though not as low as the corresponding ERDIs.

FREE TRADE MAY WIDEN THE GAP BETWEEN THE PPP AND THE EXCHANGE RATE: A DIDACTIC EXPOSITION

Following the long tradition of *pure theory of international trade*, we henceforth rule out unbalanced trade and also any trade in non-consumer goods. For any trading nation, the value of exports of 'food' equals the value of its imports of 'non-food tradables'.

ERDI* for a country which has completely free trade with Austria (that is, our reference country) may diverge from 1 even if all tradable goods' relative prices (foreign/Austrian) are the same (and equal to some constant, say 'c'). Partial PPP for the tradable consumption would here exactly equal c. But the PPP for all consumption would equal c by coincidence only. Hence ERDI* need not equal 1 – even under quite ideal conditions.

To see how demanding it is to require that ERDI* = 1, let us examine the following example. Assume the constant c equals 1 (that is, that both tradable goods have the same price in either country, as if measured in a common currency). Partial PPP (our 'exchange rate') equals 1. Moreover, assume that the share of expenditure on 'non-tradables' is the same in either country (and equals, say, r). Under these assumptions, the full PPP (and hence ERDI*) would be equal to the square root of the following expression:

$$\left[\frac{1-r+p_3^i q_3^a}{1-r+p_3^a q_3^i}\right]$$

where p_3^i, q_3^i are respectively price and quantity of non-tradables in country i, p_3^a, q_3^a and the respective price and quantity in the reference country (here, Austria). Quite obviously this expression may deviate from 1 in either direction.

The question to be asked now is whether a complete trade liberalisation – and hence equalisation of relative prices of the tradable goods must bring the ERDI*s closer to 1. (That it need not bring it to 1 we have just seen). Shortly, we shall demonstrate that this need not be the case: free and otherwise 'perfect' trade may, under imaginable conditions, widen the gap between the full PPP and the partial PPP for tradable goods.

We are not going to provide a general theoretical proof that under conventional neoclassical assumptions the presence of non-tradables may result in a growing disparity between the exchange rate and the PPP. Instead, it may be useful to examine in some detail a specific numerical example in which such an event takes place. Our starting point is a 'real-life' comparison of data for Austria and Hungary. As before, we work with our three aggregates of consumer goods derived from the ECP 1990. The real quantities consumed per capita in Austria are shown in line 1 of Table 3.2. (The first entry of line 1 is consumption of 'food', the second of 'non-food tradables', and the third of 'non-tradables'.)

Line 2 of Table 3.2 contains the comparable information for Hungary (with quantities expressed in Austrian schilling). Line 3

Table 3.2 The effects of Austro-Hungarian free trade

	Food	Non-food tradeables	Non-tradeables	Parities all consumption	tradeables
Prior to free trade					
Quantity consumed					
Austria	27.68	44.32	80.86		
Hungary	14.44	10.48	40.56		
Price levels					
Austria	1.00	1.00	1.00		
Hungary	2.50	2.78	1.36		
PPP				1.907	2.645
ERDI*				0.7210	
Under free trade					
Quantity consumed					
Austria	28.16	43.85	80.86		
Hungary	13.96	10.95	40.56		
Price levels					
Austria	0.972	1.00	0.989		
Hungary	0.972	1.00	0.511		
PPP				0.7218	1.00
ERDI*				0.7218	

Source: Own calculations. Data on quantities consumed and price levels (prior to free trade) calculated from 'Europa im Wirtschaftsvergleich', 1993.

contains Austrian respective prices (all equal 1, by construction) and line 4 the respective prices for Hungary (relative to the Austrian prices). As can be seen, relative prices of both tradable goods diverge – which of course may indicate that trade between both countries is not quite free. As such it leaves consumers in either country with less utility than might be otherwise attainable. Line 5 contains the PPP for total consumption (the first entry) and the PPP for tradables (the second entry). ERDI* (the only entry in line 6) is the ratio of the PPPs from line 5.

Before we can analyse the consequences of free trade between both countries, we have to assume in neoclassical manner that the representative Hungarian and Austrian consumers are utility maximisers. They choose the consumption bundles in such a way as to maximise the value of their respective utility functions while respecting their household budget constraints.

Assume the Hungarian consumer 'has' the following Cobb–Douglas utility function:[4]

$$0.2998\log(q_1^h) + 0.2419\log(q_2^h) + 0.4582\log(q_3^h) \tag{1}$$

where log is (natural) logarithm, q_1^h, q_2^h, q_3^h, are the quantities of goods 1, 2, 3 respectively, to be chosen by him (her). The choice is restricted by the consumer's budget constraint:

$$2.5q_1^h + 2.78q_2^h + 1.36q_3^h = 120.40 \tag{2}$$

where 2.5, 2.78, 1.36 are observed prices of goods 1, 2, 3 (see line 4, Table 3.2) and 120.396 is the total observed consumption expenditure. It can be easily verified that the maximisation of equation (1) subject to constraint by equation (2) results in values for q_1^h, q_2^h, q_3^h which were actually observed:[5] $q_1^h = 14.44$, $q_2^h = 10.48$, $q_3^h = 40.56$.

For the Austrian consumer, we assume a numerically different Cobb–Douglas utility function:

$$0.180\log(q_1^a) + 0.2899\log(q_2^a) + 0.5289\log(q_3^a) \tag{3}$$

Since Austrian prices are all 1 (see line 3, Table 3.2), the Austrian consumer's budget constraint is

$$q_1^a + q_2^a + q_3^a = 152.86 \tag{4}$$

Maximisation of equation (3) subject to equation (4) results in numerical values for q_1^a, q_2^a, q_3^a equal to the observed consumption in Austria (line 1, Table 3.2).

Under complete and perfect liberalisation of trade between both countries, Hungarians and Austrians exchange their 'endowments' of tradable goods in such a way as to maximally increase the values of their utility functions. An equilibrium exchange will emerge, with the same relative price p_1/p_2 obtaining in either country.

Let us denote the (yet unknown) equilibrium relative price by p. (In effect p is the equilibrium price of our first good, with the price of our second good equal to 1.) Because the amounts of 'non-tradables' consumed by residents in either country are not affected by the exchange,[6] either consumer's choice boils down to the determination of new values for q^1 and q^2. The Hungarian utility function for this choice has the following form:

$$\frac{0.30}{0.30+0.242}\ln(q_1^h) + \frac{0.242}{0.30+0.242}\ln(q_2^h) \tag{5}$$

while the Austrian utility function is

$$\frac{0.181}{0.181+0.29}\ln(q_1^a) + \frac{0.29}{0.181+0.29}\ln(q_2^a) \qquad (6)$$

Maximisation of equations (5) and (6) are subject to the respective budget constraints– specified with the (yet unknown) equilibrium prices and (yet unknown) total expenditure. What is known, however, is that either total expenditure depends on the common-market value of the initial endowments in both tradable goods held by either consumer. Either consumer can spend on buying, from her partner, only as much as she herself earns from selling what she owns. The Hungarian budget constraint is therefore $pq_1^h + q_2^h = 14.44 + 10.48$ and the Austrian: $pq_1^a + q_2^a = 27.68 + 44.32$.

The Hungarian (per capita) demand for good 1 equals $\frac{0.30}{0.542}\frac{14.44+0.48p}{p}$ and the Austrian (per capita) demand for good 1 equals $\frac{0.181}{0.471}\frac{27.68+44.32p}{p}$. Because total demand for good 1 must be equal to its total supply, the following condition must be satisfied:[7]

$$\frac{0.30}{0.542}\frac{14.44+10.48p}{p} + \frac{0.181}{0.471}\frac{27.68+44.32p}{p} = 14.44 + 27.688 \qquad (7)$$

Equation (7) can be solved for p. It turns out that $p = 0.9723$. This is then the relative price of 'food' (against 'non-food tradables') obtaining in Austro-Hungarian trade, and on both domestic markets. The equilibrium price is associated with slightly altered consumption patterns: Austrians consume a bit more 'food' and a bit less 'non-food tradables', and Hungarians correspondingly more 'non-food tradables' and less 'food'. The post-trade consumptions are in lines 7 and 8 in Table 3.2.

The new structures of prices and new quantities of tradables consumed in either country have to be reflected in the domestic prices of 'non-tradables'. Otherwise the domestic demand for 'non-tradables' may no longer equal its (unchanged) supply. The new price of 'non-tradables', relative to the price of good 2, in Hungary is determined from the following condition:

$$40.56 = \frac{0.4582}{p_3^h}(0.9723)13.96 + 10.95 + p_3^h 40.56)$$

where the factor 0.4582 is taken from the original utility function equation (1) for Hungary, and the numbers 13.96, 10.95 are the post-trade quantities consumed of 'food' and 'non-food tradables'. p_3^h, solving this condition, equals 0.5112. For Austria the condition for p_3^a is the following:

$$80.86 = \frac{0.529}{p_3^a}(0.9723)28.16 + 43.85 + p_3^a 80.86)$$

p_3^a = 0.9894. Equipped with full information on quantities and (relative) prices following free trade between both countries we may now re-compute full and partial PPPs – and the resultant ERDI*. Having done this we can see that free trade has increased ERDI* from 0.7210 to 0.7216. In this case the intuition regarding free trade as diminishing the gap between the exchange rate and PPP is confirmed.[8]

A Case with Free Trade Widening the Gap

Slight changes in the definitions of the utility functions can yield the post-trade ERDI* *lower* than the pre-trade one. Assume, for example, that the Austrian utility function is the same as before but the Hungarian function is now given by the following (ELES) formula:

$$U(q_1, q_2, q_3) = 0.2187 \ln(q_1-5) + 0.2700 \ln(q_2) + 0.5112 \ln(q_3)$$

The parameters appearing in the ELES utility function are so 'calibrated' that its maximisation subject to the Hungarian budget constraint specified with the observed prices and total expenditure yields demand values for our three commodities equal to the observed quantities.

To determine the effects of trade liberalisation we must repeat the procedure described above, applying new parameters for the Hungarian utility function and slightly different formulae for the post-trade consumption and the post-trade prices (in line with the ELES demand functions.) It turns out that the post-trade consumption levels are almost identical to those derived previously. (Post-trade Austrian consumption of 'food' equals 28.09, Hungarian 14.03.) The relative price of the 'food', p, equals 0.9764. Hungarian post-trade relative price of 'non-tradables' p_h^3 equals 0.5079, and the Austrian 0.9909. But the corresponding change in ERDI* goes in the other direction.

The post-trade ERDI* now equals 0.7195, which is less than the pre-trade ERDI* of 0.7210.

It may be important to make two points. First, the increase in the gap between full and partial PPPs following trade liberalisation must be attributed to the presence of non-tradables. If 'non-tradables' were yet another group of tradable goods, then its price (relative to price of 'non-food tradables' would, under trade liberalisation, be the same in both countries. Irrespective of the value of that price, PPP for the entire consumption would then equal 1 (and so would ERDI*). Moreover, trade makes 'non-tradables' in Hungary less expensive relative to the basket of the other two goods. In effect, the post-trade share of 'non-tradables' declines to 0.4560 (from the pre-trade value of 0.4582).

Second, the PPP (and hence ERDI*) value calculated here, are the Fisher-type indices. As such they are not free of their well-known deficiencies. Thus, trade liberalisation resulting in a rising gap between full and partial PPPs may reflect the imperfection of Fisher indices and not the 'actual truth'. Reservations over possible distortions due the nature of Fisher PPPs are of course valid, but as long as the actual practice of international comparisons relies on these (or other, possibly equally imperfect) measures for PPPs one has to perceive them just in these terms. Moreover one cannot rule out divergence of exchange rates and PPP occurring because of trade liberalisation even under ideal conditions, when *exact* PPPs happen to exist.[9]

THE EFFECTS OF TRADE LIBERALISATION IN EUROPE UNDER A CROSS-COUNTRY ALMOST IDEAL DEMAND SYSTEM

The Cross-Country AIDS for the 1990s ECP

Under utility functions of problematic general relevance attributed to Hungarian and Austrian consumers, free trade between Hungary and Austria could, under assumptions specified in the previous section, be expected to narrow, or widen, the gap between the PPP and the exchange rate. More definite conclusions would require application of less arbitrary utility functions. To derive such functions for separate countries one could attempt econometric analyses of relevant, national, time series. Yet, such an approach would be fraught with difficulties. First, for all post-Socialist countries the pre-1990 time series on consumption and prices are worthless for a meaningful econometric demand analysis. Because of endemic shortages and relative-price distortions inherent under the pre-1990 economic systems in Eastern Europe, the data on consumption and prices, even if not purposefully falsified by the authorities,[10] may not reveal actual consumer preferences.[11] Second, the available time series on consumption and prices for the market economies would have to be recalculated in line with the ECP-1990 definitions. No doubt that would be a task all of its own. Third, as a rule the national statistics on relative prices show rather little variation over time. This often makes the estimates of the parameters of the national demand systems derived from the time-series data rather unreliable.

An alternative approach pioneered by Henri Theil assumes the same consumer preferences across countries. Under this assumption (first suggested by Houthakker, 1957, and then maintained by many authors, including Lluch, Powell and Williams, 1977) the data provided by the International Comparison Projects are treated as a cross-section sample of observations and can be directly used for estimation of the *cross-country systems of demand functions* (see Theil and Suhm, 1981, and Theil and Clements, 1987). The approach does not require the recalculation of national statistics. Besides, the ICP data on relative prices and quantities consumed display much more variability than national time series. Theil, Seale and Fiebig (see Theil and Clements, 1987) report the parameter estimates of a cross-country system of demand functions based on data provided by International (UN) Comparison Projects for 1970, 1975 and 1980.

There are three reasons why those estimates cannot be applied in the present study. First, Theil *et al.* had 10 detailed goods, some of them combining both services and commodities to a much greater extent than we do. For example they had 'transport and communications' and 'house furnishings and operations' as single items. Any simple aggregation of their commodities may not yield a usable equivalent to our 'non-food' and 'non-tradables'. Even if this were the case, it is not quite clear how to aggregate their parameter estimates properly. Second, any application of Theil's parameter estimates in the context of the 1990 ECP would require much additional statistical work in order to bridge the 1980 and 1990 national ICP/ECP data for each country. Directly one cannot use their parameters to see how they would perform in explaining the consumption patterns in 1990, even with respect to their 10 goods. Third, the specific form of the system of demand functions adopted by Theil, which possesses many properties desirable from the viewpoints of econometric estimation and interpretation, lacks – as the Rotterdam model does – an identifiable theory of choice background. Although the statistical quality of their parameter estimates seems high and the model is capable of generating plausible price and income elasticities for the samples' observations, it is not clear at all whether it implies consumer behaviour consistent with the utility-maximisation postulate for any configuration of prices and incomes outside the original observations. In particular, one cannot be sure if that model would always imply the existence of an exchange equilibrium if two (or more) countries entered free trade.

It is of course possible to estimate the parameters of a sufficiently flexible utility-based cross-country system of demand functions consistent with our data on prices and quantities for our three goods for 1990. The AIDS, which is an obvious replacement for Theil's system, was chosen for estimation and further analysis.[12]

The AIDS equations have the following form:

$$w_i = a_i + b_i (\log M - \log P) + \Sigma_j c_{ij} \log(p_j) \qquad i = 1 ... n \qquad (8)$$

where n is the number of goods, w_i is the budget share of good i, M is the total per capita expenditure, log is (natural) logarithm, p_j is the price of good j, and P is the price index defined by

$$\log P = \Sigma_k a_k \log(p_k) + 0.5 \Sigma_j \Sigma_k c_{kj} \log(p_k) \log(p_j) \qquad (9)$$

and a_i, b_i, c_{ij} are parameters satisfying the following conditions:

$$\Sigma_i a_i = 1, \quad \Sigma_i b_i = 0, c_{ij} = c_{ji} \text{ for each } i, j, \text{ and } \Sigma_k c_{jk} = 0 \text{ for each } j \qquad (10)$$

Under equations (8)–(10) there are $n - 1$ independent equations. In the three-good case there are two independent equations and seven independent parameters to estimate. The following parameters were selected for estimation: $a_1, a_2, b_1, b_2, c_{11}, c_{12}, c_{22}$. A non-linear full information maximum likelihood (FIML) procedure was applied to the system consisting of equation (8) for 'food' and 'non-food tradables', with the variables for M taken as relative to the Austrian M. The procedure yielded the following parameter estimates (approximate standard errors are in parentheses):

$a_1 = 0.173$ (0.001), $a_2 = 0.265$ (0.001), $b_1 = -0.145$ (0.005),
$b_2 = 0.062$ (0.003)
$c_{11} = 0.135$ (0.006), $c_{12} = -0.095$ (0.003), $c_{22} = 0.165$ (0.003)

Because of equation (10) the remaining parameters take on the following values:

$a_3 = 0.562$, $b_3 = 0.083$, $c_{21} = -0.095$, $c_{13} = c_{31} = -0.04$, $c_{23} = c_{32} = -0.07$, $c_{33} = 0.11$

Due to the relatively small sample[13] and the well-known difficulties inherent in appraising the statistical significance of estimates derived via the non-linear FIML[14] these estimates must be treated as possibly unreliable – despite rather low computed approximate values for their standard errors. There is a relative shortage of published studies concerned with an estimation of the AIDS (or related systems) parameters whose results might be directly used for a comprehensive comparison with our estimates. The situation seems much better only with respect to the b parameter for food. As documented by Clements and Selvanathan (1994), various national studies yield b_1 distributed around –0.15. Theil's cross-country studies based on the ICPs yield b (for food, excluding beverages and tobacco) equal to –0.155 (for 1970), –0.154 (for 1975) and –0.140 (for 1980).[15] The sums of Theil's b parameters for food *and* alcohol and tobacco equal – 0.153, –0.153 and –0.141 respectively, reasonably close to our –0.145. There is less agreement between the sums of Theil's estimates for the a parameters (for food, alcohol and tobacco) and our a_1 (0.173). Theil's sums of parameters for 1979, 1975 and 1980 are 0.197, 0.218 and 0.228 respectively. Bearing in mind that AIDS is not functionally equivalent to the Theil's system, one can perhaps assume that our a_1 is nevertheless plausible. The comparisons between sums of b and a parameters for other goods considered by Theil and ours (for non-food tradables and non-tradables), though shaky on grounds of possibly different coverage, indicate the plausibility of the latter.

Computation of Free Trade Effects under Cross-Country AIDS

Equations (8) imply the following demand functions for q_1, q_2, q_2:

$$q_1 = \left[0.173 - 0.145 \left(\log \frac{M}{M^0} - \log(P) \right) + 0.135 \log(p_1) - 0.095 \log(p_2) - 0.04 \log(p_3) \right] \frac{M}{p_1}$$

$$q_2 = \left[0.265 + 0.062\left(\log\frac{M}{M^0} - \log(P)\right) - 0.095\log(p_1) + 0.165\log(p_2) - 0.07\log(p_3)\right]\frac{M}{p_2}$$

$$q_3 = \left[0.562 + 0.083\left(\log\frac{M}{M^0} - \log(P)\right) - 0.04\log(p_1) - 0.07\log(p_2) + 0.11\log(p_3)\right]\frac{M}{p_3}$$

where M^0 is the per capita nominal expenditure in Austria (the fixed constant) and $\log(P)$ is the log of the price index given by equations (9) specified with our a and c parameter estimates. M is the total expenditure. Hence $M = p_1q_1 + p_2q_2 + p_3q_3$.

Let us assume that K European countries, indexed 1, 2, ..., K, form the free trade area. Let us assume away any impediments to trade in 'food' and 'non-food tradables' including transport costs, and ignore trade with the rest of the world including the left-out European countries. Finally, assume the trade balance of each participant country is zero, that is there are no capital flows and no trade in goods other than the consumption ones. The law of one price makes one expect a single relative price of our two tradable goods to emerge out of trade within the area. Assuming the second good ('non-food tradables') as the numeraire (with its price set at 1), the relative price of the first good ('food') will be denoted as p. The exchange equilibrium does not necessarily equalise the prices of the third good ('non-tradables'). Their values, relative to the price of the second good, may well still vary across countries. These prices will be denoted as π^k, $k = 1, 2, \ldots, K$.

Let q_1^k be the per capita quantity of the first good consumed in country k prior to trade, and q_2^k, q_3^k the quantities of the second and the third good respectively. We identify these quantities with the ECP data on per capita consumption. In effect they represent pre-trade national supplies, or endowments.[16] In equilibrium the sums of supplies of and demands for either tradable good must be equal to each other for the whole free trade area, and the supply of the third good must equal demand for it in each participating country. The following equations must therefore hold:

$$\sum_k s_k q_1^k = \frac{\sum_k s_k \left[0.173 - 0.145 \left(\log \frac{M^k}{M^0} - \log P^k \right) + 0.135 \log(p) - 0.04(\pi^k) \right] M^k}{p} \quad (11)$$

$$\sum_k s_k q_2^k = \sum_k s_k \left[0.265 + 0.062 \left(\log \frac{M^k}{M^0} - \log P^k \right) - 0.095 \log(p) - 0.04(\pi^k) \right] M^k \quad (12)$$

$$q_3^k = \frac{\left[0.562 + 0.083 \left(\log \frac{M^k}{M^0} - \log P^k \right) - 0.04 \log(p) + 0.11 \log(\pi^k) \right] M^k}{\pi^k} \quad (13)$$

with $k = 1, \ldots, K$, where s^k is the population of country k, $M_k = pq_1^k + q_2^k + \pi^k q_3^k$ and $\log(P^k) = 0.173 \log(p) + 0.562 \log(\pi^k)$

$$\frac{[0.135 \log(p)^2 + 0.11 \log(\pi^k)^2 - 0.08 \log(p) \log(\pi^k)]}{2}$$

The system consisting of equations (11)–(13) has $K + 2$ equations and $K + 1$ unknowns: p, π^1, π^2, ..., π^K. One equation, (11) or (12), is superfluous. Unlike the equations of the previous section, the present ones are highly non-linear. Solving the system consisting of equations (11) to (13) is possible only through iterative methods. The convergence of the method used was, in all cases reported below, still very fast.

One general feature of equilibria calculated for various sets of countries forming free trade areas is that they imply rather significant changes in relative prices (post-trade vs pre-trade) in all countries. At the same time volumes of trade, relative to the existing supplies are very small for most countries, in most of the cases.[17]

The Effects of Trade under Various Free-Trade Areas

Table 3.3 summarises the results of equilibrium computations for six free-trade area scenarios:

1. Europe as a whole, including Turkey and the Soviet Union;
2. Europe, excluding Turkey and the Soviet Union;
3. Western Europe;

Table 3.3 Trade effects

	Pre-trade characteristics					Post-trade effects											
	Relative prices		Quantities, relative to Austria			All Europe		Europe-T-SU		Western Europe		EU-12		EU-6		Comecon	
	'Food'	'Non-tradables'	'Food'	'Non-food'	'Nontradables'	Rel. price 'Nontradables'	'Food' demand/supply	Rel. price 'Nontradables'	'Food' demand/supply	Rel. price 'Nontradables'	'Food' demand/supply	Rel. price 'Nontradables'	'Food' demand/supply	Rel. price 'Nontradables'	'Food' demand/supply	Rel. price 'Nontradables'	'Food' demand/supply
Germany	1.006	1.167	1.044	1.180	1.106	1.206	1.013	1.168	1.000	1.165	0.999	1.157	0.996	1.150	0.993		
France	0.940	0.950	1.052	0.992	1.220	1.018	1.023	0.978	1.011	0.974	1.010	0.967	1.007	0.959	1.004		
Italy	0.918	0.862	1.074	0.994	1.130	0.934	1.020	0.896	1.011	0.893	1.010	0.886	1.008	0.879	1.006		
Netherlands	1.042	1.121	0.899	0.896	0.996	1.149	1.004	1.106	0.998	1.103	0.997	1.094	0.995	1.086	0.994		
Belgium	1.002	0.972	0.961	1.047	1.074	1.008	1.008	0.975	1.001	0.972	1.000	0.965	0.998	0.959	0.996		
Luxembourg	0.987	0.975	1.224	1.321	1.190	1.016	1.018	0.982	1.004	0.979	1.002	0.973	0.999	0.966	0.995		
Great Britain	1.051	1.001	0.811	0.967	1.294	1.018	1.005	0.988	0.995	0.985	0.994	0.980	0.991				
Ireland	1.088	0.903	0.695	0.463	0.710	0.911	1.000	0.860	1.001	0.855	1.001	0.845	1.001				
Denmark	1.079	1.025	0.854	0.752	1.320	1.038	1.004	0.990	0.989	0.986	0.987	0.977	0.984				
Greece	0.939	0.724	0.971	0.405	0.454	0.820	1.002	0.764	1.001	0.759	1.000	0.749	1.000				
Spain	0.922	0.825	0.832	0.674	0.743	0.902	0.995	0.861	0.998	0.858	0.998	0.850	0.998				
Portugal	0.919	0.566	0.816	0.445	0.624	0.641	0.996	0.602	0.998	0.599	0.998	0.591	0.998				
Austria	1.000	1.000	1.000	1.000	1.000	1.042	1.007	1.003	1.001	1.000	1.000						
Switzerland	1.294	1.248	1.259	0.934	1.360	1.125	0.968	1.067	0.949	1.062	0.947						
Finland	1.305	1.081	0.790	0.810	1.104	0.999	0.993	0.962	0.989	0.959	0.988						
Iceland	1.455	1.032	0.952	1.004	1.140	0.906	0.986	0.875	0.979	0.872	0.979						
Norway	1.399	1.092	0.797	0.746	0.992	0.961	0.995	0.922	0.993	0.919	0.993						
Sweden	1.414	1.194	0.792	1.042	1.218	1.093	0.987	1.066	0.978	1.064	0.977						
Turkey	0.953	0.622	0.368	0.206	0.295	0.692	0.978										
Yugoslavia	0.902	0.461	0.499	0.277	0.415	0.530	0.977	0.497	0.986							0.429	1.004
Poland	0.937	0.459	0.397	0.147	0.308	0.537	0.997	0.492	0.998							0.500	0.997
Czechoslovakia	0.823	0.481	0.659	0.318	0.553	0.598	0.990	0.557	0.991							0.476	1.002
Hungary	0.897	0.487	0.522	0.236	0.502	0.580	0.995	0.536	0.996							0.387	0.999
Soviet Union	0.856	0.382	0.488	0.207	0.368	0.470	0.983										
Romania	1.054	0.547	0.467	0.188	0.277	0.569	0.998	0.527	1.003							0.467	1.014
International price of 'food'						1.103		1.008		1.000		0.982		0.963		0.870	

Source: Own calculations. Columns 1–5 are derived from 'Europa im Wirtschaftsvergleich' 1993. All prices are relative to 'non-food tradeables.' Quantities (columns 4–5) are per capita. 'Food demand/supply' (columns 7, 9, 11, 13, 15, 17) is the ratio of post- to pre-trade consumption of 'food'.

4. EU-12, the 12 EU (European Union) countries, as of 1990;
5. EU-6, the long-standing 'core' members of the EU: France, Italy, Germany, Benelux); and
6. Comecon, the former Socialist countries excluding Yugoslavia.

Information from Table 3.3 allows computation of the post-trade ERDI*s for our six scenarios. The resultant values are shown in Table 3.4. Before we comment on Table 3.4 it may be worthwhile remarking on the trade effects elicited in Table 3.3, and there are four interesting points:

1. Although trade somewhat narrows the gaps between prices of 'non-tradables' (relative to 'non-food tradables') in poor and rich countries, prices of 'non-tradables' still remain high in affluent countries and low in poor countries. Relative to 'food' the gaps between prices of 'non-tradables' in rich and poor countries tend to increase, with 'non-tradables' becoming even cheaper in the poor countries *vis-à-vis* the rich ones.
2. The broader the territorial scope of the free-trade area the greater reallocation of existing endowments. Trades of individual West European countries are the highest when all Europe, including Turkey and the Soviet Union, are free-trade partners. The trades decline with the narrowing of the free-trade area. This seems to indicate that Western Europe has indeed been quite well integrated. Apparently the endowments (domestic consumption) of tradables are much less in need of being reallocated among the West European countries.
3. The broader the scope of the free-trade area, the higher the price of 'food' (relative to 'non-food tradables'). At the same time the relative domestic prices of 'non-tradables' in individual countries also tend to be positively related to the scope of the area.
4. Scenario 1 indicates that the reallocation of endowments under all-Europe free trade would imply exports of 'food' from Eastern Europe, Scandinavia, Spain and Portugal to Western Europe. Under scenario 2, Eastern Europe (with the exception of Romania), Scandinavia, Spain and Portugal would still exchange some 'food' for the other good with the remaining Western Europe.

As can be seen from Table 3.4, free trade does not necessarily result in ERDI*s differing from 1 *less* than the pre-trade ones. In scenario 1 the

Table 3.4 Post-trade ERDI*s

	Pre-trade	Pre- and post-trade ERDI*s in Europe under various free-trade scenarios						ERDI*s under different rates in domestic supplies of change (g)		
		Post-trade scenarios						Post-change		
		1	2	3	4	5	6	g = 0.01	g = 0.05	g = 0.10
Germany	1.087	1.083	1.086	1.087	1.071	1.073		1.085	1.073	1.062
France	0.985	0.099	0.986	0.986	0.970	0.971		0.984	0.980	0.975
Italy	0.941	0.944	0.942	0.942	0.927	0.928		0.941	0.940	0.940
Netherlands	1.056	1.056	1.055	1.056	1.040	1.040		1.056	1.055	1.051
Belgium	0.985	0.983	0.985	0.985	0.970	0.972		0.983	0.975	0.970
Luxembourg	0.989	0.987	0.989	0.989	0.974	0.976		0.988	0.982	0.975
Great Britain	0.990	0.987	0.991	0.992	0.977			0.985	0.964	0.945
Ireland	0.927	0.930	0.920	0.919	0.902			0.950	0.966	0.969
Denmark	0.997	0.998	0.992	0.992	0.975			0.996	0.989	0.979
Greece	0.876	0.896	0.883	0.882	0.864			0.908	0.957	0.988
Spain	0.922	0.929	0.925	0.924	0.909			0.915	0.985	0.985
Portugal	0.779	0.791	0.785	0.985	0.770			0.772	0.855	0.868
Austria	1.000	1.000	1.000	1.000				1.000	1.000	1.000
Switzerland	1.062	1.045	1.036	1.035				1.066	1.079	1.088
Finland	0.982	0.977	0.977	0.977				0.984	0.982	0.972

Table 3.4 (Cont'd)

Pre- and post-trade ERDI*s in Europe under various free-trade scenarios

	Pre-trade	Post-trade scenarios						ERDI*s under different rates in domestic supplies of change (g) Post-change		
		1	2	3	4	5	6	g = 0.01	g = 0.05	g = 0.10
Iceland	0.935	0.925	0.930	0.930				0.936	0.938	0.933
Norway	0.968	0.957	0.955	0.955				0.973	0.976	0.971
Sweden	1.024	1.028	1.035	1.036				1.019	1.005	0.985
Turkey	0.803	0.819	**0.792**	**0.786**				0.803	0.950	0.934
Yugoslavia	0.718	0.732	0.724	**0.685**				0.718	0.846	0.840
Poland	0.706	0.731	0.715	**0.684**				0.704	0.770	0.782
Czechoslovakia	0.737	0.764	0.753	**0.675**			0.645	0.734	0.832	0.839
Hungary	0.720	0.746	0.733	**0.684**			0.689	0.717	0.790	0.801
Soviet Union	0.677	0.700	**0.620**	**0.629**			0.665	0.677	0.790	0.792
Romania	0.757	0.765	0.753	**0.771**			0.627	0.756	0.841	0.849
							0.684			

Note: All ERDI*s are against Austria. For empty places in columns for scenarios 4, 5, 6 ERDI*s are same as pre-trade (column 1). Numbers in bold print in columns for scenarios 2 and 3 are ERDI*s for countries excluded from free-trade with the remaining ones.

Source: Author's calculations.

84   *Non-tradable Goods, PPPs and Exchange Rates*

gap between exchange rate and PPP is increased, as compared with Austria, for six out of 24 countries. The choice of the reference country does not significantly affect this conclusion. Interestingly, all 'diverging' countries belong to the affluent ones (Belgium, Luxembourg, UK, Finland , Iceland and Norway).

In scenario 2 there are five 'diverging' free-trade participants (all affluent.) The poor countries excluded from free trade (Soviet Union and Turkey) also 'diverge'. The same outcome obtains in scenario 3 (five affluent participating countries and all seven poor non-participating countries 'diverge'). In scenarios 4 and 5 all countries except Germany diverge against Austria which is excluded from free trade.[18] Finally, if the former Comecon countries formed a free-trade area (scenario 6) they would all 'diverge' quite radically.

The conclusions following the findings reported in Tables 3.3 and 3.4 must of course be viewed as tentative. Still, we are willing to risk a statement that free trade need not reduce the gap between exchange rates and PPPs – even if trade brings about equalisation of relative prices of tradables across the countries involved. Under equalised relative prices of tradables and the corresponding trade flows, the domestic prices of non-tradables may change in such a way that the ratios of PPPs to the exchange rates (or ratios of prices of nontradables to prices of tradables) would actually diverge for some countries.

Of course the equalisation of relative prices of tradables happening without any actual trade being conducted, and without that trade having any effect on the domestic prices of non-tradables (which is implicitly assumed in the traditional literature) would have to narrow the gap. But it is rather hard to understand the mechanism of price equalisation without actual trade taking place. One would have to assume that domestic suppliers of various goods consult their pricing decisions (which are over *absolute*, *nominal* values) so that the *relative* prices for the whole economy emulated the foreign, or international *relative* ones. Even then there would be a problem: unless changes in prices were properly coordinated with changes in domestic supplies, prices could not be changed at will without possibly disturbing the equilibrium in the domestic market.

Persistence of the PPP/exchange rate gaps in a poor country entering free trade with an affluent one would seem to have serious policy implications. An examination of these implications is best conducted if one observes that such countries actually can have a common currency and, for most practical economic reasons, can be considered a single new state.[19] Assume it is the affluent (and much larger) country whose money becomes the common legal tender (as was the case with German unification). Unless there is a sufficient rise in labour productivity in the poor part of the new state, it would seem that its wages should be sufficiently lower. Otherwise the production costs there would be too high and massive unemployment would follow. Depressing wages, however, implies a fall in purchasing power, and in living standards. Yet, a poor country need not experience a lower PPP/exchange rate gap. This applies to our unified country. One unit of the same currency would still have different purchasing power in either of its parts. (Incidentally, this is the case with most existing countries consisting of regions with different per capita income levels.) Non-tradables may become *cheaper* in the poor part, relative to the basket of tradables. Wages may stay low without a fall in living standards – even if prices of tradables become the same in both parts. The German post-unification wage policy stipulating convergence of East German wages to the West German levels, well in excess of what was justified by labour productivity differentials, resulted in a collapse of most East German manufacturing and farming (and possibly unnecessarily high prices of services there as well). But that policy may have been unnecessary for protecting East German living standards. In any case free trade between *representative* consumers of any two countries should always make *both* better off, even without a part of the income of the rich one being transferred to the poor one by way of subsidies. That of course does not imply that under free trade no *individual* consumer would be exempt from suffering.

The results given in Table 3.4 allow formulation of some tentative hypotheses regarding the persistence of the exchange rate–PPP gaps.

1. Since World War II, there has been a tendency toward the liberalisation of foreign trade, but this need not have been conducive to the *convergence* of exchange rates and PPPs.[20]
2. Formation of free trade areas consisting of relatively affluent countries, which was not uncommon, was likely to increase the gaps between exchange rates and PPPs for the relatively poor ones.
3. Formation of freer-trade areas by poorer countries (which often feel discriminated by the affluent ones) may have definitely increased their gaps – even if the affluent countries actually did not form free-trade areas.

POSTSCRIPT 1: GROWTH MAY BE CAPABLE OF REDUCING THE EXCHANGE RATE–PPP GAPS

Relatively small PPP/exchange rate gaps for more affluent countries indicate that catching-up in income levels may be reducing the gaps. Poor countries do not have to fear, or hope for, disappearance of the gaps just because of liberalisation of trade with the affluent ones. The gaps may be expected to diminish quite automatically if these countries grow faster than the affluent ones. If free trade helps to speed growth, then of course trade would, if indirectly, accelerate the narrowing of the gaps.

The intuition asserting faster growth in poorer countries to be a powerful factor behind an eventual narrowing of the PPP/exchange rate gaps seems quite correct, if perhaps requiring further studies. The analytical framework developed in the last section may also be applied to an examination of the effects of *uniform growth* across European countries. More specifically, let us assume the per capita supplies of each of our three goods is increased by a factor $(1 + g)$, in each country. To focus attention on growth effects themselves, let us ignore foreign trade (and equalisation of relative prices of tradables). Our assumption now is that all growing supply is consumed domestically. Correspondingly, total per capita consumption (and expenditure) increases, in conventionally understood real terms, by 100g per cent everywhere. Of course relative prices clearing the domestic market will have to be changing together with growing supplies, possibly differently in various countries. Only with the Cobb–Douglas utility function the relative prices would not be affected by the magnitude of the rate of change. Quite certainly it is rather unrealistic to expect uniform growth in the supplies of our three goods, anywhere, at least for larger g. The uniform expansion path may be far from optimal. Resources used to sustain such a path might be used differently to generate supplies' growth following a possibly non-linear trajectory along which the value of the utility function will be close to maximal.

Admitting that there is an element of fiction in assuming uniform expansion paths, one can perhaps ask how such a development would affect our ERDI*s for small growth rates. With our cross-country AIDS we can calculate relative domestic prices in each country for different values of g, and the corresponding ERDI*s. The results are shown in Table 3.4 (columns 8–10). As can be seen, even under a 1 per cent rate of change the gaps would narrow in some countries.

Under 5 per cent this would be the case with all poor countries and most of the rich ones.

It is interesting to note that the narrowing takes place *without* the poor countries actually catching up, as far as per capita real income is concerned, with Austria. Absolute differences in per capita real consumption among countries are rising (while their relative positions are constant throughout the exercise). Because of a possible bias due to the rigid structure of changing supply assumed here, it is difficult to claim that growth in poor countries reduces the PPP/exchange rate gaps even if their relative position is unchanged. But such a claim certainly deserves further research.

POSTSCRIPT 2: WHY IS DEMAND FOR SERVICES LOW IN POOR COUNTRIES?

The traditional question is 'why are services cheaper in poor countries?' The traditional answer is that in poor countries services are, for technological reasons (or because of the structure of factor endowments), relatively cheap to produce. An alternative answer is yet possible: services in poor countries are cheaper because at lower income level the demand for them is relatively weak. Of course the second answer does not necessarily render the first one empirically false. Both answers may be right at the same time, though one of them may in fact be superfluous. The present Postscript may not be the right place to discuss the issue thoroughly, but it may be worth seeing some admittedly simplified argument in favour of the alternative answer.

Let us consider a country with a linear production possibilities frontier. Without any loss of generality, let us assume that the rates of production transformation are all 1 so the production possibilities frontier is of the following form:

$$q_1 + q_2 + q_3 = Y \qquad (14)$$

where q_i are (efficient) levels of per capita production of our three goods and Y is the aggregate per capita output the economy can produce (as determined by its productive resources). Unit production costs are all equal, let us say $(1 + m)^{-1}$ where m is the (uniform) mark-up on costs. The non-substitution theorem applies: here prices are all equal to 1 irrespectively of the consumer demand. But quantities demanded of our three goods would be different. According to our

AIDS formula, these quantities are given by the following expressions:[21]

$$q_1^d = Y[\ 0.173 - 0.145 \log(Y)]$$
$$q_2^d = Y[0.265 + 0.062 \log(Y)] \qquad (15)$$
$$q_3^d = Y[0.562 + 0.082 \log(Y)]$$

Let us assume the economy is growing: the set of production possibilities expands. Suppose the rates of production transformation remain at unity (that is, *relative costs are unchanged*). Equations (15) then apply, with Y being variable, and they indicate that the demand for our second and third good would also be rising. Because of a negative coefficient (–0.145) in the formula for q_1^d, the demand for 'food' could actually *decline*, at a sufficiently high level of Y. It is important that the demand for non-tradables would *always* rise faster than the *aggregate* demand for tradables:

$$\frac{q_3^d}{q_2^d + q_1^d} = \frac{0.562 + 0.082 \log(Y)}{0.438 - 0.082 \log(Y)} \qquad (16)$$

The derivative of the ratio on the left hand side of equation (16) with respect to Y is always positive. The higher the value of Y, the higher the demand for services relative to that for commodities. Under such conditions, slight modifications of the production conditions, making services even relatively *cheaper* to produce, would be unlikely to affect relative prices in favour of commodities. The opposite would be more likely. Stronger relative prices of services could be expected even if growth was associated with costs of services *falling* relative to costs of commodities. A rise in mark-up in the service sector would be one possible consequence of such a situation. And, in due time, there would be higher *wage claims* in that sector. If successful, the wage push would *adjust costs to prices*. Statistics could then indicate that services indeed tend to be relatively more expensive to produce in more affluent countries. But *causation* would be different from that traditionally proposed: prices of services would *not* be relatively low in poor countries *because of* relatively low wages in the service sector. *Wages* would be lower because of lower prices.

Conclusions

Gaps between PPPs and exchange rates reflecting the presence of non-tradable goods may, at least directly, have little to do with differences in relative labour productivity or factor endowments among nations. Under strictly neoclassical assumptions on international trade and consumer behaviour, trade need not narrow the gaps even if the law of one price holds. International exchange of tradables may change relative prices of domestic non-tradables in such a way as to actually increase the gaps. Our analysis assuming cross-country AIDS preferences over three goods ('food', 'non-food tradables' and 'non-tradables') with parameters derived from data provided by the 1990 European Comparison Project, indicates that pan-European free trade would, in some cases, even widen the gaps. The analysis also indicates that in absence of trade, growth in lower-income countries may be reducing the gaps even if the relative real income position of these countries is unchanged *vis-à-vis* the rich ones. Finally, as per capita income rises, the demand for services may become stronger relative to the demand for commodities. This may explain why services are cheaper in low-income countries.

Notes

1. The ECP's PPPs are (multilateralised) Fisher-type price indices, with prices of countries in question, relative to Austrian prices, weighted by expenditure shares.
2. Our and ECP's PPPs for private consumption could have diverged more evidently. First, because of various underlying aggregation levels. Second, because ECP's PPPs are multilateralised (through the EKS method) whereas ours are bilateral (vs Austria).
3. Actual trade among European countries is far from being free. All European countries practice elaborate protectionism. Besides, there are transport costs, information is imperfect, the market is not perfectly competitive, and price discrimination at the international level certainly exists. Henceforth all such imperfections are assumed away.
4. In applied general equilibrium models of foreign trade, it is sometimes assumed that consumers in different countries have the same preferences. This is acceptable provided the utility function is 'flexible' to allow for non-linear Engel effects and realistic substitution effects. It is wrong to presume that the same inflexible utility function (such as Cobb–Douglas or ELES) adequately represents preferences of consumers at widely different real income levels. It is acceptable to use numerically different C–D or ELES utility functions. Each such function could be viewed as a local approximation of the proper one.
5. The solutions are given by a very simple formula. If total expenditure is M, the ith price is p_i and is the factor by which the logarithm of q_i (in equation (1)) is multiplied is b_i, then one $q_i = b_i = M/p_i$. Thus, for instance, $q_1^h = 0.30\ 120.4/2.5$.

6. This assumption is marginally unrealistic, as any visitor of the Austro-Hungarian border must know. Cheap Hungarian services are not shipped to Austria – instead the Austrians invade Hungarian border towns in search of dental and other services (some of which have never been included in any statistics anywhere).
7. For simplicity we assume that Hungary and Austria are equally populous. This saves us the weighting of per capita supplies and demands with the population numbers.
8. Because the PPP calculations presented in Table 3.2 assume 'neo-classical' representative consumers in both countries, each endowed with a C–D (hence homothetic) utility function, it might seem that the exact (Konüs) PPPs should be calculated here, and not the Fisher ones. As is known (see Diewert, 1991) Fisher-type PPPs are exact only for the homogeneous quadratic utility functions. However, the two C–D functions are specified with different parameters. Existence of exact (Konüs) PPPs is not obvious here.
9. Free trade in the presence of non-tradables may have different effects on ERDI*s even if ideal PPPs exist.
10. Throughout 1990 shortages of consumer goods and services in Poland, Hungary and Czechoslovakia were already something of the past. But they were still a reality in the Soviet Union and Romania.
11. See Podkaminer, 1982 and 1988; Collier, 1986 and 1989 for the discussion of the problem.
12. AIDS was formulated by Deaton and Muellbauer, 1980. AIDS and Theil's system share many features. When there is no price variation (as in cross-section analyses of national household surveys data) both systems boil down to the same Working (1943) model.
13. Our sample consists of 25 countries. Final estimation made use of data for 23 countries. Greece and Turkey were excluded because they spoiled the fit. These two countries may differ in consumer tastes from the rest. Turkey may be different on account of its different climate and views on alcohol consumption. Quality of national statistics may have played a role, as well as distortions inherent in the ECP aggregation methods. ECP data for the Soviet Union and Romania seem wrong: they indicate higher living standards than in Poland. This is hard to believe. Falsification of Romanian and Soviet data does not surface in the estimation. Their *statistics* conform to the presumed pan-European patterns. A similar observation was made about the 1980 ECP data (see Podkaminer, Theil and Finke 1984).
14. See Chapter 3 in Theil and Clements, 1987.
15. See 'Epilogue' in Theil and Clements, 1987. Their estimation with pooled ICP results (combining data for 1970, 1975, 1980) yielded b for food equal -0.140 and for tobacco and beverages equal -0.01.
16. Unknown fractions of quantities are already present as imports from 'the rest of the world'. In the case of internationalised EU countries these fractions may be large. Calculation of exchange equilibria makes sense all the same. The equilibria represent effects of free re-trading of

quantities, parts of which were traded or consumed under less ideal conditions (for example transportation costs).

17. In many cases trades are lower than the residual values for the pre-trade supplies implied by the estimated demand functions. This poses a question: should one relate a change in consumption to the actual pre-trade consumption, or rather to the theoretical one, that is computed according to the estimated demand function? The problem would be of little importance if trades were large vs residuals. The problem was 'solved' by the assumption that demand functions for individual countries do *differ*, if insignificantly. It was assumed that each country's demand functions for the 1st and 3rd good equal the estimated demand function *plus the country-specific residuals for the 1st and 3rd good*. The modified demand function for the 2nd good equals the estimated demand function minus the expression $\dfrac{(r_1 p_1 + r_3 + p_3)}{p_2}$ where r_1, r_3 are the residuals for the 1st and 3rd goods. The modified system is consistent with utility-maximisation and can be derived from a slightly modified AIDS utility function. The results reported below allow for the modification. Equilibrium prices equate demand with actual, not theoretical, supplies.

18. About half of countries participating in free trade (scenarios 4 and 5) 'diverge' in terms of ERDI*s recalculated against Germany.

19. The common currency does not pre-empt different economic performance and policies. This is best exemplified by Belgium and Luxembourg – both using the same currency (Belgian). Belgian public debt/GDP is 133 per cent, Luxembourg's only 8 per cent.

20. Improving transportation technologies and falling transport costs must have had similar effects to trade liberalisation. Forty-five or even 35 years ago most goods were locally produced and consumed. It was not even uncommon for supplies of beer or dairy products to be hauled from producers to retailers on horse carriages. Nowadays almost everywhere in Europe the consumer can purchase foreign beer or yoghurt, manufactured hundreds of miles away.

21. Because all prices are now set at unity, all price-elasticity effects operating in the original AIDS formula through logarithms of prices now vanish.

Bibliography

BALASSA, B. 'The Purchasing-Power Doctrine: A Reappraisal', *Journal of Political Economy*, vol. 72, 1964, pp. 584–96.

BERGSTRAND, J. 'Structural Determinants of Real Exchange Rates and National Price Levels: Some Empirical Evidence', *American Economic Journal*, vol. 81, 1991, pp. 325–4.

BHAGWATI, J. 'Why Services Are Cheaper in Poor Countries?', *Economic Journal*, vol. 94, June 1984, pp. 279–86.

CLEMENTS, K. W. and SELVANATHAN, S. 'Understanding Consumption Patterns', *Empirical Economics*, vol. 19, 1994, pp. 69–100.

COLLIER, I. L. 'Effective Purchasing Power in a Quantity-Constrained Economy: An Estimate for the German Democratic Republic', *Review of Economics and Statistics*, vol. 68, 1986, pp. 24–32.

COLLIER, I. L. 'The Measurement and Interpretation of Real Consumption and Purchasing Power Parity for a Quantity-Constrained Economy: The Case of East and West Germany', *Economica*, vol. 56, 1989, pp. 109–20.

DEATON, A. S. and MUELLBAUER, J. 'An Almost Ideal Demand System', *American Economic Review*, vol. 70, 1980, pp. 312–26.

DE GREGORIO, J., GIOVANNINI, A. and WOLF, H. C. 'International Evidence on Tradables and Nontradables Inflation', *European Economic Review*, vol. 38, 1994, pp. 1225–43.

DIEWERT, W. E. 'Index Numbers', in J. Eatwell, M. Milgate and P. Newman (eds), *The New Palgrave: A Dictionary of Economics*, Vol. 2, London, Macmillan, 1991, pp. 767–80.

DORNBUSCH, R. 'Purchasing Power Parity', in J. Eatwell, M. Milgate and P. Newman (eds), *The New Palgrave: A Dictionary of Economics*, Vol. 3, London, Macmillan, 1991, pp. 1075–85.

AUSTRIAN CENTRAL STATISTICAL OFFICE, 'Europa im Wirtschaftsvergleich', *Kaufkraft in West und Ost*, Vienna, Austrian Governmental Printing Office, 1993.

HOUTHAKKER, H. S. 'An International Comparison of Household Expenditure Patterns, Commemorating the Century of Engel's Law,' *Econometrica*, vol. 25, 1957, pp. 523–51.

KRAVIS, I. and LIPSEY, R. *Toward an Explanation of National Price Levels*, Princeton Studies in International Finance no. 52, Princeton: Princeton University Press, 1983.

LLUCH, C., POWELL, A. A. and WILLIAMS, R. A. *Patterns in Household Demand and Saving*, Oxford, Oxford University Press, 1977.

PODKAMINER, L. 'Estimates of Disequilibria in Poland's Consumer Markets, 1965–1978', *Review of Economics and Statistics*, vol. 64, 1982, pp. 423–31.

PODKAMINER, L. (1988), 'Disequilibrium in Poland's Consumer Markets: Further Evidence on Intermarket Spillovers', *Journal of Comparative Economics*, vol. 12, 1988, pp. 43–60.

PODKAMINER, L. THEIL, H. and FINKE, R. 'Cross-Country Demand Functions and Centrally Planned Economies', *Economics Letters*, vol. 16, 1984, pp. 269–74.

SAMUELSON, P. A. 'Theoretical Notes on Trade Problems', *Review of Economics and Statistics*, vol. 46, 1964, pp. 145–54.

THEIL, H. and CLEMENTS, K. W. *Applied Demand Analysis: Results from System-Wide Approaches*, Cambridge Mass., Ballinger Publishing Company, 1987.

THEIL, H. and SUHM, F. E. *International Consumption Comparisons: A System-Wide Approach*, Amsterdam: North Holland Publishing Company, 1981.

WORKING, H. 'Statistical Laws of Family Expenditure', *Journal of the American Statistical Association*, vol. 38, 1943, pp. 43–56.

II

Exchange Rate Systems, Capital and Transfer Inflows

4 Real Exchange Rates and Growth after the EU Accession: The Problems of Transfer and Capital Inflow Absorption

Witold M. Orlowski

INTRODUCTION

The EU enlargement to the East is probably one of the biggest challenges that Europe will have to face during the next 5–10 years. Ten potential future member states represent more than 100 million consumers. Although the GDP produced in these countries accounts today only for a small fraction of the EU GDP, the future growth potential remains indisputable. This has already been demonstrated in the dynamic growth of trade between the EU and Central and Eastern European countries (CEECs), albeit from a very modest initial level. Last but not least, the eastern enlargement may be seen in a broad historic sense as a re-unification of two parts of Europe once divided by the iron curtain, a re-unification that should promote stability, security and prosperity throughout Europe.

At the same time, however, several serious problems arise:

- Firstly, CEECs are still in the transformation process towards market economies. The transformation and stabilisation is well advanced in some of them, while the others are still vulnerable to powerful shocks and far from the state of an effective macroeconomic control (as the latest Bulgarian crisis shows). In this chapter we argue that an effective macroeconomic policy is crucial for exploiting the benefits of EU integration.
- Secondly, the scale of financial burden connected with the eastern enlargement may create a huge obstacle to the process or, at least, an incentive to slow it down significantly. Why is the West so afraid of the East? The main role is played by relatively

recent experiences gained during the EU integration of three Mediterranean countries (MC-3), particularly during the 1990s, and by the traumatising experience of the German unification. In our view, such an approach is wrong. The German case had its special features that are not likely to appear in CEECs joining the EU (in the first place, the gigantic real appreciation of the domestic currency and fall of competitiveness due to the exchange rate set for monetary union (Siebert, Schmieding, Nunnenkamp, 1992)). As far as MC-3 are concerned, the argument is sometimes used that the per capita scale of transfers received by these countries creates the lowest possible transfer needed by CEECs (Courchene *et al.*, 1993).[1] In this chapter we argue that the role of official transfers is not as obvious as it is generally assumed. The marginal utility of transfers is continuously falling, and after reaching the level that exceeds absorptive capacities the marginal utility may even become negative (that is, transfers may become counter-productive). Therefore, the problem with CEECs is to search for an optimal rather than maximal scale of transfers.

- Thirdly, the level of development of CEECs is very low in comparison with the EU. This remark concerns both the GDP level[2] and living standards. In this chapter we argue that exploiting the EU integration for acceleration of the balanced GDP growth is the main target for CEECs. On the other hand, the temptation to rapidly increase consumption levels rather than investment (a possibility that appears together with large transfers) will be very strong, and may result in a failure of the integration process.

DOES EU ACCESSION HELP TO ACCELERATE GROWTH?

We will try to answer questions concerning possible macroeconomic problems of the EU accession of CEECs looking at the experience of MC-3, and try to assess similarities and differences between the situation of these two groups of countries.

Let us start by noticing that the MC-3 experience shows that the growth benefits resulting from EU accession can not be taken for granted (see Figure 4.1[3]). Although Spain and Portugal recorded growth rates higher than Germany over the first 6 years of accession, the accumulated growth differentials started to fall after having absorbed the initial medium-term growth effect.[4]

Figure 4.1 Cumulated GDP growth differentials against Germany after the accession of the MC-3 countries (per cent points)

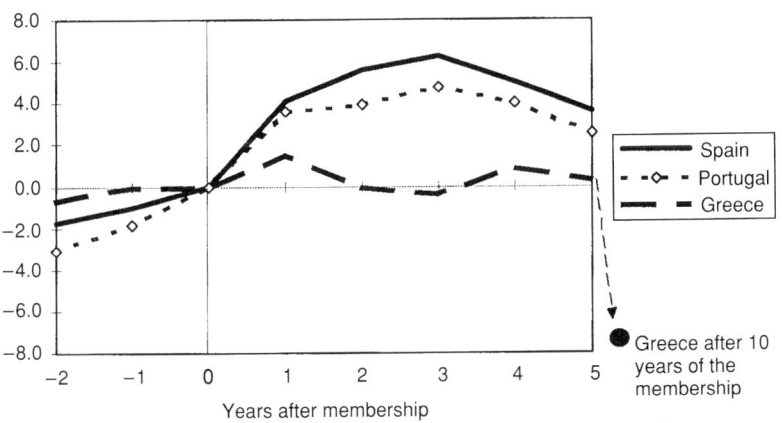

Source: Author's calculations based on IMF data.

Unfortunately, the phenomenon of accelerated growth was not experienced by Greece. During the first six years of their membership, development in Greece was not faster than the German case. The real catastrophe came during the following years, when Greece lost almost 8 per cent of the accumulated growth differentials instead of the long-term growth benefits and convergence that should be expected on the basis of the economic theory (Baldwin, 1994; Barro and Sala-I-Martin, 1995). Incidentally, the period between the sixth and tenth years of Greek membership is exactly the same as the period of the first, quite successful, years of Spanish and Portuguese membership.

Common wisdom tends to link the economic success of relatively poor countries that joined the EU with the scale of development assistance received mainly in form of transfers from the EU. The total scale of transfers, however, happens to be negatively correlated with the performance of MC-3. The lowest official transfers, hardly reaching 1 per cent of GDP in 1990 (on a net basis) were received by Spain. Portugal, performing a bit worse, received about 2 per cent of GDP in transfers. But Greece, the worst performer, got the highest transfers (exceeding 3 per cent of GDP by 1986, and growing to over 5 per cent in 1990, Figure 4.1). During the early 1990s the scale of transfers was still growing (mainly due to successful bargaining during the process of negotiations of major EU reforms), with virtually no effect on growth.

Thus, a widespread myth about the beneficial role played by EU transfers does not necessarily fit with reality. On the other hand, such a result may be astonishing. The EU transfers increase savings which the economy may use for financing growth. Moreover, they allow for the accelerated imports of modern technologies, and therefore should result in higher growth rates (Lee, 1994). Common sense suggests that the effect of the transfers can only be beneficiary. If it is not always the case, the question arises why?

INFLOWS OF TRANSFERS AND CAPITAL, AND CHANGES IN THE REAL EXCHANGE RATE

The first point is that receiving EU transfers is not the only way of mobilising foreign saving after joining the EU. If the transfers are not high enough, one can always seek private sources of capital. Improved access to the EU market, and good development prospects of the domestic market create a strong incentive for foreign direct investment (FDI). The relatively low cost of labour creates an incentive for locating exports-oriented production in the new member states, while the large scale of incomes and of the domestic market favours inward-oriented investment instead. It is obvious that CEECs, after joining the EU, can strongly benefit particularly from the first type of FDI, as well as from the other forms of increased private capital inflows.

Figure 4.2 shows that both Spain and Portugal were much more efficient in attracting private capital than Greece. The reasons may be found both in a more stable and reliable macroeconomic policy of both Iberian countries, and with a much more investment-friendly environment.[5] As we will show later, the inflow of foreign saving was also fuelled by yield differentials due to the exchange rate policy.

One should also point at the difference, from the point of view of growth, between the main forms of private capital flows. FDI undoubtedly represents the most desirable type of inflow, both from the point of view of efficiency (FDI is normally connected with the transfer of managerial and organisational know-how, new technologies, and so on) and security of the balance of payments. Both portfolio investment and foreign credits are much less welcome from both points of view.

Private capital, if attracted, can very well substitute for the lower transfers in the short and medium run. Of course, in the long run

Figure 4.2

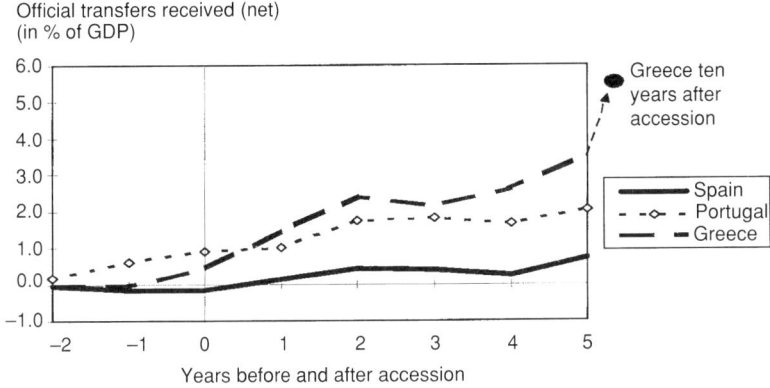

Source: Author's calculations based on IMF data.

the inflow of private capital leads to increased transfer of capital income abroad. Nevertheless, there is little doubt that private capital inflows, if properly used, can exert a positive long-term effect on growth, particularly in a country with a relative scarcity of capital. On the other hand, one can not exclude that the excessive scale of transfers may lead to the well-known crowding-out effects pushing private investors out of the market, and discouraging foreign investors.

The second point is that the increased inflow of foreign saving (both transfers, and private capital) normally leads to real exchange rate appreciation. It means that the stream of foreign exchange flowing into the country grows rapidly. Figure 4.4 shows the total of transfers and private direct and portfolio investment received after joining the EU by MC-3. A particularly strong increase was experienced by Spain. The increase in Portugal was more gradual, but steady and equally impressive if related to the size of the economy. Only Greece, unable to attract private capital and relying only on EU transfers did not experience the surge in foreign savings – not until the scale of transfers started to grow rapidly in the late 1980s.

The increased inflows must somehow be absorbed by the economies. If the supply of foreign exchange starts to grow, reserves start to grow, and the balance of payments must change to accommodate the increase. The natural reaction of markets to such a situation is a pressure to lower the price of the foreign currency, that is to increase the real exchange rate of the domestic currency. Such a reaction was

Figure 4.3 Capital inflows and the curent account for MC-3 countries before and after accession

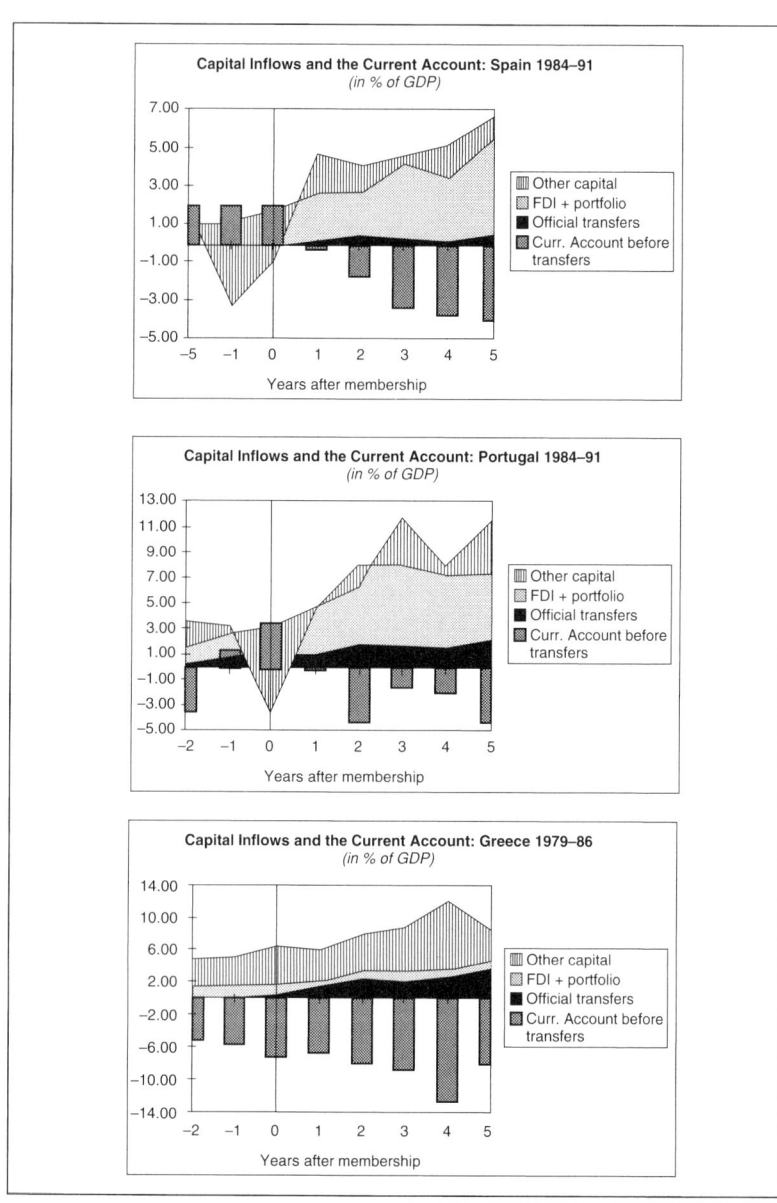

Source: Author's calculation based on IMF data.

Figure 4.4 Increased inflows of transfers and private investment to the MC-3 countries before and after accession

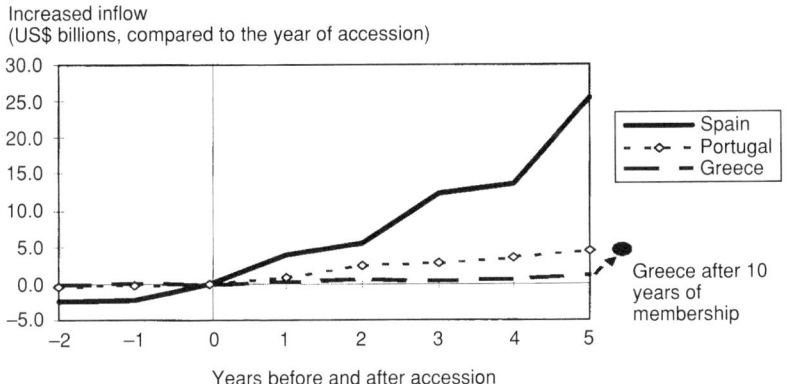

Source: Author's calculations based on IMF data.

observed in both Iberian countries and, during the first two years of EU membership, in Greece (Figure 4.4). It is only in the second half of the 1980s, after the growth of EU transfers, that Greece started to experience the same real appreciation effects again (official transfers received by Greece increased from 0 to USD 1 billion by 1985, and then grew four times as large during the next five years). Given that even modest (from the EU point of view) transfers, accompanied by private capital inflow, will most probably represent a significant share of GDP in a CEEC, and of the balance of payments turnover, one may expect a significant real exchange rate appreciation after CEECs join the EU.

The third point is that the real appreciation of currencies due to the surge in EU transfers and FDI leads to increased yields for the foreign portfolio investors. Increased portfolio investment adds to the capital inflow and eventually leads to further appreciation. The reason for this phenomenon is quite simple: MC-3 joined the EU with inflation rates, and therefore nominal interest rates, much higher than in the EU countries. The nominal devaluation was significantly slowed down, or even stopped; however, the inflation and interest rates differentials remained high. To be sure, the fall of inflation followed real appreciation, but with a considerable lag, that was mainly due to non-tradable inflation.[6] As a result, yields on domestic currency-denominated papers dramatically increased both in Spain and Portugal (in Greece the same phenomenon was

Figure 4.5   Real exchange rate development for MC-3 countries before and after accession

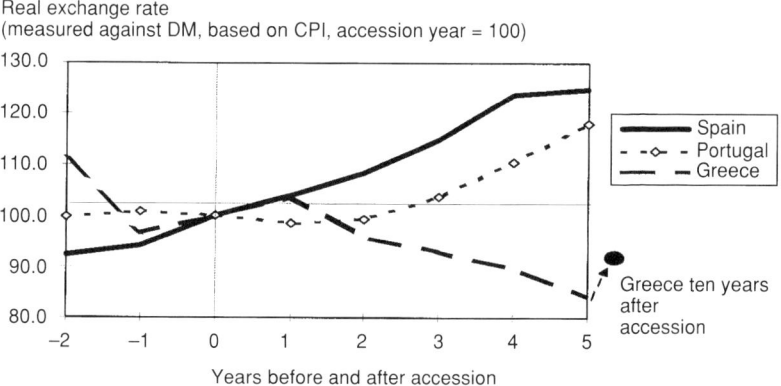

Source: Author's calculations based on IMF data.

observed only during the late 1980s, Figure 4.6). As non-tradable inflation is likely to be quite high in CEECs during the next several years (mainly due to the low level of prices of services), one may expect significant inflation rates and interest rate differentials between CEECs and the EU, leading to similar effects of increased portfolio investment, particularly after the reduction of the investment risk after accession to the EU.

The fourth point is that real exchange rate appreciation leads to lower competitiveness, and therefore to a rapid increase of imports, a slowdown of exports, and to the significant deterioration of the current account before official transfers.

The MC-3 experienced significant real appreciation either during the first years of membership or, in the case of Greece, in the period of increasing EU transfers. There is little doubt that the trade creation effects, as well as the new investment and productivity growth helped to reduce the negative effects of a stronger currency on the dynamics of exports (in MC-3 the volume of exports grew by 30–50 per cent during the period of real appreciation). However, the surge in the volume of imports was much stronger, reaching from 75 per cent in Greece to 90 per cent in Spain. Therefore, the trade deficits and current account deficits before official transfers grew rapidly, particularly in the case of Spain (deterioration of the Portuguese current account deficit was similar if related to GDP, by about 6 per cent of GDP until 1991; in the

Figure 4.6 Yields on T-bonds for Greece before and after accession

Yields on T-bonds in DM terms

[Chart showing yields from year -2 to 5 for Spain, Portugal, Greece, with a marker for "Greece ten years after accession"]

Years before and after accession

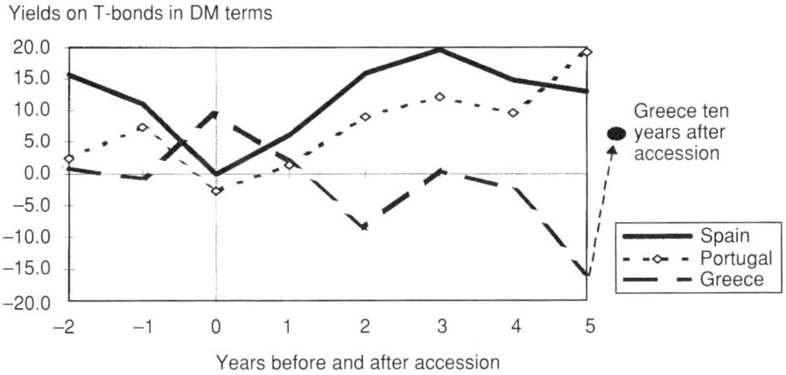

Source: Author's calculations based on IMF data.

Greek case the number was much smaller). Figure 4.7 shows the scale of the current account changes experienced by MC-3.

A similar effect, possibly smaller in absolute terms but bigger in relation to GDP, is likely to take place in CEECs (currently growing deficits of the most successful CEECs, particularly Poland, the Czech Republic, and Slovakia, suggest that the elasticity of imports with respect to the real exchange rate appreciation is very strong).

The fifth and final point is that, albeit we do not treat the trade and current account deficit as an evil, an inappropriate macroeconomic policy accompanying big deficits may lead to negative long-term growth effects. We call these 'the generalised Dutch disease'. The 'Dutch disease', as described in macroeconomics, is normally linked to the rapid improvement in terms of trade or appearance of new sources of export income, traditionally, the analysis concerns the booming natural resources sector, for example gas or petroleum exports.[7] The increased export revenue leads to real appreciation of the currency, and therefore increases production costs, lowers competitiveness and eventually hurts manufacturing exports. The evil, however, is not the higher imports and lower exports of manufactured goods: if properly used, the increased imports may be spent on accelerated imports of capital goods, and therefore may well serve long-term growth. The real problems appear when the increased revenues and, consequently, imports are used for supporting consumption (both personal, and government consumption; in the classical example of the Netherlands,

Figure 4.7 Change in MC-3 current accounts before and after accession

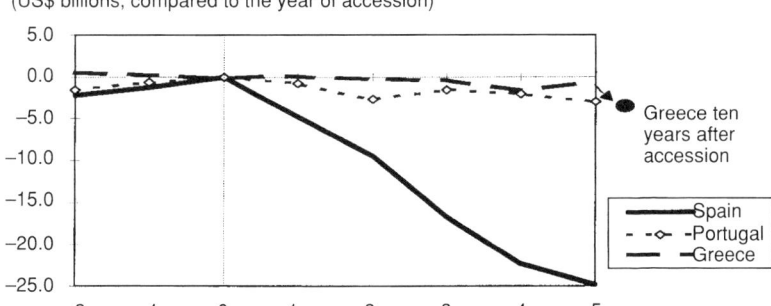

Source: Author's calculations based on IMF data.

the revenues from gas exports were used for supporting social services at unsustainable levels).

The increased official transfers, enhanced by private capital inflow (especially portfolio investment) may lead to very similar effects. The real exchange rate appreciation, resulting in increased imports, may result in increasing and maintaining excessive consumption levels, with negative effects both for economic activities and for long-term growth.[8] We consider the East German example as an extreme case of the generalised Dutch disease.[9] In our view, a risk of generalised Dutch disease is particularly strong during the accession of CEECs to the EU. To avoid this risk, a careful macroeconomic policy is necessary.

AVOIDING 'GENERALISED DUTCH DISEASE': DOMESTIC AND FOREIGN SAVING AS SOURCES OF GROWTH FINANCING

Although none of MC-3, with a possible exemption of Greece, experienced a full-scale typical 'generalised Dutch disease', the analysis of their performance may be useful in assessing the risk of this syndrome during the accession of CEECs.

The simplest indication of the use made of foreign savings is the change of the structure of imports experienced by the MC-3 group

Table 4.1 Changes in imports structure of MC-3 after EU accession

	Imports structure (%)			Change in first 6 years of membership
	1980	1985	1992	
Greece				
Machinery and equipment (SITC 7)	36.0	23.6	34.0	−12.4
Passenger cars (SITC 781)	0.8	3.2	8.7	2.4
Other machinery and equipment	35.1	20.4	25.3	−14.7
Other imports	64.0	76.4	66.0	12.4
Portugal				
Machinery and equipment (SITC 7)		21.6	38.0	16.4
Passenger cars (SITC 781)		3.9	7.9	4.0
Other machinery and equipment		17.7	30.1	12.4
Other imports		78.4	62.0	−16.4
Spain				
Machinery and equipment (SITC 7)		21.4	37.2	15.7
Passenger cars (SITC 781)		1.3	6.7	5.4
Other machinery and equipment		20.3	30.5	10.3
Other imports		78.5	62.8	−15.7

Source: United Nations, *International Trade Statistics Yearbook* 1981, 1988, 1993.

(see Table 4.1). While in both Spain and Portugal the increase in imports was accompanied by a significant shift in their structure towards capital goods, the opposite phenomenon was observed in Greece. During the first years of membership the share of capital goods fell drastically, and even after the following years the import boom did not reach the pre-accession level. It is a first indication that Greece used the additional revenue for increasing consumption rather than investment.

The ratio of investment to GDP improved considerably in both Spain and Portugal after their EU accession (Figure 4.8). At the same time, the Greek investment to GDP ratio gradually lowered from about 30 per cent before accession, to about 20 per cent just

Figure 4.8 The ratio of investment to GDP for MC-3 countries before and after accession

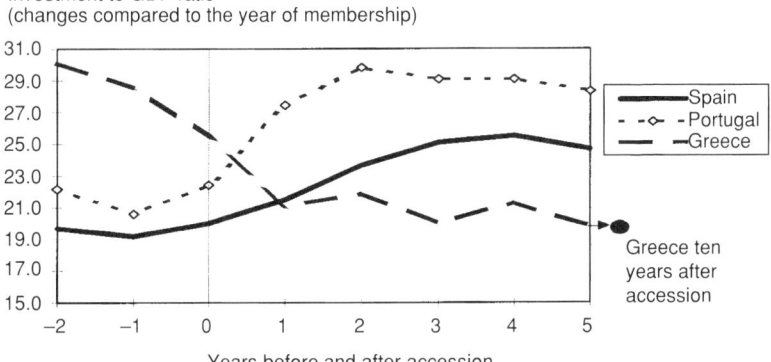

Source: Author's calculations based on IMF data

two to three years later. The ratio continued to fall, although very gradually. By the early 1990s it reduced to well below 20 per cent. At the same time the ratio of consumption to GDP, rather stable in Spain and Portugal after EU accession (around 78–79 per cent in Spain, 83–84 per cent in Portugal) was gradually growing in Greece from 80 per cent before accession, to 85 per cent during the early 1980s, and then to more than 90 per cent during the period of growing inflow of foreign savings in the late 1980s and early 1990s.

The radical growth of Greek consumption meant, of course, an equivalent fall in domestic savings. Changes of the domestic savings to GDP ratio pushed the ratio down from 20 per cent before accession to about 8 per cent in the early 1990s (Figure 4.8). This factor can explain the fall of the investment to GDP ratio observed despite growing foreign savings: simply, foreign savings were unable to compensate for the fall in domestic savings. Therefore, Greece simply did not find sufficient funds to finance its long-term investment needs. On the contrary, the ratio of domestic savings to GDP remained stable in Spain (adding up to a huge inflow of foreign saving) and even increased in Portugal. The effect of all these changes was a vigorous economic growth of both Iberian countries during the first years after accession, and a sluggish economic development in Greece.

Figure 4.9 The ratio of domestic savings to GDP for MC-3 countries before and after accession

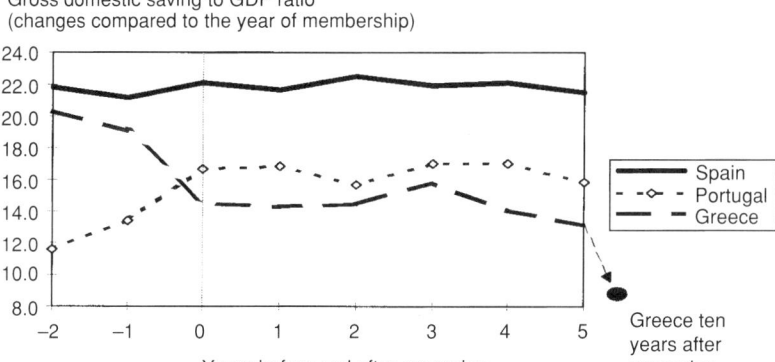

Source: Author's calculations based on IMF data.

Thus, Greece has experienced something very similar to the 'generalised Dutch disease', albeit on a much smaller scale than East Germany. The inflow of foreign savings was primarily used for releasing domestic resources from financing investment to consumption. When domestic savings fell, and a significant part of the domestic investment was to be financed by foreign savings, consumer demand started to expand rapidly (personal consumption grew during the period 1980–86 by 4 per cent annually on average, government consumption by 3 per cent, in sharp contrast with a 1 per cent average GDP increase). Despite growing domestic demand, and despite EU transfers, the aggregate level of Greek investment fell (the increase in the EU transfer-induced investment in infrastructure was smaller than the fall in private investment) as the Greek propensity to consume from the increased income proved to be stronger than its propensity to invest. By contrast, both Spain and Portugal managed to avoid a temptation to rapidly increase consumption levels. The difference in the reaction to EU accession was mainly due to differences in the macroeconomic policy applied by the MC-3 group.

The fall of domestic savings in Greece was mainly caused by the careless fiscal and monetary policy. Figures 4.10 and 4.11 show the main differences between Greece, on the one hand, and the Iberian countries on the other. An attempt to speed-up the economy by a fiscal stimulus – that was at the very core of the economic

Figure 4.10 Fiscal deficits of MC-3 countries before and after accession

Fiscal deficit (general government) as % of GDP

[Chart showing fiscal deficits for Spain, Portugal, and Greece from year -2 to year 5 before and after accession, with a separate point for Greece ten years after accession at approximately -16.0]

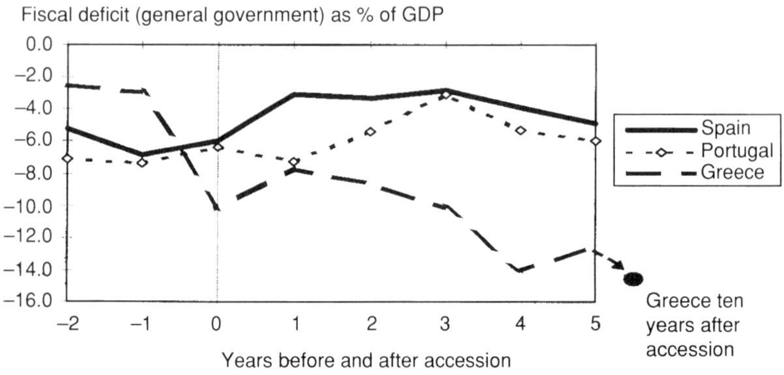

Source: Author's calculations based on IMF data.

programme of the first PASOK government – resulted in a fiscal balance deterioration from 2.5 per cent of GDP in 1980 to more than 10 per cent in 1981. The deficit dramatically increased (and, correspondingly, government consumption grew and domestic savings were reduced) with virtually no growth response from the economy. However, as foreign savings increased (mainly in the form of EU transfers, as private investors were effectively discouraged from entering the country), the deficit could be financed in a way that did not significantly accelerate inflation. Once macroeconomic control was lost, the fiscal deficit was gradually drifting towards 18 per cent in 1990; in fact, until today Greece has been unable to implement a radical fiscal adjustment programme that would allow for the release of savings from financing the public sector, to financing growth. By contrast, during the late 1980s both Spain and Portugal were applying a relatively conservative fiscal policy.

Instead of counteracting the expansionary fiscal policy, Greece's monetary policy was equally disastrous (Figure 4.10). In a hopeless attempt to revive investment (and to avoid high costs of servicing the public debt) Greece applied a permanent policy of negative real interest rates (different from conservative interest rate policies of the both Iberian countries) during the early 1980s. Investment did not react to this situation, but domestic savings did. In a nutshell, Greece did its best to reduce domestic savings through the huge fall in the public sector's savings and reduced incentives for private saving. The risk that CEECs may follow the Greek example of a careless

Figure 4.11 Real interests rates of MC-3 countries before and after accession

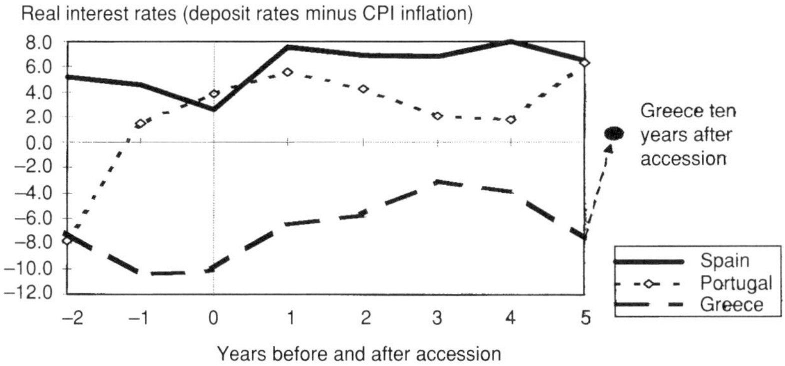

Real interest rates (deposit rates minus CPI inflation)

[Chart showing real interest rates for Spain, Portugal, and Greece from years -2 to 5 relative to accession, with a separate point for Greece ten years after accession]

Source: Author's calculations based on IMF data.

macroeconomic policy promoting consumption (at the expense of saving) after EU accession is relatively high for several reasons.

Firstly, the consumption levels are low, while the expectations connected with EU membership are high. That would create a strong pressure on the government to allow for fast private consumption growth. Secondly, the relatively big inflow of foreign saving will allow for a comfortable, non-inflationary financing of fiscal deficits. Thirdly, the slow path of public sector reform (for example the pension system) in CEECs, combined with the increase of disposable resources, may lead to a strong pressure for higher government spending. Finally, the lack of true social stability may leave the floor open for all the kinds of populist policies (for example similar to that of the first PASOK government). If these worries materialise, the generalised Dutch disease may severely hurt long-term growth prospects of CEECs.

The low domestic savings level is considered as one of the main obstacles for achieving rapid economic growth in CEECs (Sachs and Warner, 1996). As convergence of the GDP per capita level is generally seen as the most important target for CEECs during the next several decades, policies for promoting saving and investment are crucial for exploiting the benefits of EU accession. The generalised Dutch disease may severely jeopardise these prospects, confirming the position of CEECs as poor peripheries of the West European economy.

BEYOND THE 'GENERALISED DUTCH DISEASE': FOREIGN SAVINGS AND ABSORPTION CAPACITIES OF THE ECONOMIES

Let us assume, however, that a cautious macroeconomic policy will allow CEECs to avoid the risks of a generalised Dutch disease, namely to use increased disposable savings for financing investment rather than consumption. Can we feel comfortable about exploiting the EU accession benefits? Unfortunately, not yet. The key issue in the whole discussion of long-term benefits is not just a formal earmarking of funds for investment, but an efficient way of making these investments. Returns on investment are as equally important for economic growth as the size of the investment itself (Girard and Hurst, 1994). The experience of the MC-3 group shows that not only the scale of investment (in relation to GDP) was lower in Greece than in the Iberian countries, but the efficiency of investment as well (see Table 4.2).

The incremental capital–output ratio ICOR (measured against gross fixed capital formation[10]) was considerably higher in Greece than in the Iberian countries during the whole process of EU integration (particularly high values were observed in the first years after joining the EU). In our view, a couple of factors might have contributed to such an outcome:

- Firstly, the scale of EU transfers was much bigger in Greece than in the other MC-3. That makes us believe that a larger share of

Table 4.2 Efficiency of growth after joining the European Union

	Incremental capital–output ratio (ICOR)		Ratio of transfers[1] to investment	Ratio of FDI to investment	
	1981–86	1987–92	1989	1981–86	1987–92
Spain	–	6.4	4.0	–	6.8
Portugal	–	7.1	9.3	–	8.6
Greece	15.2	10.5	12.1	5.8	7.7

Note: [1]Only transfers from structural funds (earmarked for investment).
Source: IMF, European Commission, author's calculations based on World Bank data.

investment was spent on public projects such as costly infrastructure investments. This type of investment, based on a bureaucratic game rather than economic analysis, is characterised by the low average and falling marginal utility[11] (in some cases public investment may even become counter-productive, as some East German examples show[12]).
- Secondly, even outside the public service sector, the state-owned enterprises (SOEs) played a much larger role in the Greek economy than in the Iberian countries. The share of SOEs in total investment in Greece was below 9 per cent before accession, but grew to 23 per cent by the mid-1980s. By contrast, in Portugal this share decreased from 21 per cent before accession to 15 per cent three years later, and in Spain from 12 per cent to 9 per cent (World Bank, 1995).[13] Again, one may expect lower returns on the investment projects of SOEs than in the private sector.
- Thirdly, foreign involvement in the investment process in Greece was initially (during the first years after the accession) significantly smaller than in the Iberian countries (one may expect higher returns on the investment projects financed by FDI than by the domestic private sector, mainly due to the transfer of new technologies and the know-how connected with FDI).

As a general conclusion we could say that the ability of the economy to absorb increased investment in an efficient way has its limits. Only a limited number of private investment projects can assure sufficient returns that make the investment reasonable from the long-term growth viewpoint. However, the demand for additional investment projects claimed by SOEs and especially by the public service sector does not seem to have such strict limits, as the risk envisaged by firms involved in these projects is much smaller. Therefore, with high public investment the economy can easily exceed its real absorptive capacities (in the extreme case, with public investment that has returns close to zero, there is almost no difference between investment and consumption – both do not influence long-term growth).

In our view, a high share of EU transfers in the total inflow of foreign savings (as observed in Greece) creates an incentive to exceed the absorptive capacities of the economy through the excessive scale of low-return public investment. The second factor that plays a crucial role is the structure of the economy, for example the degree of privatisation. Both factors may have a particularly strong impact on CEECs' accession to the EU (given a continuously high share of SOEs in the economy, and the most likely significant scale, in relation to GDP, of EU transfers). It is crucial that an appropriate structural policy, mainly aimed at privatisation, demonopolisation, and public service sector reform counteracts this danger.

Notes

1. The rationale behind this argument is that, as the level of development of CEECs is lower than in MC-3, CEECs will need more transfers than MC-3.
2. Ranging, in purchasing power terms, from 17 per cent of the EU average in Romania, to about 40 per cent in the Czech Republic (World Bank, *World Development Report 1996*).
3. Sources of data used are: World Bank, *World Tables 95*; IMF, *IFS Yearbook 96*; EU, 1993.
4. Mainly investment-led, see Baldwin, 1994.
5. See Sampedro *et al.*, 1983. Actually, the first PASOK government in Greece did its best to scare away the majority of potential investors through a strongly anti-European and anti-market rhetoric used in the electoral campaign in 1980.
6. Temporary persistence of non-tradable inflation despite real appreciation is a normal feature in the period of opening economies with initially suppressed non-tradable prices. Such a phenomenon was observed both in CEECs, and in East Germany. In the latter case the monetary union that created a unified market, presumably with a single price, almost immediately reduced the tradable inflation to West German levels. However, the non-tradable prices in eastern Länder were still growing rapidly during the whole period 1990–93. As a consequence, the differentials between CPI rates for both parts of Germany reached a peak of more than 7 points in 1992 (inflation in western Länder 4 per cent, in eastern Länder over 11 per cent). It was only 4–5 years after the monetary union that the CPI differentials started to disappear (Orlowski, 1996).
7. See Corden, 1984.
8. The crucial role of saving and investment in CEECs growth is discussed in Sachs and Warner, 1996.
9. For further discussion see Orlowski, 1996.
10. The incremental capital–output ratio (ICOR) is defined as $\text{ICOR} = \dfrac{K_1 - K_{t-1}}{GDP_1 - GDP_{t-1}}$ that is, as a ratio of the increment of capital stock K between period $t-1$ and t to the GDP growth achieved during the same time. This ratio, usually estimated for longer periods (in shorter periods it can strongly fluctuate) shows by how many units the capital stock should be increased so that GDP can be increased by one unit. Due to statistical problems connected with the measuring of capital stock, a simplified formula is usually used taking gross fixed capital formation accumulated over the analysed period as a proxy for

the growth of the capital stock (the measure obtained in this way is higher than the real ICOR, because replacement investments are not deducted from total outlays).
11. For statistical verification see Barro and Sala-I-Martin, 1995.
12. See Siebert, Schmieding and Nunnenkamp, 1992.
13. The main reason for the decrease of the importance of SOEs in both Iberian countries was a privatisation programme that followed EU accession (*Les Privatisations en Europe*, 1993). By contrast, in Greece the first years of membership were marked by a re-nationalisation programme, that resulted in the increase of the share of SOEs in non-agricultural GDP from 6 per cent in 1979 to 17 per cent in 1986.

Bibliography

BALDWIN, R. E. *Towards an Integrated Europe*, London, CEPR, 1994.
BARRO, R. J. and SALA-I-MARTIN, X. *Economic Growth*, New York, McGraw-Hill, 1995.
CORDEN, W. M. 'Booming Sector and Dutch Disease Economics: Survey and Consolidation', *Oxford Economic Papers*, no. 36, 1984, pp. 359–80.
COURCHENE, T. et al. 'Stable Money–Sound Finances', *European Economy*, no. 53, 1993.
EUROPEAN COMMISSION 'The Economics of Community Public Finance', *European Economy*, no. 5, 1993.
GIRARD, J. and HURST, C. 'Investment and Growth: Quality versus Quantity', *EIB Papers*, no. 23, 1994, pp. 39–55.
LEE, J.-W. 'Capital Goods Imports and Long-Run Growth', *NBER Working Papers*, no. 4725, 1994.
ORLOWSKI, W. M. *Droga do Europy. Makroekonomia wstepowania do Unii Europejskiej (The Road to Europe. Macroeoconomics of EU accession)*, ZBSE, Warszawa (in Polish; the English translation in printing), 1996.
DA SILVA LOPEZ, J. (ed.), *Portugal and EC Membership Evaluated*, London, Pinter, 1993.
WRIGHT, V. (ed.), *Les Privatisations en Europe*, Poitiers, Actes Sud, 1993.
SACHS, J. D. and WARNER, A. M. *Achieving Rapid Growth in the Transition Economies of Central Europe*, Warszawa, CASE, 1996.
SAMPEDRO, J. L. and PAYNO J. A. (eds), *The Enlargement of the European Community. Case Studies of Greece, Portugal and Spain*, London, Macmillan, 1983.
SIEBERT, H., SCHMIEDING, H. and NUNNENKAMP, P. (1992), 'Lessons from German Unification', paper presented to the conference of the IMF and National Bank of Austria, Baden, Austria, 15–18 April 1991.
WORLD BANK *Bureaucrats in Business. The Economics and Politics of Government Ownership*, Oxford, Oxford University Press, 1995.

5 Capital Inflows and Convertibility in the Transforming Economies of Central Europe

Lucjan T. Orlowski[1]

INTRODUCTION

Central European transforming economies have all experienced considerable capital inflows once their initial inflation shock expired and their national income started to grow. These capital inflows are induced by both domestic and external economy conditions. The economic reforms in these countries have increased demand for money and have improved productivity. These improvements in domestic economy conditions have invited capital inflows from abroad. In addition, international interest rates have been falling since 1994, which promoted capital allocations in Central European countries still perceived as emerging market economies by international capital investors.

This study focuses on the principal causes of capital inflows and on the economic consequences of possible sterilising actions. It is not aimed at reporting or examining in detail sterilisation operations of individual central banks. Rather, it intends to alert monetary authorities in transforming economies about possible economic consequences of large capital inflows and various tools of their sterilisation. The role of external factors is emphasised and the dangers of reversed capital outflows are discussed. Economic consequences of large capital inflows and sudden reversed outflows are examined in the context of fixed and more flexible exchange rate systems. Exchange rate flexibility is favoured for the purpose of rationalising capital inflows. Flexible rates allow for some nominal currency appreciation or depreciation cushioning the dangers of inflows and sudden outflows. High inflation, real currency appreciation and trade and current account deficits are less likely to persevere under flexible exchange rates. Furthermore, flexible rates improve the structure of inflows because, by introducing more uncertainty about future currency changes, they discourage speculative inflows.

Against this background, countries of Central Europe willing to join the European Union are discouraged to further advance the capital account convertibility. They need to strengthen their financial infrastructure and to improve the system of banking supervision first. At the same time, they have to pursue a comprehensive policy of disinflation. They are also advised not to introduce a currency peg with a narrow band or without the band too early.

The analysis focuses on policy problems and practices of Poland, Hungary and the Czech Republic only, since these countries have experienced most of the capital inflows to transforming economies of Central Europe and since they are also prime candidates for a future accession to the European Union.

The following section examines main causes of capital inflows as they are articulated by both the theoretical and the empirical economic literature, along with their impact on selected macroeconomic variables. Methods of sterilisation of these inflows, their costs and economic consequences are then discussed, followed by the empirical analysis of policy responses to capital inflows in the three examined countries. The concluding section attempts to articulate some policy advice for these countries in the context of their future accession to the European Union.

LARGE CAPITAL INFLOWS: PRINCIPAL CAUSES AND EXPECTED EFFECTS

The emerging market economies undergoing liberalisation and deregulation are likely to experience a wave of large external capital inflows. The principal causes of these inflows to developing countries and their economic effects have been extensively investigated in the economic literature (Folkerts-Landau and Ito, 1995; Ul Haque, Mathieson and Sharma, 1997; Schadler, 1994). These net inflows have contributed to a surge in foreign reserves in a number of Latin American, Asian and Central European countries. They have generated potential for higher investment and for an accelerated economic growth but, at the same time, they have created problems with real currency appreciation, deteriorating current account deficits and aggravated inflationary pressures. These dangers have been particularly strong in countries where the risk of reversal of capital inflows into sudden net outflows is high. Consequently, large external capital inflows must be managed effectively in these countries so that they do not cause permanent disturbances in the real GDP growth and in external balance of the economy. At the same time, they can be productively used by government, financial, and business institutions to ensure a sustained, high level economic growth.

Before analysing specific economic effects of these inflows in the transforming economies of Central Europe, it is helpful to elaborate their principal causes and effects as identified by both the theoretical and the empirical economics literature. These causes and effects largely depend on their composition. There are sizeable, sometimes contradictory effects on the real sector of investment capital as opposed to speculative capital inflows. A surge in short-term and medium-term portfolio investment may have a more disruptive impact on the economy than long-term portfolio and foreign direct investments. Furthermore, the real effects of capital inflows largely depend on the exchange rate system and on institutional constraints (the degree of financial markets depth, capitalisation and regulation, and the advancement and the competitiveness of financial institutions).

Despite considerable differences in the institutional and macroeconomic framework accompanying large capital inflows, some general *benefits* from these inflows can be identified. In general terms, they lead to a higher degree of capitalisation of financial institutions and markets that normally expand a borrowing, lending and investing potential of domestic banks and their customers. The greater access to international financial markets helps to enrich modern technology of financial institutions in terms of their asset and liability management. It leads to an expanded diversity of financial instruments, including the introduction of financial derivatives, that contributes to the knowledge and expertise of financial managers in emerging market economies. If long-term inflows of both portfolio and direct investment capital prevail, they contribute to higher productivity of domestic capital and labour and to a better allocation of capital through the link to international capital markets. The depth and capitalisation of financial markets and the improved investors' confidence are considerably enhanced by foreign portfolio capital inflows.

Inflows of external direct and portfolio capital are likely to generate a number of undesirable side effects. The *dangers* of these inflows have been explicitly identified in the economics literature. The boost in inflation and real currency appreciation are the most direct negative effects of large capital inflows. The domestic currency real appreciation is likely to exert pressures on current account deficits, thus it may cause a more or less permanent damage to the international competitiveness of exports.

The economic literature that draws on the empirical research on emerging market economies experiencing large capital inflows (Folkerts-Landau and Ito, 1995; Ul Haque, Mathieson and Sharma, 1997) concentrates on three principal *causes* of net capital inflows in these countries. Each of these causes has distinguishable implications on the duration, destabilising effects, and inflation. The first of them is an *autonomous increase in domestic money demand* that stems in practice mainly from financial deregulation and modernisation of financial institutions that ultimately leads to an expanded range of savings and borrowing instruments for businesses and households. Because such an increase can be viewed as a one-time, temporary phenomenon, it may not have a significant impact on the long-term growth of real income. Nevertheless, it is an important source of intermediation and bank capitalisation causing some positive, durable effects for domestic financial markets.

The second factor is also internally induced. It is an *increase in domestic productivity of capital*. A sustained, long-term increase in productivity is likely to generate inflows of direct investment and medium-term and long-term portfolio investment. Capital inflows stemming from a long-term productivity growth contribute to a sustained high growth of real income. They assist the development of small businesses providing new sources of credits.

The first two causes of external capital inflows are induced by changes in the national economy. They are described in the literature as 'pull factors' inducing capital inflows, due to their domestic roots. By contrast, the third cause stems from external conditions and is referred to as a 'push factor'. The dominant external cause of large capital inflows to emerging markets are *declining international interest rates*. International portfolio investors and speculators dissatisfied with low returns on domestic securities seek higher returns elsewhere. To balance the declining risk on domestic securities they find incentives to enter more volatile, higher risk emerging financial markets.[2] A specific structure and predominant directions of these inflows depend on adjustments in international yield curves. In general terms, if yield curves in highly developed industrial economies decline, strong capital inflows to emerging markets are likely to accelerate. Correspondingly, yields on Brady bonds increase, as measured by the rising Brady bonds return index. The index is a good proxy measure of intensity of external capital inflows to emerging markets since there is a strong correlation between these two variables (BIS, 1996). In addition, if international yield curves are getting steeper thus showing declining short-term in relation to long-term interest rates, speculative capital inflows to emerging markets will prevail. Adversely, if international yield curves are getting flatter although still declining, there is a chance to attract more medium-term and long-term portfolio investment and direct investment capital to the emerging markets.

Experiencing a greater degree of openness to international capital flows, the monetary authorities of emerging market economies have almost no control over the 'push factor'. Even if they impose short-term, strong sterilisation measures, they risk a sudden reversal of capital flows if international interest rates exhibit a cyclical increase. Calvo, Sahay and Végh (1995) convincingly prove that sterilised capital inflows to emerging market economies are not sustainable in the long-run and are best replaced by exchange rate appreciation. These large capital inflows are likely to be followed by reversed, destabilising outflows. The ability to regulate capital flows to emerging market economies by their governments is very limited. Their directions and magnitude strongly depend on monetary policy decisions of the US Federal Reserve, the Bank of Japan, and the Bundesbank and, in the future, on the European Central Bank (ECB). Monetary authorities in emerging markets may consider forming a coalition or a forum, coordinated perhaps by the International Monetary Fund (IMF), aimed at negotiating international interest rate movements. By having a consolidated voice, they will be relieved from otherwise ineffective and costly sterilisations. International coordination of interest rates may be aimed at discouraging speculative attacks on emerging markets and their currencies.

The economic effects of capital inflows strongly depend on the recipient country exchange rate system. Under *flexible exchange rates*, all large capital inflows regardless of their cause induce a domestic currency nominal appreciation. This, in turn, causes a major realignment of relative prices. Prices of imported goods decline relative to prices of domestic goods and, consequently, prices of tradables decline relative to prices of non-tradables. Assuming that absolute prices of tradables remain constant due to a sustained internal demand, while relative prices of tradables decline, capital inflows under flexible exchange rates are likely to alleviate inflationary tendencies in the national economy. The dynamic extension to this process can be explained in terms of the Balassa–Samuelson effect.[3]

This concept implies that the prices of non-tradables in poorer economies are lower than in well-developed economies due to a lower productivity of resources, while prices of tradables are roughly the same through open international trade. The declining inflation resulting from capital inflows under flexible exchange rates accompanied by comprehensive economic reforms (deregulation, liberalisation, macroeconomic stability, and privatisation) results in a lower uncertainty about relative prices and encourages direct investment. These conditions improve domestic productivity, mainly in the tradable goods sector. These results are likely to occur as dynamic, lagged effects of economic reforms and they become apparent once the so called 'corrective inflation' expires. In sum, disinflation brought by economic reforms together with capital inflows are likely to raise the relative price of non-tradables in emerging market economies. Because the productivity gains occur mostly in the tradable goods sector, the domestic currency is likely to appreciate in real terms since a large increase in real wages will raise the relative price of non-tradables.

The dynamic extensions to the Balassa–Samuelson effect help to further explain that large capital inflows induced by higher domestic productivity may have a neutralising impact on inflation under fixed exchange rates as well, depending upon the speed of adjustments between productivity gains, average costs, profit margins and prices. If capital inflows are caused by higher domestic productivity under fixed exchange rates, they will initially induce higher wage demands and some inflation. Yet, they will be ultimately followed by a higher domestic supply of goods if the productivity growth outperforms the nominal wage increase. This interaction is generally achieved under fairly tight domestic fiscal and monetary policies that ensure positive real interest rates and higher national savings. Consequently, inflation in the long run is likely to assume a diminishing path. Sterilisation of capital inflows is not justified in the long run since the initial inflation resulting from early inflows under fixed exchange rates may be self-correcting. If under fixed exchange rates capital inflows are induced by a sustained increase in domestic money demand, they will not be inflationary. They will satisfy the initial money demand increase by keeping the equilibrium money balances at a stable level and maintaining the money multiplier unchanged.

There are always strong inflationary effects of capital inflows under fixed exchange rates if these inflows are induced by declining international interest rates. Moreover, since lower external interest rates promote inflows of short-term, speculative capital, inflationary shocks in emerging market economies may be significant and destabilising. The surge in inflation stemming from the inflows may quickly lead to a large real appreciation of the domestic currency that may have a damaging effect on export, on domestic industrial production, and on the GDP. Even in this case central banks should think twice whether they need to sterilise large capital inflows. Without sterilisation inflationary shocks may be initially deep. However, if the government stabilisation policy is credible and the climate for new business activity is favourable, they will be self-correcting in the long run. Only if the government economic policy is not credible due to persistent real currency appreciation and growing trade and current account deficits, some sterilisation may be indispensable. It shall be remembered here that the common cause of low policy credibility in the transforming economies of Central and Eastern Europe is the extensive central bank financing of government budget deficits.

In sum, fixed exchange rates cause a significant problem of asymmetric information for central banks in emerging economies. The leading international central banks controlling the reference currencies have a better knowledge about international interest rates and money balances and have more influence to control them. The asymmetry problem exposes emerging markets' central banks to a high sensitivity of domestic monetary variables to international interest rates. If these rates decline, pro-inflationary and destabilising capital inflows may persevere. They are triggered by the fixed rate that diminishes expectations of speculators about the nominal exchange rate, thus encouraging speculative capital inflows to emerging markets. Any reversal of international interest rates may quickly convert the inflows into large, destabilising outflows.

A model of large capital inflows induced by a growing domestic money demand to open economies and their impact on domestic money balances, interest rates and exchange rates is presented in Figure 5.1. In this model, large external capital inflows are induced by an increase in domestic real money demand from MD_0 to MD_1. In the case of asymmetric information and imperfect asset substitutability between domestic and foreign markets, the domestic equilibrium interest rate R, assuming that the interest rate parity condition (IPC) holds, will be equal to:

$$R = R^* + \frac{E_1 - E_0}{E_0 + \rho} \qquad (1)$$

Figure 5.1 The impact of capital inflows on domestic money balances, interest rates and exchange rates

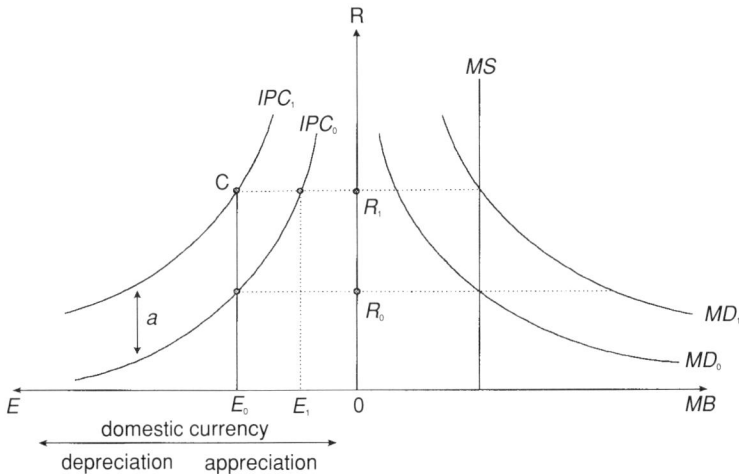

E = exchange rate stated as domestic currency value in foreign currency terms
MD = real money demand R = domestic equilibrium interest rate
MS = real money supply
MB = domestic real money balances
IPC = interest parity condition

The formula presents the risk-adjusted domestic currency return on foreign currency deposits. E_1 is the expected equilibrium exchange rate, E_0 is the initial or fixed exchange rate, R^* is the foreign interest rate, and ρ is the risk premium attributable to imperfect substitutability between foreign and domestic assets. If both foreign and domestic assets were perfect substitutes, ρ would be zero. The imperfect substitutability assumption is appropriate and realistic for emerging market economies. Their risk premium follows the relationship:

$$\rho = B - A \qquad (2)$$

where B is the value of government debt and A are central bank assets.

Higher domestic demand for money MD_1 will eventually result in an upward pressure on domestic equilibrium interest rates at R_1. Capital inflows in the magnitude equal to the difference $A_1 - A_0$ will shift the

IPC function to IPC_1 generating a new equilibrium at point C between the interest rate differential $R^* - R_1$ and the expected appreciation of the domestic currency $(E_1 - E_0)/E_0$. The new equilibrium domestic interest rate is determined by:

$$R_1 = R^* + \frac{E_1 - E_0}{E_0} + \rho(B - A_1) \tag{3}$$

If the central bank wants to maintain the fixed exchange rate at E_0 and to prevent the excessive currency appreciation to E_1, it must arrange a sterilised sale of foreign assets in the magnitude implied by vector a. That would eventually leave the domestic money supply unchanged, but drop the IPC line back to IPC_0. The new equilibrium interest rate is corrected to the R_0 level corresponding to:

$$R_0 = R^* + \frac{E_1 - E_0}{E_0} + \rho(B - A_2) \tag{4}$$

where A_2, approximately equal to A_0, is the new level of central bank assets.

A choice of the exchange rate system has a considerable impact on the duration and composition of capital inflows and outflows. Under the fixed exchange rate system or the managed float, capital flows are difficult to control; central banks are committed to convert foreign currency to local currency and vice versa. Under flexible rates this commitment is weakened (Sachs, 1996). Moreover, currency convertibility for capital transactions under fixed exchange rates poses a serious risk of considerable nominal undervaluation (in the case of prevailing inflows) or overvaluation (in the case of net outflows) of the domestic currency as reflected by the difference between E_0 and E_1 in Figure 5.1. These distortions urge central banks to sterilise if the banks are committed to targeting the exchange rate in the monetary policy system.

Specific central bank responses to capital inflows or outflows have a 'signaling effect' on the economy (Bartolini and Drazen, 1997). If the central bank wants to express commitment to exchange rate stability it must undertake frequent sterilising actions. Alternatively, the central bank could allow the domestic currency to depreciate and to relax the fixed exchange rate in order to correct the current account deficit. The relaxation of the currency peg accomplished either through the assumption of a clean float or through widening the band of permitted fluctuations sends a signal about the central bank's willingness to devalue the currency. This, in turn, is likely to induce large speculative outflows, but it may improve the structural composition of external capital in the economy leading to the advantage of direct and long-term portfolio investments over short-term capital.

Following the path of these developments one may argue that large capital inflows under fixed exchange rates are likely to increase expectations of an exchange rate policy reversal if the economic agents detect a real currency appreciation and deterioration in trade and current account balances. These expectations are triggered if a domestic currency belongs to an integrated currency system and a coordinated exchange rate mechanism, such as the European Exchange Rate Mechanism (the ERM). The monetary authority cannot change the exchange rate system or devalue the currency in this case. Investors and speculators have the right to expect a largely undervalued currency attacking it with large inflows. After a certain time lag, they may expect an excessively overvalued currency in the presence of strong inflationary pressures induced by earlier inflows. The frequency of speculative attacks and the risks of their sudden reversals are pervasive under the fixed exchange rate system.

This rule has been confirmed by the empirical experiences of Latin American and Asian countries where large capital inflows were followed by speculative attacks and reversed outflows when a deterioration of current account balances became apparent or when international interest rates began to rise (Calvo, Sahay and Végh, 1995). The empirical research confirms that fixed exchange rates considerably expose a country's capital account to the risk of reverse movements in international interest rates and yield curves. The declining international interest rates, or the 'push factor', have contributed to accelerated capital inflows to emerging markets, especially in the period 1995–96 (Bank for International Settlements, 1996). But rising external interest rates in 1994, and to some extent in the second quarter of 1997, induced extensive speculative attacks on these markets and large capital outflows.

The deviation between the fixed rate and the market equilibrium rate has a significant impact on the composition of capital flows. The larger the difference, the shorter maturity and the higher risk capital prevails. Moreover, if the financial markets in the emerging economies are already well-developed as implied by their high capitalisation rates in relation to GDP, their absorptive capacity is certainly larger. In this case, they are likely to receive a large volume of speculative capital inflows. The potentially damaging effect on the economy of sudden reversed outflows is more severe in this case due to the large scale of the expected capital flight.[4] Consequently, offsetting interventions by central banks of emerging market economies do not make much sense; they normally do not have enough accumulated foreign currency reserves to counteract aggressive, decisive outflows. Daily turnovers in international currency markets (estimated by the BIS to reach USD 2 trillion in March 1996) are simply overwhelming in relation to limited foreign currency reserves in emerging market economies, even if only a small portion of these turnovers involves capital transactions in emerging markets.

As noted before, the fixed exchange rate system involves a considerable asymmetric information between central banks and suppliers of capital in the countries of base currencies on the one side, and domestic central banks and suppliers of capital in emerging market economies on the other. The asymmetry affects the structure of the so called 'pecking order' of capital flows as examined by Razin, Sadka and Yuen (1996). If capital investors consider the currency peg sustainable, foreign direct investment will prevail over more risky portfolio debt and the riskiest portfolio equity investment. If the peg sustainability is questioned, the short-run capital will be in a standby position and ready to fly out.

Adoption of full capital account convertibility and fixed exchange rates by emerging market economies must be accompanied by an efficient banking system and by an effective financial supervision (Diaz-Alejandro, 1985). These two conditions effectively cushion the country's exposure to sudden reversed outflows. This exposure depends mostly on the *de facto* rather than on the *de jure* opening of the capital account (Milesi-Ferretti and Razin, 1996). The *de facto* opening is a function of internal incentives to export capital that are strongly related to the risk-adjusted rate of return differentials as a direct function of political and economic stability. Although the greater capital convertibility increases exposure to adverse external shocks, it provides a strong disciplining role on domestic policies. This function may be too rigorous for countries undergoing active structural adjustments, increasing bank capitalisation, and expanding domestic credit. In this case, effective capital controls would have to be imposed to ensure a sustained monetary policy credibility. These capital controls ought to be applied as precautionary or preventive measures. The policy credibility would be hurt if they were applied as corrective, or *ex-post* instruments.

The above analysis leads to a conclusion that economies with relatively well-developed financial markets and, correspondingly, with a high degree of substitutability between domestic and foreign capital are more exposed to reversals in capital flows and they are more dependent on changes in international interest rates. The changes in external interest rates are transmitted to adjustments in domestic interest rates to a magnified degree, considering that emerging countries must keep appropriate risk margins between domestic and international interest rates.[5] A more favourable situation takes place when large capital inflows to emerging markets are induced by a sustained growth of productivity. In this case, the structural position of foreign capital allocations is much better, and foreign direct investment and long-term portfolio investment are likely to prevail.

The principal causes of capital inflows play an important role for the directions of their impact on domestic interest rates. If induced by the 'pull factors', capital inflows result in increasing domestic interest rates (as shown by Figure 5.1). They increase the risk-adjusted interest differential with foreign monetary centres. Adversely, domestic interest rates normally decline if capital inflows are induced by 'push factors'. In the dynamic analysis, the path of capital inflows may have an automatic stabilising impact on domestic interest rates. The internally-induced inflows initially increase the risk-adjusted interest rate differential. This, in turn, is likely to invite short-term capital inflows contributing to a narrower differential. This path has, however, some influence on the structural composition of capital inflows or on the 'pecking order'. At the beginning, long-term direct and portfolio investment may prevail, but toward the end of this path, short-term capital inflows gradually increase their share. A sustained, long-term-oriented monetary policy ought to be designed and pursued to ensure a stabilising impact of capital inflows in the long-run.

Another noteworthy structural feature of large capital inflows is their impact on foreign currency deposits in the banking system and, ultimately, on the currency substitution (Ul Haque, Mathieson and Sharma, 1997). If induced by higher autonomous domestic demand, foreign capital inflows cause a declining share of foreign currency deposits, they are quickly exchanged into domestic currency and satisfy the rising domestic money demand. On the contrary, if induced by declining international interest rates, the large capital inflows will cause an infusion of foreign currency deposits seeking higher domestic yields. The impact of capital inflows attracted by higher domestic productivity on the share of foreign currency deposits in total bank deposits is highly uncertain. The empirical research shows little connection between these variables (Folkerts-Landau and Ito, 1995). Under fixed exchange rates these reactions are stronger than under flexible exchange rates, where the latter cushion the impact of capital inflows on the composition of money balances. The rising currency substitution in emerging markets resulting from capital inflows attributable to declining international interest rates may cause an illusion of rapidly improving bank capitalisation and a strong increase in broad money balances. Monetary authorities and bankers ought to recognise the temporary nature of this capital and their vulnerability to reversed outflows.

In conclusion, the structural composition of large capital inflows and reversed outflows in emerging market economies is important for the determination of their specific economic effects. Capital inflows induced by a higher autonomous money demand are dominated by short-term and medium-term portfolio assets. They may contribute to higher domestic interest rates and to a simultaneous real currency appreciation. With a certain time lag, they may have a negative impact on the real economy causing a deterioration of trade and current account deficits and a reduction in aggregate demand. More desirable effects are generated by capital inflows induced by growing domestic productivity. They are dominated by foreign direct investment and long-term portfolio investment. Their real effects depend on the absorptive capacity of the domestic economy and on the regulatory environment. By contrast, the highest risk of destabilising effects and sudden reversals into outflows exists when capital inflows are induced by declining international interest rates. Expanded capital convertibility in the presence of a weak financial supervision aggravates destabilising effects of these capital inflows and increases the risk of speculative attacks on the currency and on capital account balances.[6]

THE AVAILABLE POLICY RESPONSES

Before examining the tools available to Central European countries and their practices with various methods of sterilisation of capital inflows, it is helpful to overview the main sterilisation instruments developed by world central banks. The Central European countries have already expanded internal markets for government securities and have introduced open-market operations. This allows them to sterilise capital inflows using a variety of instruments including offsetting open-market sales of government securities. In general terms, sterilisation of external capital inflows must reduce other components of the central bank monetary base since the inflows increase the foreign currency assets of the central bank. The practical experiences of emerging markets central banks indicate that sterilisation through *open-market sales of securities* is highly ineffective for halting capital inflows in the long run. These operations only temporarily cushion the effects of capital inflows, but they cannot correct their long-run underlying causes. Specific cases of sterilisation examined by the IMF[7] – including Chile in 1990, Colombia in 1991, Indonesia in 1991–93 and Malaysia in 1991–93 indicate that during sterilisation periods their international reserves were rising further rather than declining. The reserves expanded even more when sterilisation efforts were abandoned. The suspension of sterilising open-market sales left a much higher degree of market exchange rate volatility. During sterilisation periods, short-term interest rates increased dramatically and, especially in the case of Colombia, open-market paper notes rose significantly in relation to the monetary base.

The fallacy of sterilisation through open-market sales can be further confirmed by the experience of Argentina that had very large capital inflows after the April 1991 Convertibility Plan reform. The Argentine central bank applied the fixed peg of one peso to one USD and introduced a quasi-currency board and exchange rate-based monetary policy. The Central Bank of Argentina did not sterilise spectacular capital inflows that followed the stabilisation programme. Despite the absence of sterilisation, Argentine interest rates converged to world levels and inflows levelled off by 1993.[8]

Nevertheless, central banks may consider applying open-market sales for the purpose of sterilisation of capital inflows as a short-term, corrective measure. Their use is limited when financial markets are underdeveloped and short-term Treasury bills, central bank paper, or commercial paper are imperfect substitutes for medium- and long-term equity and fixed-income assets of investors. Therefore, despite the rise of short-term interest rates resulting from open-market sales, there is no automatic switch to fixed income and equity short-term securities. Instead, sterilisation may risk inducing further inflows of short-term, speculative capital.

Open market sales impose a heavy quasi-fiscal net cost.[9] This is because the government imposes a debt-service cost on its own budget through emission of a large stock of securities aimed at lowering liquidity (Aizenman and Guidotti, 1994). Moreover, they may lead to operating losses of central banks since they increase their foreign assets that normally earn lower interest rates than domestic short-term securities sold by central banks. These losses can reach severe levels that may require recapitalisation of central banks. This method of sterilisation may also have a perpetual effect. Open market sales increase the advantage of domestic over foreign interest rates, and the wider interest rate differential may ultimately trigger further external capital inflows.

Alternatively, central banks may consider raising their key lending rates (Lombard and discount rates) or increasing the ratios of required reserves for the purpose of sterilisation of large capital inflows. These two instruments are highly inflexible. Central banks ought to avoid using them since their changes disturb the strategic asset and liability management of member's commercial banks. Their frequent adjustments may ultimately hurt the credibility of central banks, especially if they are inconsistent and go in different directions. Changes in central bank key interest rates or ratios of required reserves reveal strong signals about the monetary policy directions of the banks. If the signals are inconsistent, the policy credibility is hurt. Central banks in emerging market economies generally have a tendency towards a discretionary rather than a rules-based monetary policy. They normally lack experience and expertise to judge whether disturbances in money balances have a temporary or a permanent nature. Disturbances related to capital inflows are mostly temporary and self-correcting, and do not require sterilising actions.

Increases in central bank lending rates and in minimum reserve requirements have strong signaling effects about central bank monetary policy only if they are used infrequently. Under such conditions, they have a potential to discourage speculative inflows. However, they increase a risk of sudden reversed outflows because central banks openly admit having a problem with the destabilising effects of inflows. In this case, higher minimum reserve requirements and central bank lending rates may backfire and induce large speculative outflows. On the positive side, higher central bank lending rates involve a lower fiscal cost than open-market sales, since discount rates are normally lower than market interest rates. Because of their inflexibility, discount and Lombard rates ought to be used only in severe cases and usually only at early stages of large capital inflows. These policy tools can be used if capital inflows have a strong impact on the real appreciation of the domestic currency which may sharply deteriorate trade and current account balances. Lifting the discount and/or Lombard rates would signal the central bank's commitment to support the exchange rate. However, if investors and speculators read it as a problem revealed by the central bank, they may be willing to pull their capital from domestic to foreign assets.

Frequently changed, higher ratios of required reserves create a number of negative side effects in emerging market economies. They certainly disrupt strategic asset and liability management of banks forcing them to keep excessive reserves due to the policy uncertainty, and they impose a heavy tax on emerging banks that is likely to result in disintermediation (Calvo, Leiderman and Reinhard, 1994). Empirical research on the subject generally agrees that these ratios are already too high in emerging market economies and they impede the task of capitalisation of emerging banks. Moreover, their cost to the government is high if they are held in the form of remunerated requirements which cause central banks to pay interest on these reserves. The paid interest on these reserves is roughly equal to market interest rates. Therefore, the resulting fiscal cost of remunerated required reserves is approximately equal to the cost of open-market sales. Pursuing a discretionary monetary policy, central banks do not hesitate to frequently change these ratios. Consequently, member banks are forced to keep extra required reserves which inhibit their lending operations and lower their profitability. This has a negative impact on economic growth. It also puts domestic banks in a highly disadvantageous position when they openly compete with branches of leading international banks. In sum, central banks shall use adjustments in their key lending rates and in statutory reserve requirements infrequently and only when they wish to send a strong signal about their commitment to stabilise the exchange rate and the capital account.

Among more flexible tools of sterilisation, central banks may consider *shifting public sector deposits from commercial banks to the central bank* as applied, for instance, by Malaysia in April 1990 (Folkerts-Landau and Ito, 1995, p. 84). All Malaysian government deposits in the banking system were withdrawn and placed in the money market operations (MMO) account of the central bank. This method does not involve higher fiscal costs since the interest paid on MMO accounts is generally lower than interest rates on government deposits at commercial banks. However, it is yet another highhanded regulation by a central bank because it impedes asset and liability management of commercial banks. Their total liabilities become unpredictable.

A more flexible and relatively effective tool of sterilisation are *foreign currency swaps*, both short-term and medium-term. These swap arrangements involve central bank selling excess foreign currency reserves at a spot foreign exchange market with a simultaneous forward repurchase contract at a specified future date. This tool has by definition only a temporary nature due to limited maturities of forward contracts in the economies fighting inflation and having rather unstable market interest rates. There is normally a limited forward trading of only partially convertible domestic currencies. However, if forward repurchasing contracts on foreign currency are available, central banks ought to consider using them for sterilisation of capital inflows (forward repurchases for sterilisation of inflows and forward selling contracts for a defense against excessive outflows). The use of foreign currency swaps using the forward contracts is justified by two reasons. First, sterilisation should be normally only temporary, not exceeding three to four months, which is a feasible time span for forward contracts involving emerging market currencies. Second, forward contracts can always be rolled-over if a longer period of sterilisation is required. Spot sales with forward repurchases of reserve currencies can effectively unload large capital inflows. Applications of these swap transactions at least temporarily reduces the central bank's monetary base and overall domestic money balances. These contracts effectively sterilise inflows if their pricing guarantees a greater forward premium than the interest rate differential, thus providing incentives to commercial banks for capital outflows. Foreign currency swaps ought to be viewed as supplementary tools to some, perhaps limited, monetary tightening by other means, primarily through open-market sales. If there is a significant domestic currency forward discount related to high inflation expectations and the expected currency depreciation within a wide band of fluctuations, these swaps will be very costly for central banks.

Foreign exchange swaps have serious disadvantages as well. If central banks do not offer competitive margins on these transactions, member banks have incentives to sell foreign currency in exchange for domestic currency. This practice may be widespread if the banks' monitoring and supervision systems are inefficient. Commercial banks actions would undermine efforts of central banks to sterilise capital inflows in this case. In essence, sterilisation of inflows via swaps is effective when used together with other means of monetary tightening to ensure favourable forward premiums and when commercial banks act accordingly and do not undermine central bank's efforts. The forward premiums are certainly smaller and the swaps less costly when the domestic currency fluctuates within a relatively narrow band of permitted fluctuations. The band widening will increase the cost of these contracts to the central bank.

Alternatively to foreign exchange swaps, central banks can sterilise capital inflows by offering their own outright forward exchange facility. However, they can only do it when domestic forward markets and government security markets are very well-developed. These contracts expose central banks to high fiscal costs since these banks have to pay large forward premiums on foreign currency exceeding interest rate differentials.

Another method of sterilisation of inflows is the *exchange rate band widening*, as applied by Chile in 1992, Colombia in 1993, Poland in 1995 and the Czech Republic in 1996, among others. A wider band of permitted exchange rate fluctuations allows some room for nominal currency appreciation that eventually decreases prices of imported goods. This may relax inflationary pressures and diminish the need for sterilisation. The band widening reduces expectations of the domestic currency's continuous undervaluation, and exposes speculators to a greater risk of currency fluctuations. Consequently, it improves the risk structure of capital inflows. In order to generate desirable effects of a wider band, central banks must explain to the public that the band widening is an integral part of the policy of disinflation and the bank will not give in to the calls for subsequent devaluations commonly voiced in practice by export lobbies. The band widening shall be applied mainly at early stages of large capital inflows so that it will effectively reduce the degree of currency undervaluation and subdue inflationary pressures. If a wider band is applied at a late stage when possibilities of reversed outflows emerge, it may open more room for speculative capital outflows increasing the degree of uncertainty about the nominal exchange rate. The breaking point in this cycle is a recognition of a negative impact on trade and current account balances of the real domestic currency appreciation. In sum, a wider band sends a signal of more uncertainty about the central bank's exchange rate policy that may induce speculative capital outflows. Using band widening is not feasible when the country prepares to join a common currency system; in this case, the band of permitted fluctuations is predetermined and is expected to be narrower, not wider, in the future.

Perhaps the most effective instrument of dealing with capital inflows is a *relaxation of restrictions on capital outflows*. This can be accomplished by elimination of surrender requirements for foreign currency receivables, by the encouragement of investment abroad through tax incentives, or by allowing foreign investors to issue local currency bonds in the domestic market. A further encouragement of outflows can be accomplished through a reduction of restrictions on foreign firms' profit remissions, a reduction of a minimum maturity on foreign loans, encouragement of pension funds to hold a larger portion of their portfolios in foreign assets, lowering the ratio of required reserves on foreign currency deposits in relation to the ratio on domestic currency deposits, and liberalisation of investment in foreign assets by domestic residents. These tools have been effectively used for the purpose of encouraging capital outflows by Chile (between 1990–92), Colombia (1990–94), Mexico (1991), the Philippines (1994), Sri Lanka (1993), Thailand (1991, 1994), and the Czech Republic (1994–96) (Folkerts-Landau and Ito, 1995, pp. 101–2).

Interest rate equalisation taxes have the most durable impact on the encouragement of capital outflows; they have been effectively used by Brazil since 1993. Their purpose is to levy a higher tax on inflows relative to the tax on outflows that would yield a noninflationary proportion of capital balance transactions. Application of this tool has at least two serious pitfalls. First, a higher tax on inflows significantly increases the total cost of capital in the economic system, thus it distorts a proper allocation of economic resources. Second, this instrument is very dangerous in the case of sudden reversed outflows and it may trigger speculative attacks on the domestic currency. This is mainly because adjustments in the tax structure have a longer action-decision lag than the time of a sudden speculative capital flight. Relaxation of restrictions on capital outflows has backfired in several cases in practice, because it sent a positive signal about the currency strength that raised confidence of international investors about the country's capital market and further boosted external capital inflows (Bartolini and Drazen, 1997).

The empirical literature on capital inflows to emerging market economies (Folkerts-Landau and Ito, 1995; Schadler, 1992; Bartolini and Drazen, 1997) seems to conclude that direct sterilisation of large inflows is rather ineffective. This particularly holds true when the inflows are induced by domestic, or 'pull' factors. Adjustments in central banks' interest rates, mandatory reserve ratios, or prolonged applications of open market sales and foreign currency swaps are all very costly for monetary authorities. They involve not only direct quasi-fiscal costs, but they are likely to hamper the real economy growth, primarily investment, consumption and export. The best method to break the transmission of large capital inflows into inflation is fiscal tightening. A mix of loose fiscal and tight monetary policies has always contributed in practice to large capital inflows (Schadler, 1993). However, a careful analysis of empirical studies seems to indicate that this mix has also increased a danger of sudden reversed outflows. A large budget deficit contributes to inflationary pressures that over time add to the real currency appreciation and to deterioration of trade and current account balances. When international investors realise that the central bank is no longer able or willing to sterilise inflows receiving no help from fiscal tightening, a sudden reversed outflow is likely to occur. This implies that an effective control over fiscal policy is the best method of 'sterilisation'.

Another effective method is to permit a nominal currency appreciation by increasing flexibility of exchange rates. Policy-makers ought to realise that greater exchange rate flexibility increases uncertainty of speculators about expected changes in the currency value. Speculative capital inflows in the case of flexible exchange rates may be not as severe as in the case of fixed rates where expectations of a continuous undervaluation are more apparent. An expanded exchange rate flexibility contributes to a healthier structure of capital inflows increasing the share of long-term and diminishing the share of short-term inflows. Consequently, it reduces the risk of sudden reversed capital outflows.

Emerging market economies alone can do very little to change the stream of large capital inflows or outflows. If international interest rates decline, as in the period 1995–96, very likely as a result of the US Federal Reserve monetary easing, international investors seek higher returns in emerging markets' securities. Central banks of emerging market economies should absorb this capital at the lowest possible cost to the economy. A corresponding fiscal tightening is more than welcome to help them. Adversely, signals that industrial countries' central banks begin monetary tightening induce large portfolio capital outflows from emerging markets that ought to have by then enough reserves to defend their currencies. Such massive speculative outflows from emerging markets took place in 1994 and to some extent in the second quarter of 1997 as a result of monetary tightening by the US Federal Reserve. Considering a massive volume of this capital flight that by far exceeds available foreign currency reserves in central banks of emerging markets, there is almost nothing these banks can do to reverse the trend. The IMF and the World Bank's International

136 *Capital Inflows and Convertibility*

Finance Corporation (IFC) with the help of leading central banks of industrial countries should create a special emergency assistance facility aimed at covering at least a portion of the costs of sterilisation of capital inflows to emerging market economies.

THE EVIDENCE FROM CENTRAL EUROPEAN ECONOMIES ON CAPITAL INFLOWS AND THEIR SUDDEN REVERSALS

Monetary authorities in countries of Central Europe are concerned with the problem of large capital inflows, their implications on stability and growth, appropriate response methods, and with the danger of sudden reversed outflows. During the course of their economic liberalisation, stabilisation and privatisation programmes in the first half of the 1990s, Central European countries have attracted large net inflows of direct and portfolio capital. The value of portfolio investment in these countries in 1995 alone reached USD 12.5 billion and the stock of foreign direct investment (FDI) by the end of the same year amounted to USD 38 billion. They have also started to engage in security emission in international capital markets, borrowing this way in 1996 USD 3.5 billion (1.7 in new bonds, 1.6 in stocks and 0.2 in shares). These countries should more extensively engage in the future emission of short-term and medium-term securities as well, primarily the Euro commercial paper (ECP) and Euro medium-term notes (EMTN). The value of capital inflows to Central and Eastern European countries as a share of total capital inflows to emerging market economies is not very large. However, it constitutes a large share of their national income. These inflows are undeniably fruits of economic reforms in these countries and they are beneficial for their continued growth, but they create serious problems as well. In the most general terms, they add to inflation and to trade and current account deficits in these countries. These dangers have diversified magnitudes in different transforming economies of Central and Eastern Europe in response to their different approaches to privatisation, current account and capital convertibility, and monetary policy targeting and implementation including exchange rate systems.

This analysis focuses only on the Czech Republic, Hungary and Poland as countries affected most significantly by problems with capital inflows and, at the same time, as countries planning a future accession to the European Union (EU). Most recent available

Table 5.1 Selected economic indicators and capital flows

	Czech Republic	Hungary	Poland
Real GDP growth rate in 1996	+4.4	+3.0	+7.3
Annual CPI inflation rate, April 1997	+6.7	+18.6	+15.3
Foreign direct investment 1996 stock USD bn (per cent of GDP)	7.2 (13.7)	15.0 (34.2)	12.0 (10.4)
Foreign direct investment 1996 one year flow in USD bn	+1.4	+4.3	+5.2
Foreign currency reserves March 1997 stock USD bn (per cent of GDP)	11.7 (26.2)	9.8 (22.4)	21.1 (18.2)
Foreign currency reserves 1996, one year flow USD bn	–1.6	–2.3	+7.1
Current account balance 1996 in USD bn	–4.5	–1.2	–1.1
Current account balance (per cent of GDP)	–8.6	–2.7	–0.9
Central government budget balance in 1996 (per cent of GDP)	+0.1	–2.0	–2.5
REER* 1996	131.9	98.6	110.1

Note: * REER is the real effective exchange rate index, trade weighted index 1992 = 100 vis-á-vis 21 countries, based on industrial producer prices (as compiled by the National Bank of Hungary).
Sources: Business Central Europe May 1997, and The National Bank of Hungary, The Czech National Bank, The National Bank of Poland – monthly and annual reports.

economic indicators that pertain to external capital flows and their economic repercussions in these countries are presented in Table 5.1.

The three examined countries have experienced FDI inflows to various degrees. Hungary has attracted the highest stock of these inflows in nominal terms and as a share of its GDP, which share is double that in the Czech Republic and approximately three times higher than in Poland. Over the most recent one-year period, FDI inflows to Poland have considerably accelerated while those to the Czech Republic have been slowing down. In 1996, for the first time in recent years, the Czech and the Hungarian foreign currency reserves declined, while Poland's reserves considerably increased. This shows a subdued pace of net inflows in Hungary and in the Czech Republic, but much accelerated in Poland. Yet, Poland is getting closer to the others in terms of the proportion of these reserves to the GDP as a reflection of their impact on inflation and income growth.

Capital inflows along with the applied exchange rate formula have played a major role in various degrees of domestic currency real appreciations. The Czech koruna (CZK) has appreciated considerably, by 32 per cent, in real terms in the period 1992–96. Capital inflows and a prolonged peg without crawling devaluation have contributed to the koruna's strength. The Hungarian forint (HUF) has experience a mild real depreciation in the same period as a result of more effective sterilisations by the Bank of Hungary and the strong rates of crawling devaluation, currently at a monthly rate of 1.1 per cent as of March 1997. The real currency values have a significant impact on current account deficits. The Czech deficit has reached an alarming proportion of over 10 per cent of the country's GDP, the Hungarian deficit is getting closer to this level and the Polish deficit in 1996 follows a surplus in 1995. This questions the sustainability of capital inflows and brings a danger of reversed outflows. The deteriorating trade and current account deficits result from a combination of many systemic, structural and growth-related factors, among them continuously strong, positive GDP growth rates. In particular, the Polish brisk economic recovery has contributed to the reversal of the current account surplus into a deficit in 1996. A strong pressure on the deficit is exerted by high inflation which adds to the real currency appreciation. The Polish zloty (PZL) has appreciated in real terms by 10 per cent since 1992 as shown by the REER index. The index set at 100 in 1992 gives a realistic picture of the degree of real currency appreciation (or depreciation) since the initial shock of corrective inflation in all three countries that was related to price liberalisation and to the erasure of the monetary overhang already expired by the end of 1991. The CZK real appreciation stems from the prolonged fixed peg and is still advancing despite the widening of the band of permitted fluctuations by the Czech national bank (CNB) to plus–minus 7.5 per cent on 28 February 1996.[10]

The Czech currency stability has attracted large capital inflows, yet it has made it difficult to lower the rate of inflation running at a level close to 9 per cent. This level is too high in relation to corresponding inflation rates in the US and in Germany, to which currencies the Czech koruna was pegged (65 per cent DM and 35 per cent USD in the basket) until 26 May 1997. This has contributed to the growing real currency appreciation and to the large current account deficit. These factors have only recently caused a slower growth rate of FDI inflows and a reduction in foreign currency reserves. The CNB has intervened in foreign exchange markets to stabilise the currency and to prevent the reversed outflows, but these interventions cannot fix the growing external imbalance problem. Foreign exchange investors and speculators did react to the questionable sustainability of the Czech koruna fixed rate, launching massive speculative attacks on the koruna on 21–23 May 1997. To avert the attack, the CNB used over USD 2 billion of its foreign currency reserves (equivalent to roughly 4 per cent of the annual GDP) to support the CZK. But the foreign exchange market intervention was not sufficient to restore confidence in the CZK, and the CNB had to declare a free float of the CZK on 26 May 1997. By mid-June, the CZK regained stability both in DM and in USD terms.

The Czech fixed exchange rate and the highest (among the three analysed countries) degree of capital account convertibility may be at least partially blamed for a wrong structure of external capital inflows. The relatively high share of short-term capital inflows has exposed the country to potentially more damaging effects of sudden reversed capital outflows. The total capital account balance of the Czech Republic in 1996 closed with a USD 4074 million surplus, which was less than half of the 1995 surplus. A net flow of foreign direct investment reached USD 1388 million in 1996, almost half of the 1995 amount; both short-term and long-term portfolio investment was USD 725 million, 47 per cent less than in 1995 (CNB: *Monthly Bulletin*, April 1997). There was a significant change in other short-term capital (mostly speculative) net flows. While in 1995 short-term capital showed a net inflow of USD 1052 million, it was reversed into a large net outflow in 1996 of USD 898 million. In addition, CNB foreign currency reserves declined in 1996 by USD 1.6 billion. These numbers show a dramatically deteriorating capital balance position in addition to a large USD 4.1 billion current account deficit in 1996.[11]

Poland and Hungary have been able to avert similar dangers by applying a forced crawling devaluation. At the end of 1997, the monthly rate of crawling devaluation against the basket stood at 1.0 per cent for Poland and 1.1 per cent for Hungary. This solution is, however, useless and counterproductive in the long-run, because crawling devaluation is a serious source of indexation of wages and prices and keeps these countries' inflation running above the annual rate of 15 per cent.[12] Consequently, crawling devaluation has little effect on the real appreciation or depreciation of the national currency in the dynamic adjustment scenario.

For the purpose of improving the structure, or the 'pecking order', and cushioning inflationary effects of capital inflows, the Polish exchange rate system is perhaps superior to the Czech and the Hungarian systems. Poland widened the band of permitted currency fluctuations to plus–minus 7.0 per cent in May 1995, soon after capital inflows started to accelerate, while the Czech Republic delayed the move until 28 February 1996, after the expiration of the large wave of capital inflows. As a result of the band widening, short-term portfolio capital inflows to the Czech Republic considerably decreased (CNB 1996 *Annual Report*, p. 31). This proves a strong impact of the 'push factor' on capital balances of the Czech Republic. The Hungarian band of plus–minus 2.25 per cent may be too narrow. A wider band would increase uncertainty of exchange rate fluctuations. It would, therefore, discourage short-term capital inflows and reduce a risk of speculative outflows.

It is no coincidence that capital inflows to these countries accelerated in 1995 and in the first half of 1996 together with the increased capital flows into emerging market economies. This was largely influenced by the 'push' factor, or by declining international interest rates in developed industrial countries. International investors began seeking higher returns in emerging markets, becoming interested in their securities and in Brady bonds (Bank for International Settlements, 1996). The push factor was induced mainly by the US Federal Reserve monetary policy easing in the presidential election year of 1996. Correspondingly to declining returns on industrial countries fixed income securities, the Brady bonds total return index rose to 141 per cent in 1996 (January 1996 = 100), and accelerated further to 145 by March 1997. Its correction was experienced only after the March 1997 monetary tightening by the Federal Reserve: the index fell to 135. The index changes are strongly correlated to the directions of capital flows to emerging market economies and ought to be closely followed by investors in securities of Central European countries in transition as well.

To defend their economies from speculative capital inflows, Central European monetary authorities have used a variety of sterilisation methods. Unfortunately, the inflationary consequences of rising capital inflows in 1994–96 unfolded rather quickly since the monetary growth largely attributable to external capital inflows exceeded the coincident inflation, with the exception of Hungary where the National Bank of Hungary (NBH) applied tight control over domestic credit. Hungarian domestic credit actually declined in 1996

Table 5.2 Growth of broad money and inflation rates

		1994	1995	1996
Hungary:	M2 growth rate	13.0	18.5	16.1
	CPI inflation	21.2	28.3	19.8
Czech Republic:	M2 growth rate	19.9	19.8	9.2
	CPI inflation	10.0	9.1	8.8
Poland:	M2 growth rate	38.2	35.0	32.7
	CPI inflation	32.2	27.8	18.5

Note: Broad money aggregates include foreign currency deposits.
Sources: The Czech National Bank, the National Bank of Hungary (NBH), the National Bank of Poland – monthly reports.

by 8 per cent in nominal terms. Comparisons between growth rates of broad money, including foreign currency deposits, and inflation rates are presented in Table 5.2.

The data show strong inflationary pressures stemming from monetary growth in Poland and in the Czech Republic. In these two cases monetary growth rates by far exceeded the predetermined targeted levels. For instance, the upper bound of the M2 growth rate for the Czech Republic in 1994 and in 1995 was 10 per cent, while the actual percentage growth of this aggregate was twice bigger. This implies a strong monetary pressure from capital inflows. On the contrary, by imposing a tight control over domestic credit, the NBH cushioned inflationary consequences of foreign capital inflows and prevented real currency appreciation.

Accelerated capital inflows to Central European countries also resulted from the progress in privatisation. Czech mass privatisation attracted large inflows of direct investment in 1994 and in 1995, particularly from Germany. Moreover, Central European countries taking advantage of generally low international interest rates have further contributed to large capital inflows by borrowing in international capital markets. Their total borrowing in 1995 reached USD 6.7 billion which more than doubled the amount borrowed in 1994 (USD 3.7 billion). The final general factor that contributed to large capital inflows by these countries in 1995 and in 1996 was expansion of the current account convertibility to the degree satisfying Article VIII of the IMF Articles of Agreement, as a prerequisite for OECD membership. Poland reached Article VIII current account convertibility status on 1 June 1995, the Czech republic on 1 October 1995, and Hungary on 1 January 1996.

The expanded current account convertibility was accompanied by a significant easing of restrictions on capital account convertibility (Backé, 1996). On their way to OECD membership, these countries signed OECD Codes of Liberalisation of Current Invisible Operations and of Capital Movements. The latter involves commitment to a far-reaching liberalisation of direct investment, real estate operations, portfolio investment, credit operations and other selected capital operations (deposit accounts, foreign exchange operations, life assurance, personal income transfers, and so on). By mid-1997, all three countries were maintaining minimal restrictions on FDI in selected strategic sectors. They are restricting foreign involvement in real estate investment with the exception of that part of residential investment related closely to FDI. Restrictions on portfolio investment are minor, mostly related to permission requirements for purchases of money market securities, negotiable instruments and derivatives by non-residents. Capital outflows have also been considerably liberalised.[13]

Direct investment by foreign residents is not severely restricted. Foreign real estate purchases by residents are limited to ECU 50 000 by Poland and Hungary, but unlimited for the Czechs. Czech residents can invest abroad without limits, although only through authorised banks. Poland fully liberalised institutional resident investment in foreign securities at the end of 1996, but Hungary still restricts investment abroad by domestic residents to highest rated securities of OECD countries only. Both Poland and Hungary restrict investment in foreign money market instruments. Outward credit operations have been fully liberalised in all three countries by their new Foreign Exchange Acts, but at least one resident is required to participate in these transactions. There are some restrictions left on outward portfolio investment; repatriation of foreign exchange earnings from such investment is required in all three countries. Domestic residents are not allowed to open foreign bank accounts except for the case of Poland, where the country's citizens staying abroad or foreign branches of Polish banks can do so without prior approval.

In addition to these standard measures, there are some country-specific restrictions. The Czech Republic extended deposit requirements for inward capital transactions in 1997. Hungary keeps extensive restrictions on short-term capital inflows and its banks have the right to delay inward credits exceeding USD 50 million for up to three months. Purchases of shares of existing banks by non-residents require approval in the Czech Republic only. Domestic securities can be admitted to foreign capital markets with approvals in the case of Poland and the Czech Republic, but without any restrictions in the case of Hungary. The remaining legal restrictions on capital convertibility ought to be normalised for these countries in their preparation programmes for accession to the EU. Their elimination should, however, proceed with caution for the reasons discussed in the next section.

Sterilisation of large capital inflows has been widely applied by central banks of these countries in the period 1995–97. Banks have used a variety of sterilisation methods rather than concentrating only on the most effective tools, and their policy implies a very discretionary and experimental approach to monetary policy which can be explained by the limited experience of monetary authorities with policy formulation and implementation based on indirect policy instruments under the new, decentralised system. Outright open market sales have been widely used by all three banks: the National Bank of Poland (NBP), the National Bank of Hungary (NBH), and the Czech National Bank (CNB). They have had little impact on the intensity of capital inflows. The NBP and the NBH have extensively applied adjustments to the ratio of required reserves to the extent that has introduced enormous uncertainty about statutory reserve requirements in the banking system. The NBH changed the ratio of required reserves for domestic and foreign currency deposits 10 times between January 1995 and June 1996, starting from a 12 per cent requirement on domestic deposits, raised gradually to 17 per cent in June 1995, then reduced in several steps to 12 per cent in June 1996. The NBP raised the ratio of required reserves in February 1997, at the wrong time, since trade and current account balances had already started to deteriorate and a possibility of large reversed outflows became more apparent in the first half of that year.

The ratio of required reserves has served as the main tool for sterilising capital inflows, especially in Hungary. Monetary authorities in Central Europe ought to remember that large adjustments of this ratio are very costly for them since they have to charge simultaneously both (higher) interest rates on foreign currency and (lower) rates on domestic currency liabilities. For example, the spread between these two rates in Hungary reached a peak of 9.5 per cent on 1 February 1996. Large changes in the statutory reserve requirements do not help commercial banks to maximise profits and to finance the economy and they impede their strategic asset and liability management. They put domestic banks in a disadvantageous position compared to foreign banks that are not bound by similar strict requirements.

To weaken inflationary consequences of large capital inflows, the NBH repaid over USD 2 billion of its external debt in 1996. It decided to do so despite low international interest rates which normally do not favour such operations. The debt repayment was the main reason for the reduction of the NBH foreign reserves in 1996.

Central banks have used traditional instruments of sterilisation as well. In all banks the stock of repos had a diminishing tendency in 1995–96, while the stock of reverse repos kept rising. Banks frequently used the differential between interest rates on repos and interest rates on reverse repos as a response to currency speculation.[14] All three central banks have already introduced forward currency swap facilities and they are gradually diminishing the minimum maturity on forward transactions. As a strong policy signal responding to capital inflows, Poland and the Czech Republic used currency-band widening. In addition, Poland used a one-time currency revaluation by 6 per cent against its five-currency basket on 22 December 1995. The revaluation combined with the continuous crawling devaluation can be interpreted as a case of monetary policy inconsistency in Poland.

The CNB responded aggressively to large capital inflows as well. The CNB raised reserve requirements, although less frequently than the NBH, and it has also increased discount and Lombard rates several times since 1994. These polices have been assessed as counter-productive. Higher interest rates resulting from increases in CNB lending rates actually triggered further capital inflows (Brada and Kutan, 1997). The CNB also acquired foreign exchange reserves from the banking system in 1994 and repaid the USD 1.1 billion stabilisation loan from the IMF, although it had a lower interest rate than the implicit cost of acquired foreign exchange reserves by the CNB. Furthermore, it imposed a number of restrictions on short-term capital inflows in 1995. Specifically, it introduced a fee of 0.25 per cent on its foreign exchange transactions with commercial banks in April, and it imposed a quantitative limit on net short-term liabilities of banks to non-residents in August 1995. The impact of net capital inflows on the CNB monetary policy can be divided into two different periods. In 1993–95, increases in CNB foreign exchange reserves were larger than the rate of increase of the entire monetary base, proving that the central bank had to significantly reduce domestic money creation in response to external capital inflows. The ratio of the change in the central bank's net foreign assets to the change in monetary base, or the *sterilisation ratio* for the CNB, was consistently larger than unity in that period, although it declined from 1.49 in 1993, to 1.44 in 1994 and further to 1.12 in 1995. This situation was sharply reversed in 1996 when the decline rather than a growth in net foreign assets of the CNB was compensated by domestic money creation. Correspondingly, the sterilisation ratio reached a negative value of –2.46 (Hrncir, 1997).

A full analysis of sterilising operations goes beyond the technical limits of this study. All three countries have sterilised large capital inflows extensively using a variety of methods. In general terms, their responses suggest a discretionary and expensive methodology of sterilisation that resembles a 'trials and errors' approach.

CONCLUDING REMARKS: CAPITAL ACCOUNT CONVERTIBILITY IN PREPARATIONS FOR ACCESSION TO THE EUROPEAN UNION

All three examined Central European countries are still classified as emerging market economies by international investors. This exposes their capital markets to considerable external capital inflows or reversed outflows, and their defense tools against speculative capital are very limited. This conditionality will continue once these countries start preparations for accession to the European Union. The accession programmes ought to take into consideration that the EU eastern enlargement involves emerging market economies, vulnerable to changes in international capital markets. It this respect, the eastern enlargement will be very different from the admission of selected Southern or Northern European countries in the past.

Accession programmes should not require full capital account convertibility in these countries (Backé and Lindner, 1996). They are still too vulnerable to international capital market shocks and they do not have sufficient defensive mechanisms at their disposal. The European Commission and the future European Central Bank (ECB) ought to provide assistance to the candidate countries' central banks for sterilising or cushioning their economies from large capital inflows and sudden reversed outflows. However, governments of Central European countries need to remember that the best method of neutralisation of large capital inflows and the improvement of their pecking order is a sound fiscal policy accomplished primarily by cuts in government consumption. Ministries of finance ought to share equal responsibility with central banks for the quality of capital inflows and their inflationary effects. The examined countries will require more time to improve domestic productivity through continuous reforms, so that the higher domestic productivity invites more external long-term portfolio capital and direct investment and ultimately improves the pecking order of capital inflows.

These countries need to build the required conditions for capital convertibility. They include a further institutional development of the banking sector and a much better prudential supervision (Diaz-Alejandro, 1985; Backé, 1996). The degree of competition among domestic banks ought to be increased. To be able to effectively use modern sterilisation techniques, particularly currency forward swaps, their financial markets need to be further developed, and it is absolutely essential to give them some time for disinflation. Only under conditions of low inflation (say, not exceeding 5 per cent), will their domestic nominal interest rates be low, and forward currency rates will not include excessive premiums which currently make sterilisation with currency forward swaps very expensive for monetary authorities. Furthermore, some inflation is rational and indispensable during their continuous process of structural adjustments (Orlowski, 1995). These countries need to build credit serving the purpose of structural changes and, at the same time, they need to increase intermediation and capitalisation of their financial institutions. Increasing monetisation of the national economy always involves some inflation as implied by the monetarist view. A faster growth of money balances than the growth of real output always leads to higher inflation (assuming constant velocity of money).

Consequently, their admission ought to be viewed as a special case and the Maastricht monetary convergence benchmark shall not apply. Instead, they are expected to articulate and to implement a long-term programme of disinflation as their competitive structures are built into their economic systems. Correspondingly, Central European candidates should not adopt fixed exchange rates in the beginning of their preparations for accession to the EU. One of the arguments against fixed rates emerging from this study is that the currency peg (or board) and the exchange-rate-based monetary policy do not contribute to the favourable structure of external capital inflows and increase the risk of speculative outflows. On the contrary, more flexible exchange rates favour more long-term portfolio and direct investment capital inflows and increase the uncertainty of exchange rate fluctuations for speculators.

The candidate countries will be well-advised to join the ERM-II system, thus being treated as 'outs' or future members of the Union who do not belong to European Monetary Union and the Euro system (Wyplosz, 1996). This will give them room for some degree of exchange rate flexibility. Further capital inflows under such conditions will not be translated into excessive real appreciation of their currencies, and will not significantly damage their trade and current accounts. To take advantage of a high degree of currency flexibility these countries ought to adopt a wide band of permitted fluctuations in the order of plus–minus 15 per cent. Yet, such a wide band can only be applied when the 1997 wave of speculative capital outflows expires and chances for net inflows emerge.

Notes

1. Professor of Economics, Sacred Heart University, 5151 Park Avenue, Fairfield, CT 06432. USA. Fax +1 203 230 9860; E-mail: Orlowski@sacredheart.edu; Paper to the conference *Opening up for Foreign Capital – Risks and Benefits for Transition Economies* at the Kiel Institute of World Economics, Kiel, Germany, 30–31 May 1997. This version: June 1997. The author wishes to acknowledge support from the Institut für Wirtschaftsforschung in Halle, Germany, and is grateful to Hubert Gabrisch and Thomas Linne who have provided valuable comments. The author remains solely responsible for the content.
2. In general terms, declining interest rates in 1995 and in 1996 were induced by a successful worldwide disinflation and by monetary easing by the US Federal reserve prior to the November 1996 presidential election in the US. These lower interest rates accelerated large capital inflows to emerging market economies. See the Bank for International Settlements report for a detailed empirical investigation of these developments (BIS, 1996, pp. 15–23).
3. For the background literature see Balassa (1964) and Samuelson (1964).
4. The Czech Liquidity Crisis of May 1997 supports this argument.
5. Specifically, the increase of the federal funds rate target from 5.25 to 5.5 per cent by the US Federal Reserve in March 1997 that signaled the US monetary policy reversal from the expansion in 1995 and 1996 induced large, unbalanced capital outflows from emerging market economies in the second quarter of 1997 (BIS preliminary information).
6. In addition to external interest rates other global economy factors are likely to affect the directions of capital flows to and from emerging market economies as well. For instance, deregulation of financial markets in Europe and their increasing integration evolving with

preparations for European Monetary Union can be expected to lower transaction costs of capital transfers and exchange rate risks. The integrated EU capital market will be, therefore, more attractive for allocations of international mutual funds and other portfolio investments at the expense of emerging markets. International business cycles in various regions play a strong role in determining capital movements as well. Expectations of strong economic recoveries in the US or in the EU at least temporarily attract more capital inflows to leading industrial countries. It is essential for Central European countries to be able to sustain high rates of economic growth preventing capital outflows in the near future.

7. For a detailed analysis see Folkerts-Landau and Ito (eds) (1996), pp. 80–94.
8. Foreign currency reserves of the Central Bank of Argentina and the Argentine stock market advanced spectacularly in the period 1991–4. Most of these capital inflows were of private capital returning to Argentina in the presence of credible economic reforms ending hyperinflation. Before 1991, the value of private capital invested abroad was roughly equal to the total external Argentine debt.
9. The quasi-fiscal net cost is in this case equal to the difference between the interest earned on foreign currency reserves and the costs of financing the sterilisation.
10. See Orlowski (1997) for a detailed description of the evolution of exchange rate system in these transforming economies.
11. Data source: the Czech National Bank 'Report on Monetary Development in the Czech Republic for the Period January–September 1996', CNB, Prague, pp. 19–22.
12. Orlowski (1997), Dabrowski (1997), the National Bank of Hungary 1995 *Annual Report* (p. 62) argue that the crawling devaluation contributes to indexation in economies in transformation and considerably adds to inflation.
13. The suspension of borrowing rights of domestic currency for non-residents by the CNB on 22 May 1997 shall be viewed as a temporary solution only.
14. For a more detailed analysis, see the National Bank of Hungary 1995 Annual Report, pp. 64–7.

Bibliography

AIZENMAN, J. and GUIDOTTI, P. 'Capital Controls, Collection Costs and Domestic Public Debt', *Journal of International Money and Finance*, vol. 13, no. 1, 1994, pp. 41–54.

BACKÉ, P. 'Progress Towards Convertibility in Central and Eastern Europe', *The Austrian National Bank: Focus on Transition*, no. 1, 1996, pp. 39–66.

BACKÉ, P. and LINDNER, I. 'European Monetary Union: Prospects for EU Member States and Selected Candidate Countries from Central and

Eastern Europe', *The Austrian National Bank: Focus on Transition*, no. 2, 1996, pp. 20–45.

BALASSA, B. 'The Purchasing Power Parity Doctrine: A Reappraisal', *Journal of Political Economy*, vol. 72, no. 4, 1964, pp. 584–96.

BARTOLINI, L. and DRAZEN, A. 'Capital-Account Liberalization as a Signal', *The American Economic Review*, vol. 87, no. 1, 1997, pp. 138–54.

BANK FOR INTERNATIONAL SETTLEMENTS, *International Banking and Financial Market Developments*, Basel, August 1996.

BRADA, J. C. and KUTAN, A. M. *Trade, Exchange Rate and Macroeconomic Policies for the Transition to Capitalism in the Czech Republic: Almost the Classical Receipe and Almost the Classical Results*, Arizona State University, Department of Economics, 1997. Mimeo.

CALVO, G., LEIDERMAN, L. and REINHARD, C. M. 'Capital Inflows and Real Exchange Rate Appreciation in Latin America: The Role of External Factors', *International Monetary Fund Staff Paper*, vol. 40, 1993, pp. 108–51.

CALVO, G., SAHAY, R. and VÉGH, C. *Capital Flows in Central and Eastern Europe: Evidence and Policy Options*, International Monetary Fund Working Paper no. WP/95/57, Washington D.C., 1995.

THE CZECH NATIONAL BANK, *Report on Monetary Development in the Czech Republic for the Period January–September 1996*, Prague, 1996.

DABROWSKI, M. *Macroeconomic Policy to Promote Disinflation and Growth*, paper to the conference 'Economic Scenarios for Poland' at the Center for Social and Economic Research, CASE, Warsaw, 18 January 1997.

DIAZ-ALEJANDRO, C. 'Goodbye Financial Repression, Hello Financial Crash', *Journal of Development Economics*, vol. 19, 1985, pp. 1–24.

FOLKERTS-LANDAU, D. and ITO, T. (eds), *International Capital Markets: Developments, Prospects, and Policy Issues*, International Monetary Fund, Washington, D.C., 1995.

HRNCIR, M. *Capital Flows and the Banking System: The Czech Experience*, paper to the conference 'Opening up for Foreign Capital, Risks and Benefits for Transition Economies', at the Kiel Institute of World Economics, 30–31 May 1997, mimeo.

MILESI-FERRETTI, G. M. and RAZIN, A. *Current-Account Sustainability*, Princeton University Department of Economics: Princeton Studies in International Finance, no. 81, October 1996.

ORGANIZATION FOR ECONOMIC COOPERATION AND DEVELOPMENT 'Financial Market Trends' no. 66, Paris, March 1997.

ORLOWSKI, L. T. 'Preparations of the Visegrad Group Countries for Admission to the European Union: Monetary Policy Aspects', *The Economics of Transition*, vol. 3, no. 3, 1995, pp. 333–53.

ORLOWSKI, L. T. 'Exchange Rate Policies in Transforming Economies of Central Europe', in L. T. Orlowski and D. Salvatore (eds), *Trade and Payments in Central and Eastern Europe's Transforming Economies*, London, 1997, pp. 123–44.

RAZIN, A., SADKA, E. and YUEN, C.-W. *A Pecking Order Theory of Capital Inflows and International Tax Principles*, International Monetary Fund, Working Paper WP/96/26, Washington, D.C., 1996.

SACHS, J. D. 'Economic Transition and the Exchange Rate Regime', *The American Economic Review: AEA Papers and Proceedings*, vol. 86, no. 2, 1996, pp. 147–52.

SAMUELSON, P. 'Theoretical Notes on Trade Problems', *Review of Economics and Statistics*, vol. 46, May 1964, pp. 145–54.

SCHADLER, S. 'Surges in Capital Inflows: Boon or Curse?' *Finance and Development*, vol. 31, no. 1, 1994, pp. 20–4.

UL HAQUE, N., MATHIESON, D. and SHARMA, S. 'Causes of Capital Inflows and Policy Responses to Them', *Finance and Development*, vol. 34, no. 1, March 1997, pp. 3–6.

WYPLOSZ, C. *Monetary Options or the 'Outs'*, paper to the conference 'Monetary Policy in Transition: Strategies, Instruments and Transmission Mechanisms', The National Bank of Austria, Vienna, 18–19 November 1996.

6 Exchange Rate Policy, Fiscal Austerity and Integration Prospects: The Hungarian Case

Jens Hölscher and Johannes Stephan[1]

INTRODUCTION

Hungary prides itself on being one of the 'hottest' candidates for EU membership in the next round of EU enlargement. It bases this on the fact that, amongst all post-socialist economies, the Visegrád-four have proceeded comparatively further in systemic transformation and economic development than other post-socialist economies. Moreover, in 1992/93, Hungary, together with Poland and the then CSFR, had signed 'Europa Agreements', which can be interpreted as a preliminary step to accession agreements. In fact, Hungary is the country which started as the earliest with systemic reforms in some form of a 'third way'. This can be highlighted not least by the introduction of a two-tier banking system already in 1987, which envisaged, but failed to achieve at this early stage, the hardening of Hungary's 'soft budget constraint' (Kornai, 1986).

Hungary's strategy for systemic transformation and economic development relied to a significant extent on state subsidies for fiscal policy, in order to fight detrimental effects of premature integration and liberalisation ('transformational recession': Kornai, 1993), and secondly on domestic as well as international capital markets for the financing of reforms and economic policies (a capital import-based strategy). For as long as the Hungarian economy produced sufficient foreign trade surpluses and attracted sufficient foreign direct investment, this policy seemed to be sustainable. However, in 1993 and more so in 1994, the economic situation strongly suggested the non-viability of this approach: budget deficits rose alarmingly and domestic demand kept on rising despite reductions in production. The current account deteriorated to a massive deficit in 1993 and capital imports had to increase more than ten-fold to be able to meet liabilities from foreign trade and budgetary needs, which aggravated the burden of foreign indebtedness on Hungary's economy.

Effected by these developments, forint-inflation began to pick up again after having already been reduced from its maximum of 35 per cent per annum for the year 1991 to some 17 per cent per annum for the first quarter of 1994. In addition, the necessary steps of exchange rate devaluations again increased in number and extend from 1993 onwards. Having been considerably successful in monetary stabilisation, redirection of foreign trade to western markets and finally the reversal of economic contraction, Hungary's reformers had to observe an exceedingly unstable financial situation (as suggested). Consequently, the IMF in late 1994 was reluctant to agree to a renewed three-year loan and further borrowing, which questioned Hungary's up-to-then record as a 'model debtor' on international capital markets.

In light of these developments, Hungary's newly-elected coalition government drafted a shift in transformation and development strategy in late 1994, the 'austerity programme', to counter the 'double deficit problem' (Erdös, 1995) of the large general budget and current-account deficits. The programme was implemented in March 1995, and primarily consisted of considerable budgetary cuts which aimed at curbing the disproportionate rise in domestic demand, a shift in the exchange rate strategy, and measures of renewed but careful protection and export promotion.

In its first part, this chapter briefly describes economic developments in Hungary that necessitated the implementation of some measures of fiscal austerity and the immediate reactions of the central bank's monetary policy to the emerging 'double deficit problem'. After then giving an overview of the austerity programme itself, we then assess the initial effects of the package during 1995. Finally, we try to evaluate the influence of this programme's measures for the prospects of EU membership in terms of systemic transformation and conditions for economic growth: whilst on the one hand the programme effected a slowdown of economic growth, it aimed at improving long-term conditions for economic development, though falling short of providing a consistent new strategy for systemic transformation and economic development for Hungary.

THE HUNGARIAN SCENARIO

The most striking experience with the Hungarian systemic transformation is that its gradual approach to a 'third way' of economic organisation started at a time where economic governance and control in all other CEE countries remained ideologically determined by socialist paradigms. However, this 'systemic goulash' remained inherently inconsistent, as it allowed some free market-determination of prices and quantities, some competition, some private entrepreneurship and some foreign trade with the West, whilst retaining the 'soft budget constraint' not least *vis-à-vis* the state-owned sectors.

It is rooted in these inconsistencies that Hungary, well before the final shift to a competitive system and economic integration with the West from 1990 onwards, accumulated a high level of foreign debt and experienced 'creeping' inflation. Whilst Hungary was commonly expected to suffer less from systemic reforms and to endure a shorter period of transitional recession due to its early start, foreign indebtedness and inflation proved to be a considerable hindrance to a fast catch-up to western levels of economic development and welfare.

The Foreign Position

The level of Hungary's gross foreign debts *vis-à-vis* economies with convertible currencies, that is 'hard' debts, had already reached nearly USD 20 billion in 1988 and, following from that, rose to USD 31.7 billion by March 1995 (NBH, 1995b, p. 96).

In line with the bilateral rescheduling of its foreign debts towards longer maturities, and due to significant rises in export earnings, Hungary, until 1992, managed to reduce its annual debt service obligations and subsequently debt service indicators improved gradually. From then onwards, though, this tendency reversed, offsetting prior achievements by the end of 1994 (NBH, 1995b, pp. 95, 240). Independent from that, official reserves stagnated in 1994 at USD 6.8 billion, sufficient to cover some seven months of imports of goods and services (see Table 6.1).

Parallel to the gradual redirection of foreign trade towards Western markets from the mid-1980s onwards, Hungary managed to retain a slightly positive trade balance in its balance of payments until the end of 1991. During 1992, however, the balance turned negative and deteriorated to USD 3.2 billion in 1993 and USD 3.6 billion in 1994,

Table 6.1 Hungary's foreign position (in USD millions)

	1990	1991	1992	1993	1994	1995
Current account (convertible currencies)	127	267	324	−3 455	−3 911	−2 480
Capital account (convertible currencies)	−689	2 453	437	6 091	3 255	7 012
Gross foreign debt	21 270	22 658	21 438	24 560	28 521	31 655
Official reserves (gold and forex.)	1 166	4 017	4 381	6 738	6 769	12 011
Debt service indicator[1]	49.0%	32.2%	31.2%	38.6%	48.7%	43.8%

Note: [1]Debt service as total debt service (credit amortisation and gross interest payment) in relation to exports of goods and services.
Source: National Bank of Hungary.

mainly attributable to falling export figures in the balance of payments for convertible currencies (NBH 1995a, p. 212). The current account developed accordingly.

Resulting from the gradual introduction of free convertibility for the forint, a new source for foreign debts emerged: international financial markets became an important source for primarily, of course, the state budget (although organised by the Hungarian central bank), but increasingly also for private entrepreneurs and investors in Hungary; and the fraction of foreign debts owed by the private sector rose from 14 per cent in 1990 to over 25 per cent in 1995 (NBH, 1995b, p. 19).

State Budget

In addition to its foreign indebtedness, Hungary's economy faces another considerable imbalance: the state budget. In the face of a young emerging tax system, revenues did not suffice to cover the immense financial needs of the general government during transition. Whilst revenues from consumption taxes initially fell in real terms until 1992, and whilst income taxes only grew very slowly and payments by economic entities (for example corporate taxation) fell in real terms, expenditure for social security and other central budgetary institutions, as well as for the servicing of the stocks of domestic and foreign debts increased disproportionally.[2]

Table 6.2 Hungary's state budget (in HUF billions)

	1990	1991	1992	1993	1994	1995
Central government balance	−1.4	−114.1	−201.8	−181.8	−276.4	−292.6
Social security funds	−0.6	−9.3	−17.3	−30.3	−35.0	−47.1
Extra-budgetary funds	−1.3	+ 4.3	+ 3.7	+ 35.1	+ 0.5	−10.0
Local governments	n.a.	n.a.	+ 12.0	−16.9	−48.3	−12.3

Note: The figures for 1990 and 1991 differ slightly in terms of methodology. Especially, privatisation income is not being considered in budgetary revenues from 1992 onwards.
Source: National Bank of Hungary.

Outside the government's budgetary items, the position of the social security funds had already deteriorated in 1992, and the budgetary situation of the local governments constantly worsened. In comparison to the year before, extra-budgetary funds in 1994 received a mere 50 per cent of transfers from the central budget. The subsequently emerging deficits had to be financed mainly by auctions of state bonds and securities, but as well, to some degree, by monetisation via the central bank (see Table 6.2).

With the gradual adoption of a market-type financing of the budget in the course of the reform processes, and the subsequent reduction in the central bank's involvement in budgetary revenues, Hungary's underdeveloped domestic capital markets were placed under an increasing burden which must have added to the rising level of real interest rates. While the deficits remained sustainably low until 1990 (peaking at HUF 55 billion in 1989), the year 1991 marked the beginning of high-level deficits, peaking to over HUF 320 billion for the fiscal year 1994.[3] In line with concurrent state budget deficits, gross state debt rose to 88.8 per cent of GDP by December 1994 (NBH, 1994, pp. 56–7).

The Dispute over the Development of Domestic Demand

In assessing the reasons underlying this unbalanced development, opinions differed greatly. The National Bank of Hungary was convinced that 'growth of domestic demand had to be curbed in order to improve the current account, primarily by cutting the excessive financing requirement of the general government ... In light of that,

Table 6.3 Changes in the structure of Hungary's domestic demand (percentage change to previous year)

	1993	1994		1993	1994
Production	−0.6	+1.5	Final consumption[1]	+2.0	+0.4
			Gross accumulation	+3.4	+3.0
Import[1]	+3.4	+4.9	Exports	−2.6	+3.0
Supply factors	+2.8	+6.4	Demand factors	+2.8	+6.4

Note: [1] Excluding Russian military equipment.
Source: NBH, 1994, p. 21.

cutting enterprise demand for credit was unavoidable' (NBH, 1994, p. 19). In contrast to that, the government held that the current account deficit in 1993 had been the expected and necessary result of Hungary's economic 'take-off', and the weak export performance was exacerbated by an unfavourable development of external markets and adverse weather conditions in regard to agricultural production. Therefore, the balancing of the current account had to be achieved by a future expansion of exports with the additional help of growing domestic demand and investment.

In respect to the foreign deficit, the government accepted that the previous accumulation of foreign debts could not be continued. The current account deficit of HUF 3.9 billion in 1994 was to be reduced to some HUF 2.5 billion, an amount which the government assumed could be financed by use of the inflow of foreign direct investment and direct foreign borrowing by the private sector. The government planned to freeze foreign indebtedness of the public sector (which included the central bank's position), whilst privatisation revenues were to account for one-third of public expenditure (some 9 per cent of GDP).

Table 6.3 sheds some light on the development of Hungary's domestic demand, distinguished as supply factors which constitute supply of goods and services in the domestic economy, and demand factors which determine demand for domestically produced or imported goods and services.

In 1993, the volume of aggregate demand rose by some 2.8 per cent, whilst domestic production was down by 0.6 per cent. Subsequently, the volume of imports had to rise by 3.4 per cent in order to fill the gap between domestic demand and domestic production. Regardless

Table 6.4 Development of consumption and investment
(Previous year = 100, changes in real terms)

	1990	1991	1992	1993	1994	1995
Consumption of households	96.4	94.4	100.0	101.9	99.8	93.4
Consumption of government	102.6	97.4	104.9	127.5	87.3	97.0
Total consumption	97.3	94.9	100.6	105.4	97.7	93.9
Gross fixed capital formation	92.9	89.6	97.4	102.0	112.5	95.7
Gross capital formation	95.8	78.9	97.6	132.3	119.8	106.3

The figures assume that the respective previous years had the value of 100.0. Consumption of households in 1991 was 94.4 if it was 100 in 1990 and so on. This obviously implies that the figures minus 100 (in the example above: 94.4 − 100 = −5.6) represent percentage changes. Most of the Hungarian statistics presents their figures in 'previous year = 100', but you can change the table into 'percentage changes' if you prefer.
Source: HCSO, 1995, p. 224.

of the fact that in 1994 the rise in aggregate demand was accompanied by a rise in domestic production, the economy still had to import an increasing amount of goods and services.

The composition of aggregate demand exhibits a significant structural change: whilst exports picked up in 1994 after having fallen in 1993, final consumption nearly stagnated in 1994 after having grown considerably in 1993. This development is also observable in the fraction of accumulated consumption in GDP: the ratio rose steadily until 1993 to 88.4 per cent, but fell in 1994 to 85.3 per cent. Consequently, the fraction of accumulation of fixed capital in GDP rose slightly from 18.7 per cent in 1993 to 19.7 per cent in 1994, although having already reached 20.7 per cent in 1991 (NBH, 1994, p. 172, own calculations).

A breakdown of consumption and accumulation into its individual components (Table 6.4) shows that consumption of households merely stagnated in real terms, whilst the rise in 1993 is attributable to government consumption, when its value rose by 27.5 per cent in real terms.

The quantitatively most important reason for the disproportionate rise in domestic demand during the years 1993 and 1994, however, can be found in the rise in capital accumulation, a real investment boom: gross fixed and gross capital formation rose by 2 per cent and 32.3 per cent respectively during 1993, and 12.5 per cent and 19.8 per cent respectively during 1994.

158   *Exchange Rate Policy and Integration: Hungary*

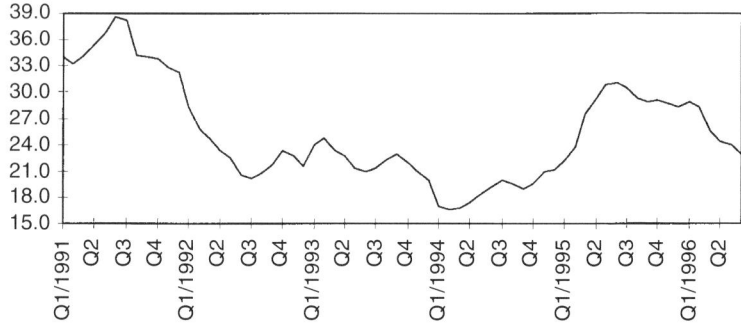

Figure 6.1   Hungarian inflation

Source: National Bank of Hungary.

Prices and Exchange Rates

Since the remarkable success in stabilising the forint's real value between 1991 and 1993, inflation fell steadily from its peak at nearly 39 per cent per annum (in monthly figures) during the third quarter of 1991, to its minimum level of 16.5 per cent during the first quarter of 1994. From the second quarter of 1994 onwards, however, the rise in consumer prices began to accelerate again (Figure 6.1).

This renewed monetary destabilisation can be traced back to mainly two roots: whilst having remained clearly below the rate of inflation, nominal rises in wages and earnings in 1994 effected increases in real terms of over 6 per cent (gross) and 8.5 per cent (net) and thereby contributed to the disproportionate rise in aggregate demand over aggregate production (in Figure 6.2). It can, in addition, be assumed that the destabilising potential of both the rising level of foreign indebtedness and constantly accumulating budgetary deficits effected a reduction in individuals' trust in the credibility of the forint's still emerging and fragile monetary constitution, possibly even giving rise to a destabilising preference of individuals to divert their monetary assets to other means of more stable value (capital flight).

This coincides with the observation that

> households increasingly preferred foreign exchange as a form of savings. This was especially true for the second half of 1994 when the surplus of household foreign exchange accounts

Figure 6.2 Development of earnings (nominal figures)

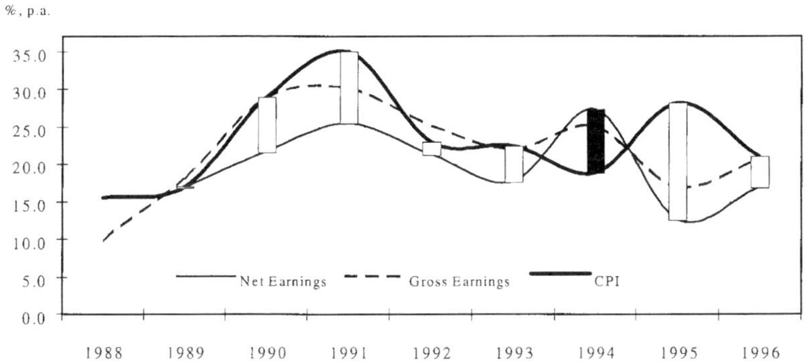

Source: National Bank of Hungary.

(USD 486 million) was much larger than in the same period of the preceding year (USD 307 million). (NBH, 1994, p. 108)

During that year, foreign exchange savings deposits increased by 43.5 per cent, whereas forint deposits declined in real terms. The central bank concluded: 'The *crowding-out effect of foreign currencies increased*, owing to the almost constantly present, periodically intensifying devaluation expectations' (NBH, 1994, p. 60). The italics appear in the original text, not our emphasis.

After having achieved some stability in the nominal exchange rate, necessary realignments started to pick up in terms of frequency and extent of devaluation from mid-1994 onwards, when inflation, too, began to rise again (Table 6.5). This development cannot be attributed to a discrete step towards convertibility, since restrictions on capital transfers had mostly been lifted already during 1992. Neither does the widening of the free floating range of the forint from 0.5 per cent to 1.25 per cent in August 1993 seem to have significantly effected this inability of exchange rate policy to sustain the stability of the nominal exchange rate any more.

Rather, the strikingly parallel development between the accumulation of foreign debts and budgetary deficits on the one side, and of prices and the exchange rate on the other, underpins our case that the early Hungarian transformation strategy of 'overspending' domestically by use of foreign markets (capital import-based strategy) was unsustainable in the long term and forced a reorientation in Hungary

Table 6.5 Forint exchange rate devaluations and average market exchange rate changes against the pegged currency basket

	Dates and rates of official devaluation against central rates of the currency basket[1] of forint pegging							Accumulation over the year	Average market exchange rate changes
1990	31 January 1.0	6 February 2.0	20 February 1.0					5.0	16.1
1991	7 January 15.0	8 November 5.8						20.8	16.4
1992	16 March 1.9	23 June 1.6	9 November 1.9					5.4	7.9
1993	12 February 1.9	26 March 2.9	7 June 1.9	9 July 3.0	29 September 4.5			14.2	10.9
1994	3 January 1.0	16 February 2.6	13 May 1.0	10 June 1.2	5 August 8.0	11 October 1.1	29 November 1.0	15.9	15.6
1995	3 January 1.4	14 February 2.0	13 March 9.0	Rest of year[2] 13.8				26.2[2]	26.9

Note: [1]The basket was based on the currency composition of foreign trade until 8 December 1991, of equal share of US dollar and ECU until 1 August 1993, of equal share of US dollar and DM until 15 May 1994, and since then of 70 per cent of ECU and 30 per cent of US dollar.
[2]From 16 March onwards, the forint followed a pre-announced crawling-peg system of daily devaluations. The accumulated yearly rate of official devaluations for 1995 is therefore an estimate.

Source: National Bank of Hungary.

in late 1994, coinciding with the shift in parliamentary power. Before we can turn our attention to the specifics and extent of this reorientation, the reaction of monetary policy shortly before the introduction of the 'austerity-programme' to these adverse developments will be briefly outlined, in order to demonstrate the extent of a Hungarian policy deficit, bearing in mind that the central bank's stabilisation efforts in late 1994 were not able to re-establish monetary stability and will have effected, if any, a contraction of economic activity via high level interest rates associated with a restrictive monetary policy.

The Response of Monetary Policy in 1994

In the face of rising inflation in early 1994, the National Bank of Hungary aimed at executing a more restrictive monetary policy: it contracted the terms and volume of foreign exchange and government securities repurchase agreements with commercial banks and increased the relevant central bank interest rates. During 1994 the repo rate rose by 8.25 percentage points, repo transactions were limited to a minimum maturity of 15 months (up from prior one week arrangements), and the central bank base rate rose from 22 per cent to 25 per cent on 15 June (NBH, 1994, p. 25).

As a further measure, the forint was devalued by 8 per cent from its central rate *vis-à-vis* the currency basket of pegging at the beginning of August 1994. 'This measure, however, was not coupled with the necessary fiscal adjustment ... the devaluation did not slow down the growth of imports, and it failed to make an appreciable change in exports as well' (NBH, 1994, p. 24). In order to retain external competitiveness by preventing the appreciation of the forint in real terms, the currency had to be repeatedly devalued again: by 1.1 per cent in October 1994 and by 1 per cent in November 1994, raising total market devaluation in 1994 to 15.6 per cent.

Combining these stylised facts on Hungary's economic situation during the period before the introduction of the austerity-programme, it becomes apparent that the underlying economic situation (growth in economic activity: production and fixed investment) showed promising sign of recovery. This, however, at the expense of the financial situation: the state budget's deficit was worsening and the development of inflation did not grant any margin for a Keynesian policy of demand management either via central bank monetisation or additional borrowing (but would have rather necessitated a budgetary surplus). The shift from a merely balanced foreign position in 1993 to unsustainable current account deficits from 1994 onwards induced a parallel development of capital imports, which resulted in a further rise in Hungary's foreign indebtedness, which in turn further destabilised the exchange rate.

There was neither a margin to reduce foreign indebtedness nor to release the burden of high interest rates on domestic capital markets, but by improving the external trade balance and by reviewing the size but also the structure of budgetary expenditure. Any further restricting of monetary policy would not have had the potential to solve any of the underlying problems and would even have failed in fighting its symptoms. This is the reason for the necessity of a shift in Hungary's approach to systemic transformation and economic development.

THE AUSTERITY PROGRAMME AND ITS INITIAL EFFECTS

The austerity package focused on the two main aspects of macroeconomic disequilibrium: improving foreign trade and balancing the state budget. The underlying theoretical and conceptual assumptions in favour of fiscal austerity as well as positive foreign trade balances are *to make room to ease monetary policy*: a 'double surplus' would allow for a significantly lower level of interest rates, which would still be consistent with monetary stability and would better promote economic growth and hence 'catch-up' development.

The Main Features of the Programme

The austerity programme consisted mainly of the following measures:[4]

Budget

- Social welfare cuts, including means-testing of child allowances, charges for outpatient care and new university tuition fees.[5]
- A strict ceiling on wage increases for public sector workers, resulting in real wage losses (19 per cent nominal), pensions developed accordingly.
- Expansion of the category of incomes to which the 44 per cent social security contribution applies.
- An expected increase in returns from privatisation.

- Redistribution of budgetary revenues from local councils to the central budget in order to increase central control over government expenses.
- The central government deficit was planned not to exceed 3 per cent of the official GDP forecast (the original budget at the beginning of the year 1995 calculated a deficit of 5.4 per cent of GDP).[6]

Foreign trade

- The adoption of a crawling-peg system from the end of March 1995 onwards (pre-announced regular steps of currency devaluation: maximum devaluation of 1.9 per cent per month until July 1995, then 1.3 per cent).
- Several small and one major step (9 per cent) of forint devaluation during January to March 1995.
- The customs code imposed a new 8 per cent surcharge on all imports (excluding capital imports), and reduced the value of imports without licence requirements.
- In the agricultural sector: export subsidies and higher import tariffs.
- In the car production industry: restriction of car imports to those older than four years from January 1995 onwards.
- Increased export promotion through the Economic Development Fund, and further tax preferences for investors in the export sector, and export financing through the Hungarian Export Credit Insurance Bank and the Hungarian Export–Import Bank.

Monetary policy[7]

- Reduced financing requirement of the central bank for the budget (monetisation).
- The central bank base rate rose from 25 to 28 per cent in February 1995.
- Minimum reserve requirements on deposits for commercial banks rose from 12 to 16 per cent in May 1995.
- The central bank stopped granting forint loans against the bank's foreign exchange deposits in January 1995.
- The shortest maturity for forex deposits was raised from 15 months to 3 years in January 1995.

ASSESSMENT: INITIAL EFFECTS OF THE PROGRAMME

Already towards the end of 1995, the austerity programme seemed to be showing positive results:

> Due to the comprehensive fiscal and monetary adjustment measures considerable shifts have taken place in the income distribution and in the main proportions of the macro-economy. These are: shifts in the net financial position of the government and business sector in favour of the latter; in the absorption of GDP between domestic and external sector in favour of exports; in the income position from the household sector to the enterprise sector ... (NBH, 1996b, p. 1)

Hungary's macroeconomic data for the year 1995 suggest further improvements: export sales nearly doubled and the trade deficit fell to USD 2.8 billion (down from USD 3.6 billion in 1994).[8] Hungary's foreign debt kept on rising, although at a slower pace. Whilst the rise in gross foreign debts persisted in the course of 1995, Hungary's foreign reserves rose to USD 12.0 billion (equalling some 9 months of imports). Privatisation income amounted to around USD 2.9 billion (NBH, 1996b, p. 2), the fraction of revenue for the government, however, being only 1.19 billion (Vági/Szakadát, 1996, p. 35), which corresponded to the budgetary target. The general government deficit, therefore, rose to only HUF 370 billion, bringing down the fiscal deficit to approximately 6.2–6.5 per cent of GDP (down from 8.1 per cent in 1994, NBH 1996b, p. 2). Also, the share of the central government deficit in GDP fell from 6.3 per cent to some 5.5 per cent (Vági/Szakadát, 1996, p. 2).

Due to fiscal austerity during the year 1995, expenditure in almost all categories of the central budget rose slower than during the year before. Its contribution to social security declined in real terms after having enjoyed a nominal rise of nearly 60 per cent in 1994. Debt service and interest payments, the highest item in the rank (consuming approximately one-fourth of total expenditure), rose again by over 40 per cent, after nearly doubling in 1994 and remained sensitive to the rate of nominal interest (NBH, 1995b, p. 114). Deflating the rise in total central government expenditure with the underlying rate of inflation, the real value of budgetary expenditure in 1995 actually fell by some 6 per cent after having risen by some 3 per cent in 1994 (Table 6.6).

Table 6.6 Development of central government expenditures (percentage change to previous year)

	Total central government expenditure	Industrial policy[1]	Benefits through social security	Debt service and interest payments	Transfers to central government	Transfers to local government	Transfers extra budgetary funds
1994	22.0	41.5	59.8	94.7	−11.2	11.9	−50.7
1995	21.7	25.3	6.4	40.8	23.1	14.4	−41.6

Note: [1] Production, housing and export price subsidies plus investment expenditure.
Source: National Bank of Hungary.

The upward trend of prices seemed to be stopped or even reversed, inflation began to fall back again from its peak of 31 per cent per annum for June 1995 to 28.2 per cent per annum for December 1995.[9] Household wages in the private, as well as in the public, sector declined in real terms over the year 1995. Despite the central bank's more restrictive stance on monetary policy during the year 1995, real interest rates on personal loans fell from 7.4 per cent in January 1995 to 1.7 per cent in June, and real interest rates on business loans came down from 10 per cent to 5.1 per cent. The *ex-post* macroeconomic real interest rate fell from 8.4 per cent in 1994 to only 4.1 per cent in 1995. In July 1995, the overnight repo money market rate fell by one percentage point to 32.5 per cent, and in August again to 31.5 per cent (EIU, 3/1995, p. 13). This development is to some degree attributable to the reversal in the rise of inflation in mid-1995, in combination with expected lower price rises for the near future, and might furthermore indicate improved capital market access in domestic as well as foreign markets, and possibly a lower interest rate spread in line with the improvement of banks' portfolios. GDP continued to increase by 1.5 per cent in 1995, although at a significantly slower rate (down from 2.9 per cent in 1994).

The newly-introduced exchange rate regime of a 'crawling-peg' had been designed to stabilise expectations on foreign exchange markets. Whether it is also able to prevent the appreciation of the real exchange rate (which constituted the aim of the preceding regime), depends on the (politically motivated) extent of pre-announced steps of devaluation. However, the new scheme will only be able to improve credibility if policy restricts itself to the pre-announced rates and dates. Whilst Nuti (1995, p. 21) takes the opinion that this regime 'deserves serious consideration in the case of post-communist economies', Erdös (1995, p. 13) dismisses this concept and rather prefers the acceptance of revaluation in real terms. Only if this policy succeeds in replacing the risk-premium on the interest rate parity to convertible currencies by a risk-free, pre-determinable premium, will this concept come to Hungary's advantage. Elsewise, it might serve as 'stabilisation of instability'.

In as far as the March austerity-programme aimed at a break with the 'overspending', it assisted Hungary to develop in a more sustainable manner. However, the central bank's attempt to execute some kind of 'financial repression', hence curbing investment, aggravated the retarding effects on Hungary's economic growth. In addition, the programme remained inconsistent as it failed to acknowledge the relation between capital imports, foreign indebtedness and monetary destabilisation. It therefore did not face up to the challenge to re-define Hungary's strategy of systemic transformation and economic development.

FISCAL AUSTERITY AND EU CONVERGENCE

Growth in Central-East Europe is the precondition for economic integration and, subsequently, for a tendency to catch up to levels of GDP per capita income in the European Union. 'Any study of integration should begin by observing that economic growth ... is both the aim of, and a constraint upon, instruments promoting integration' (Kaser, 1996, p. 208; also refer to Kornai, 1994, for this argument), in as much as insufficient growth in the catching-up region worsened the prospects for integration and the effects of integration (detrimental effects of premature integration).

In the case of Hungary, as probably one of the first accession countries, the crucial question in this context is how far the austerity programme might have on the one hand constrained growth and thereby potentially delayed Hungarian EU membership, and on the other hand improved the conditions for a future sustainable 'catch-up' development.

An orientation of the degree to which every percentage point of economic growth matters is provided by Baldwin's calculations (1994, p. 178): assuming a rate of annual growth of 4 per cent, then 19 years would be needed to achieve budget neutrality within the existing EU funding allocation system; a rate of 10 per cent would still lead to a duration of eight years. Whether or not the assumptions of these calculations are realistic, they clearly show the general relevance of the austerity programme, which could even turn out to have been counterproductive in respect to the Hungarian (political) aim of early EU membership.

In this respect, Table 6.4 indicates some relevant answers: whilst consumption had been a prime target in the austerity programme, the 1995 growth figure (−6.1 per cent) still compares well to the respective figure for 1994 (−2.3 per cent). The opposite holds true for gross fixed and gross capital formation: after having enjoyed a boom until 1994, they suffered a substantial decline in 1995, which may well be held as a result of the austerity programme. In any case, these figures provide strong explanatory power for the weak positive economic growth in Hungary following the introduction of the March package. Immediately following the execution of the programme, Hungary's economy was curbed: whilst the economy still grew at a healthy pace of 2.9 per cent in 1994, economic growth declined to an annual rate of only 1.5 per cent in 1995 (Figure 6.3).

Hungary's accession does not directly depend on the fulfilment of the Maastricht criteria: no reference hereto had yet been made. Reference can, however, be made to the 'Europa Agreements', which were designed and still today form the legal basis for the prospected accession of the Visegrád countries to the EU. The Maastricht criteria aim at the determination of convergence in the monetary field and were formulated to draw back on indisputable criteria for a decision over the participation of member economies in the venture towards a

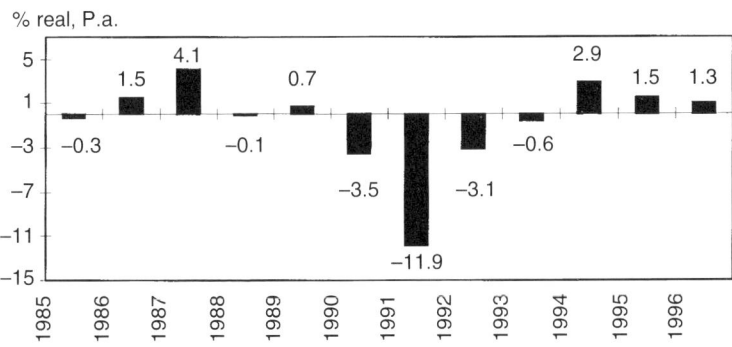

Figure 6.3 Development of real GDP

single currency. The prospected Hungarian EU membership has nothing to do with the currency union so far, but aims in the first instance at Hungary's participation in the single market, possibly to benefit from the EU's various structural funds. Here, obviously, the relevant convergence criteria would have to assess the competitiveness of production on domestic and foreign product and factor markets.

In this chapter, however, we argue that real economic integration for insufficiently converged economies does not automatically exhibit (welfare)benefits from a reallocation of resources amongst members along the patterns of 'comparative advantages', but rather tends to effect a reinforcement of 'absolute disadvantages'.[10] The reason lies in the fact that the pattern of 'comparative advantages' necessarily has its roots in prices, the determination of which between different currency areas is subject to the exchange rate and is subsequently quite independent of the respective factor and resource endowments: this is the essence of the concept of 'comparative costs'.

Any evaluation of EU membership for Hungary has therefore to carefully observe the conditions of the monetary regime under which real integration takes place: with perfectly flexible exchange rates to be ruled out as virtually impossible in the European context, the Hungarian monetary constitution will have to exhibit sufficient stability to warrant a fixed or pegged exchange rate without resulting in unsustainable real exchange rate revaluations.

How then does the Hungarian economy compare to those of contemporary members of the EU with respect to the monetary convergence criteria, laid out in the Maastricht-treaty? The level of Hungary's general government debt was typically high right from the outset of transformation and subsequently it already exceeded the criterion in 1988. The continuous rise in state debt is not only due to ordinary budgetary expenditure, but also has its roots in various other government commitments in bonds: Housing Fund Coverage Bonds aiming at placing the system of financing housing on a market basis; bonds related to the consolidation schemes; bonds issued to purchase the rouble debt owed by the NBH; and bonds issued to finance the two social security funds. Furthermore, the government keeps accumulating debt against the central bank through forint devaluations. With respect to the prospected EU membership, the current trend in government debt in relation to GDP would therefore have to be reduced considerably and finally reversed (see Table 6.7).

Table 6.7 The Maastricht convergence criteria:[1]
Hungary in comparison with EU economies

Year-end, 1995	Government debt (per cent of GDP)	Government deficit (per cent of GDP)	Inflation rate[2] (per cent p.a.)	Government bond yields[3] (per cent p.a.)
Maastricht criterion	max. 60	max. 3.0	max. 3.1	max. 8.5
Luxembourg	6.0	−1.5	1.9	7.2
Denmark	71.9	1.6	2.3	8.3
Ireland	81.6	2.0	2.4	8.3
Germany	58.1	3.5	1.5	6.9
France	52.8	4.8	1.7	7.5
Finland	59.2	5.2	1.0	8.8
United Kingdom	54.1	5.8	3.1	8.3
Netherlands	79.7	4.0	1.1	6.9
Austria	69.0	5.9	2.0	7.1
Belgium	133.7	4.1	1.4	7.5
Sweden	78.7	8.1	2.9	10.2
Portugal	71.7	5.1	3.8	11.5
Spain	65.7	6.6	4.7	11.3
Italy	124.9	7.1	5.4	12.2
Greece	111.8	9.1	9.0	17.3
Hungary	88.0	6.5	28.2	31.0

Note: [1]The criterion of a minimum of 2 consecutive years of stability within the exchange rate mechanism obviously does not compare directly and is therefore not exhibited in the table.
[2]Inflation rates for EU economies are approximated by use of Eurostat's standardised method of IICP, for Hungary by use of the central bank's consumer price index.
[3]Interest rates are measured on the basis of long-term government bonds.
Sources: EMI (1996, p. 54) and National Bank of Hungary.

The same applies to the budget: the balance shows a remarkable recovery from substantial year-on-year deficits (financed mainly by bonds and T-bills), which reached its maximum of 8.3 per cent of GDP in 1994. Whilst this reduction is attributable to the ambitious budgetary cuts of the austerity programme, it remains to be seen whether the Hungarian government is able to sustain this ambitious level of fiscal austerity in general, and of social spending in particular, until GDP picks up to a much stronger level. As, in addition, the development of nominal interest rates bears important significance for the budget, a falling level will ease the burden of returning to a balanced budget

(Hungary today has to accumulate some 3 per cent per GDP surplus in the primary budget to achieve a balanced budget).

Inflation will remain high for the time being, certainly well above the critical Maastricht value for some years to come; it departed from a level below 10 per cent in 1987, when price, currency and trade liberalisation led the rate of inflation to rocket up to its peak of 35 per cent per annum only four years later. The development of long-term government bond yields will, next to inflation, depend on the future growth of the economy, which might well remain low. Having reached their maximum in August 1995 (35.3 per cent), they are currently falling slowly, but will certainly not come close to Maastricht levels for some years to come.

This quite pessimistic assessment can be mirrored against Kornai's early assessment (December 1994) of the Hungarian 'macroeconomic tensions' of inflation, unemployment, the budget deficits and the balance-of-payments deficit and the 'policy-package' devised to meet these tensions, in which he, as a general theme, stresses the category of 'lasting growth as top priority' (Kornai, 1994).

CONCLUSION

Hungary constitutes an example of a small open economy with a fragile balance-of-payments position: whilst its strong positive balance-of-payments items (tourism, administered capital imports and foreign direct investment: Landesmann and Pöschl (1996, Figure 7.3, p. 150) allowed the economy to run significant deficits in visible trade from 1993 onwards, the subsequently aggravating burden of foreign indebtedness forced policy-makers into measures of ambitious fiscal austerity and improved external competitiveness.[11] Relatively weak initial currency undervaluation (in terms of ERDI: *ibid.*, p. 154) might let the negative effects of (premature) integration remain low, producing better catch-up results (in terms of GDP per capita) in a scenario of intensified integration, but less positive ones for a scenario of full EU membership (*ibid.*, Table 7.5, p. 158).

In the aftermath of the austerity programme, it is not a surprise that economic growth was curbed. This situation calls for active trade policy on the European side, in order to ease Hungary's balance-of-payments position, rather than the protection by the European Union against imports from Eastern Europe. The minimum would be the tolerance of Hungarian trade policy (effecting Hungarian export surpluses) in order to overcome balance-of-payments pressure.[12] The political economy of integration shows that such an asymmetrical 'protectionist' strategy can probably be implemented easier from the outside, rather than from the inside, of a free trade area.[13] Political arguments in favour of a rapid accession should therefore be carefully weighed against economic facts.

Notes

1. Helpful comments of Péter Bod, in particular for shedding some light on controversial data surveys, are gratefully acknowledged.
2. With regard to its role, it is noteworthy that in 1994 Hungary's primary balance was actually in surplus at some HUF 40 billion, after having been in deficit for the years before (NBH, 1994, p. 54).
3. In the course of the years 1992 to 1994, an additional burden was put on the state budget via two consolidation schemes (loan and bank consolidations), both of which were designed to solve the problem of 'bad assets' in commercial banks' portfolios. Non-performing assets were exchanged against interest-bearing consolidation bonds to an overall value of HUF 350 billion. Interest payments are estimated to have reached some HUF 90 billion in 1995, equalling some 5.8 per cent of budgetary expenditure, or more than 2 per cent of GDP.
4. See EIU, 1/1995, pp. 18–25, 2/1995, pp. 14–20, 3/1995, pp. 11–16.
5. Some cuts (in child, sickness and maternity benefits) had been annulled due to a constitutional court ruling in June 1995. This triggered further cuts elsewhere, though: spending on local government and on a university in Budapest have been reduced and family welfare benefits, due in November 1995, have been postponed to January 1996 (EIU, 3/1995, p. 13).
6. Already after the first quarter of 1995, though, the deficit reached a level, which suggested that the target would not be met, not even the original one. This further reduction in planned budget deficit is owed to the IMF's requirement to reduce the deficit from 5.5 per cent of GDP in 1994 to 3 per cent by 1996 (EIU, 3/1995, p. 12).
7. The aim of monetary policy was to squeeze up to HUF 170–180 billion of liquidity out of the domestic financial sector (to reduce consumption and improve the country's external balance).
8. Whilst cuts in budgetary expenditure are certainly attributable to to the 'austerity programme', faster export and slower import growth in the 1995-figure may also stem from exchange rate expectations in the wake of the announcement of the March-package. The authors want to thank Mr. J. Vincze from the NBH for his kind indication for the possible existance of this effect in Hungary during this time.
9. The reversal of the price trend is especially remarkable, as some administered prices were raised in early 1995: telephone and telegram

charges rose by 20 per cent, mail charges by 15 per cent, rail fares by 20 per cent, petrol by 4.9 per cent and compulsory motor insurance by 9.6 per cent. Furthermore, energy prices, as recommended by the World Bank in 1994, have been increased immensely to bring Hungary's prices nearer to world levels: on average, the price for electricity rose by 31.5 per cent and that of gas by 21 per cent.
10. Integration, therefore, has to find a 'policy-balance betweeen a selective protection of domestic employment and the achievement of comparative advantages' (Kaser, 1996, p. 209).
11. 'Real devaluation' as an instrument to alleviate the balance-of-payments constraint on growth (*ibid.*, p. 145).
12. A theoretical analysis of this conception can be found in Hölscher, 1997.
13. The most striking historical precedence is Germany in the 1950s (see Hölscher, 1997).

Bibliography

BALDWIN, R. *Towards an Integrated Europe*, London, 1994.
EIU (Economist Intelligence Unit), *Hungary: Country Reports for the 1st, 2nd and 3rd Quarter 1995*, London, 1/2/3/1995.
EMI (European Monetary Institute), *Annual Report for 1996*, Frankfurt a.M., 1996.
ERDÖS, T. 'Problems in the Regulation of Aggregate Demand. Inflation, Disturbances of the Internal and External Equilibrium', *Kopint-Datorg International Workshop 'Re-evaluating Economic Reforms in Central and Eastern Europe since 1989*, Budapest, 15–16 September 1995, mimeo.
EC (European Commission), *First Report on Economic and Social Cohesion*, Office for Official Publications of the European Communities, Luxembourg, 1996.
HCSO (Hungarian Central Statistical Office), *Yearbook 1995*, Budapest, 1995.
HÖLSCHER, J. 'Economic Dynamism in Transition Economies: Lessons from Germany', *Communist Economies and Economic Transformation*, vol. 9, no. 2, 1997, pp. 173–81.
HÖLSCHER, J. and STEPHAN, J. 'Export-Oriented Development and Income Creation in Hungary', in J. Backhaus and G. Krause (eds), *On the Political Economy of Transformation: Country Studies*, Marburg, 1997, pp. 47–71.
KASER, M. 'Integration and Homogeneity in the Transition Economies', in J. Hölscher *et al.* (eds), *Conditions of Economic Development in Central and Eastern Europe*, Marburg, 1996, pp. 207–28.
KORNAI, J. 'The Soft Budget Constraint', *Kyklos*, vol. 39, no. 1, 1986, pp. 3–30.
KORNAI, J. *Transformational Recession: A General Phenomenon Examined through the Example of Hungary's Development*, Discussion Paper no. 1, Collegium Budapest, Institute for Advanced Study, Budapest, June 1993.

KORNAI, J. *Lasting Growth as the Top Priority: Macroeconomic Tensions and Government Economic Policy in Hungary*, EBRD Working Paper no. 15, London, December 1994.
LANDESMANN, M. and PÖSCHL, J. 'Balance-of-Payments Constraints Growth in Central and Eastern Europe', in M. Knell (ed.), *Economics of Transition*, Cheltenham, 1996, pp. 134–67.
NBH (National Bank of Hungary), *Annual Report*, Budapest, 1994.
NBH (National Bank of Hungary), *Annual Report*, Budapest, 1995a.
NBH (National Bank of Hungary), *Monthly Report for November 1995*, Budapest, 1995b.
NBH (National Bank of Hungary), *Monthly Report for June 1996*, Budapest, 1996a.
NBH (National Bank of Hungary), 'Highlights of the Year 1995: Brief Summary of Macroeconomic Developments on the Basis of Preliminary Data', *Internal Report*, Budapest, 1996, mimeo.
NUTI, D. M. '*Inflation, Interest and Exchange Rates in Transition*', CIS-Middle Europe Centre Discussion Paper Series, no. 22, London, December 1995.
VÁGI, M. and SZAKADÁT, L. 'Industrial Policy in Hungary since 1989', International Workshop 'The Role of Industrial Policy in the Transition in Central and Eastern Europe', London, 19 January 1996, mimeo.

III
Sectoral Adjustment Issues

7 Adjusting the Common Agricultural Policy for an EU Eastern Enlargement: Alternatives and Impacts on the Central European Associates

Klaus Frohberg and Monika Hartmann

INTRODUCTION

Ten of the Central European countries expressed their intention to become members of the European Union (EU) and signed the Association Agreements. In these treaties the EU stated its interest to grant these countries, called the Central European Associates (CEAs), such membership. Some of the reasons for seeking membership are market-related while others are determined by political factors. To the former belong economic development, efficiency, security of market access, competitiveness and stability in economic policy settings. The latter comprise aspects such as historical links, political security and stability and observing minority rights.

Integrating the CEAs into the EU will be a formidable task. This is partly due to the economic situation of the countries seeking membership, which differs substantially from that of the EU member states. Moreover, the EU must also prepare itself for this enlargement. Even without the possibility of integrating, the new countries' pressure is mounting for changing the institutions of the EU and some of its policies. The addition of the CEAs makes such changes unavoidable if the EU will not stake its efficacy, efficiency and competitiveness. The pressure for reform is considerable, not only in the area of institutions but also with respect to the Common Agricultural Policy (CAP). This results from the importance of the agricultural sector in the CEAs on the one hand, and the high level of protection in the EU on the other. Thus, integrating the CEAs without changing the CAP can be regarded as an unrealistic alternative.

Given these facts, this chapter discusses alternative reform strategies for the CAP and their likely impact on the joining countries. In the following section we provide a listing of the driving forces behind adjusting the CAP and the structural policies of the EU, of which the EU eastern enlargement is only one. Thereafter, options for these policies are stated, and in the final section the impacts of these policies on the CEAs are considered.

PRESSURE ON ADJUSTING THE CAP

Several external and internal factors can be identified which hamper or ease the adjustment of the CAP to the new situation over the next years. Some of these forces are developing outside the EU and are hardly to be changed by EU agricultural policies. These are long-term world market trends, the GATT commitments set during the Uruguay Round and the start of new agricultural trade negotiations scheduled for 1999. Other factors are operating internally. Nevertheless, some of them are also rather autonomous and can only be influenced partly. To these internal factors belong negotiating the financial framework of the EU budget due in 1999, simplifying the administration of the CAP and integrating the CEAs.

Long-term World Market Trends

The development of world markets in the long run is determined by several factors. On the supply side this is especially related to technical progress, while the expansion of agricultural land and irrigation are of minor relevance. Estimates indicate that in the future only about 10 per cent of all additional output may stem from additional land being used for cultivation, and 5 per cent from expanding irrigation. This reveals the importance of technical progress for future supply. Particularly in regions where at present, due to a discrimination of agriculture, productivity is low (for example in many developing countries), a relatively elastic supply response can be expected in the medium to long run (Henrichsmeyer, 1996, p. 101).

On the demand side income and population growth are the main determinants. Forecasts reveal a rapid increase of food demand over the next decades caused by changing consumption patterns in connection with rising incomes per capita and population growth. If the increase in demand exceeds that of supply, the secular trend of declining relative world market prices for agricultural products could be lessened, stopped or even reversed. Most researchers working in the field of long-term developments in agricultural markets assume that agricultural prices stay constant relative to those of non-agricultural commodities in spite of the more recent price rises in cereals and protein meals. These were caused by a relatively scarce supply of cereals during the period 1995/96 due to unfavourable weather conditions in important production regions. This trend certainly has simplified and will very likely continue to facilitate liberalising agricultural policies throughout the world including the EU (see for example McCalla, 1997).

GATT Commitments According to the Marrakesh Agreement and Development of EU Markets

For the first time in history, GATT succeeded in the Uruguay Round by including agriculture in the negotiations and by curbing the escalation of agricultural protectionism. The main agricultural provisions of the Marrakesh Agreement resulting from these negotiations, which all signatory states[1] must meet within six years from 1995 onwards, are the following:

- Product specific reduction of the volume of subsidised agricultural exports by 21 per cent and of 36 per cent of the amount of export subsidies (reference period is 1986–90);
- A 20 per cent reduction of domestic support at aggregated level (aggregate measure of support, AMS); payments not linked to production are excluded (reference period is 1986–88);
- Conversion of all non-tariff trade barriers into customs duties (tariffication) and their reduction by an average of 36 per cent, but by at least 15 per cent for each tariff position (reference period is 1986–88);[2]
- Reduction of customs duties for a quota to ensure minimum market access for product groups amounting to 3 per cent of the domestic consumption initially, and 5 per cent in the year 2000.

Due to the agreement the scope for setting agricultural policies in the future is narrowed in all signatory countries. In addition, protection might even need to be reduced in some countries to fulfill the GATT requirements. This holds especially for the end of the implementation period. In the following, sets of those policies areas are discussed in which adjustments in the CAP are necessary in order to adhere to the GATT bindings.

Some first calculations (see Bundesministerium für Errährung, Landwirtschaft und Forsten (Federal Ministry of Food, Agriculture and Forestry), 1996, and references cited there) reveal that due to the reduction of agricultural protection already performed in the CAP reform, the obligations in the areas of internal support, market access, newly bound tariffs and export subsidies will impose no conflicts. However, the bindings with respect to the volume of exports might very likely pose problems for the following products: wheat and wheat flour, cheese and a number of other milk products, sugar as well as beef. This implies that adjustments in these markets initiated by the CAP reform of 1992 are not yet sufficient to comply with the GATT commitments. Only if the EU is willing to refrain from using export subsidies, no further reduction in export quantities will be necessary.

New Negotiations of the Marrakesh Agreement

For 1999, a new mini-round of negotiations on the agricultural topic of the Marrakesh Agreement is scheduled. One of the major items of discussion will be an enhanced movement to more market-oriented agricultural policies. That means that border protection will be reduced further. Export subsidies will also decline beyond their current level. In addition, pressure on the EU to accept an elimination of the 'Blue Box' will increase. This holds especially since the USA has now effectively decoupled their former deficiency payment system and thus no longer needs the Blue Box. Therefore, domestic transfer payments will have to become entirely decoupled from production, otherwise these payments could no longer be excluded from the calculation of the aggregate measure of support. This, however, would involve a substantial further cut in the level of subsidisation. Finally, it is expected that sanitary as well as phyto-sanitary measures and environmental issues in agricultural trade will be given great emphasis in the new negotiations.

Financial Framework of the EU Budget

Expenditures of the EU Commission are subject to some specific rules and guidelines. Their function is to prevent drastic changes in the annual spending habits of the Commission. The last agreement on these regulations, reached in 1992, covers the period 1993 to 1999. It needs to be negotiated again in 1999 and is likely to be changed unfavourably for agriculture.

The EU budget is financed by two main sources: the overwhelming share is paid by member states, complemented by common external tariff receipts as the second major source. Regarding payments by member states, the contribution consists of a 1.0 per cent levy on a set of goods and services on which value added tax (VAT) is imposed. This VAT base is harmonised among all member states and comprises about 50 per cent of the total gross national product (GNP). The total amount transferred to the Commission is limited to 1.27 per cent of Community GNP. Any difference between the budgetary needs and the other receipts obtained from the member states is covered by payments based on a uniform rate of GNP. Common external tariffs are collected by the member states, which pass on 90 per cent of these receipts to the Commission and retain 10 per cent to pay for collection costs.

Also, the spending side of the EU budget has to follow some rules. Expenditures on the CAP are constrained by the so-called agricultural guideline, which stipulates that spending on the CAP is to increase less (74 per cent) than the average economic growth in the EU, thus annually reducing the agricultural budget in comparison to other spending items. The agricultural guideline functions as a legal limit.

Table 7.1 shows the change in relative spending for various budgetary items between 1992 and 1999. To the structural funds

Table 7.1 Allocation of commitment appropriations, 1992 and 1999, in per cent

Budget item	1992	1999
CAP	53.1	45.7
Structural funds	27.9	35.7
Internal spending; e.g. R&D	6.0	6.0
External funding, e.g. aid	5.5	6.7
Administration	6.0	4.6
Reserve	1.5	1.3
Total	100.0	100.0

Source: Swann, 1996, p. 165.

belong the European Social Fund (ESF), the European Regional Development Fund (ERDF), the guidance part of the European Agricultural Guarantee and Guidance Fund (EAGGF) and the Cohesion Fund. Structural funds absorb an increasing share of the total EU budget, while agricultural spending declines from 53 to 46 per cent. In absolute terms – especially when expressed in current prices – outlays on agriculture might still increase. Spending on administration is also to decline in relation to the total budget. In 1996, outlays on agriculture were below the ceiling even with the unforeseen payments due to BSE. This can primarily be explained by favourable world market prices for major agricultural commodities exported by the EU. This development reduced export subsidies for dairy products and cereals to a large extent. In the case of the latter, payments could be completely suspended for some time and were even replaced by an export tax.

It may be possible that agriculture will have to cope with a further decline of relative spending at the EU level. A gradual increase in importance of the outlays for structural funds can be observed for the current period of the financial framework (see Table 7.1), and there is mounting evidence that this trend will continue in the next financial period. Agriculture is faced with the problem that in the future relatively more emphasis is placed on polices fostering regional development and maintaining the environment. The discussion on adhering more to the subsidiarity principle is still continuing and might lead to an even stronger reduction of agricultural spending at the EU level.

Simplifying the CAP

Administering the CAP became a very complex and costly task, and, over time, agriculture became increasingly regulated. This was partly due to the various stages of enlargement of the EU since the new member states frequently added other problems caused by their agricultural structures which often differed from that prevailing in the EU. The CAP, originally designed for six member states, now covers 15 countries and has to do its job properly in regions as diverse as Lapland and Andalusia.

This not only means that bureaucracy had to grow overproportionally, but also farmers have to spend a considerable amount of time on filing applications to get public support and on ensuring their compliance with the numerous regulations imposed on them. Thus, the CAP has to become simpler, not only easier to be implemented but also less prone to irregularities.

Integration of the CEAs

From a political point of view, an integration of the CEAs into the EU seems very likely, but will be a difficult task for several reasons. One of them is to align agricultural policies in a way which minimises the adjustment burden for both the EU and the CEAs, assures that the enlarged EU with 25 member states adheres to all international commitments, like the Marrakesh Agreement or its successor, and requires budgetary outlays which are politically feasible. These aspects render it very likely that the CAP will be adjusted so as to grant markets a larger role in providing farmers' income. Currently, a considerable share of farmers' income is provided through government support.

Extending the CAP to countries in which agriculture is a relatively large part of the economy will put considerable strain on the EU budget. The incentive for farmers in the CEAs to increase their output would be substantial (see for example Hartmann, 1995). This holds even if adjustments in input prices are considered. Consequently, exports would likely increase considerably. Those, however, could be sold on world markets only at subsidised prices.

Some long-term projections of the impact on CEAs' exports were published by the EU Commission at the end of 1995 (EU Commission, 1995). According to these figures, the CEAs would almost double the EU's surplus in cereals by 2010 as compared to what the Commission forecasts for the year 2000. The increase in the production of oil-seeds would be absorbed by domestic markets, and sugar would not cause a problem since it would still remain in deficit. In contrast, beef surplus would be untenably high. Under the assumption that the CEAs would be granted milk quotas comparable to those of the EU, milk production would also lead to more surplus.

These developments would not only be very costly and hard to justify to the public in the current member countries, more important they would violate the GATT commitments. The GATT bindings for those CEAs which are already members of the World Trade Organisation (WTO) are quite different from those for the EU. For example, for a number of commodities bound tariffs are lower in the CEAs than in the EU. Adapting EU bound rates would increase the protection of the corresponding associated country. Of even greater relevance are the export subsidy commitments. Countries which have not yet recorded export subsidies for a product in the base period in their country's schedules are prohibited to use this policy measure for those products now (*Agra-Europe*, no. 153, p. 2). Therefore, it would be impossible to have these countries adopt EU agricultural policies without violating the commitments agreed on in Marrakesh. Third parties of GATT are very likely to disagree with such an infringement.

In addition, the conditions laid down in the WTO regulations for creating or enlarging free trade areas are much tighter than they used to be in GATT. Paragraph XVI of the Marrakesh Agreement requires all members of the WTO to adapt their laws, regulations and administrative procedures in accordance with the commitments of this organisation. This also holds for establishing free trade areas. Now, there is institutional pressure for treating all commodities important for trade equally in an agreement on free trade. Thus, excluding agriculture partly or totally from an integration arrangement is no longer possible, and hence also is not on option in the case of an EU eastern enlargement.

ALTERNATIVE SCENARIOS FOR A CAP REFORM

The discussion above shows clearly that the continuation of the CAP in its present form is no alternative since it would violate the GATT commitments. Thus, the process of reforming the CAP has to be pursued further for internal and external reasons, of which the integration of the CEA is only one factor, although an important one.

Two broad areas for policy reform can be distinguished: first the agricultural market policy, and secondly the structural policies of the EU. Although the largest part of the latter is generally not considered as belonging to the CAP, both policy areas are closely interrelated. Besides, it seems to be in particular the EU structural policies which are of great importance for the CEAs.

Agricultural Market Reform

With respect to an agricultural market reform, three broad alternatives are presently being discussed. The first option would focus on a continuation of the reform of 1992 by:

- further reducing administered prices for those products already covered by the reform, mainly grain and oilseed;
- lowering price support for those commodities excluded so far in the agricultural reform; and
- granting compensatory payments for reduced market support.

A second option would be more radical in favouring:

- an elimination of price support or, at least, an adjustment of administered prices close to world market prices;
- a removal of quotas and other quantity measures;
- a further decoupling of compensatory payments and their gradual reduction; and
- direct income payments and compensation for environmental and cultural services of agricultural production financed at a national level with or without EU co-financing.

Finally, as a third option the EU could also manage to stay within the GATT bindings by:

- introducing quantity measures and stabilisation schemes like imposing production quotas on beef and sheep markets; and
- tightening the quantity control on milk and sugar markets as well as increasing set-aside obligations.

No doubt this third alternative would lead to an isolation of the EU in the worldwide movement towards greater market orientation in agricultural trade.

A brief overview is provided in the following with respect to different policy measures that could be undertaken on those agricultural markets where problems are most likely to occur (see also the earlier discussion on pp. 183–4), that is, grain, beef and milk. However, it should be noted that reforms undertaken in one market will very likely induce policy responses in other markets in order to prevent distortions in competition among the agricultural commodities. Hence, similar reforms would also be needed for other agricultural products.

Grain and beef

In the grain and beef market, the GATT obligations will be violated if no additional measures are taken. Beyond this, a further decoupling of the compensatory payments seems necessary since in the mini-round of agricultural negotiations beginning in 1999, a more restrictive definition of decoupled income support is expected to be focused on (see p. 180).

One policy option discussed presently is to further adjust grain and beef prices to the world market price level. This price decline could be compensated by direct payments. The payments, however, should be successively reduced over time and, in accordance with the principle of subsidiarity, be transferred to the national level. This reform would reduce or even eliminate the need for:

- export subsidies; and
- quasi-obligatory set-aside for grain acreage and thus lead to voluntary set-aside at lower costs.

Problems concerning agricultural production in marginal areas could be mitigated by ecological and structural measures (see the discussion on structural policies, below).

An alternative to this more liberal policy option would be a considerable increase in the quasi-obligatory requirements for set-aside of cereal acreage and, in the case of beef, the implementation of quotas to assure that the GATT bindings will not be violated. After 1999, a further decoupling of the compensatory payments is inevitable.

Milk

Several alternatives for reforming milk policies are conceivable (see Frenz, Manegold, Salamon, 1997). They range from a complete liberalisation of the European milk market without compensation, to a continuation of the present milk quota system, though by considerably tightening the supply control. In the following the two policy options in the centre of the present time discussion will be presented.

The first option implies a conversion of the present price support into direct payments. These payments should be structured similarly to those for grain and beef (see above). Prices of dairy products would be reduced gradually but substantially towards world market price levels. Hence, in this case a removal of the quota is not necessary; it no longer will be binding and will thus lose its value. However, the latter is a problem in itself. Quotas have to a certain extent been capitalised in the EU since they were bought by newcomers or by farmers who have expanded their production. Lowering prices towards world market levels would thus eliminate property values and would be equal to a breach of trust between farmers and politicians. Thus, direct payments would have to be implemented not only to compensate for reduced price support but also to cover the property value included in the quota. Payments to all dairy farmers would produce considerable pressure on the EU budget. However, to ensure that only those who paid for the quota will be compensated seems almost impossible.

In addition, such a reform of the dairy policy will induce a reallocation of milk production in the EU, which would move to those producers and regions which are highly competitive in this sector. This might not be approved by the EU for distribution and/or regional considerations. In this case, social, structural and environmental adjustment measures would be necessary (see the following section). The major advantage of this reform option would be that, due to the removal of the price gap between the EU and world market prices, the need for export subsidies would vanish. In addition, consumers would benefit from lower prices. Finally, this alternative would be compatible with the 1992 reform measures on the grain and oilseed markets.

A second alternative for reforming the dairy policy is the transformation of the quota system as it currently exists into an ABC-scheme similar to the sugar market. This would result in a three-price tear. Producers would receive high price support only for an A-quota supply, which would equal sales of milk at market prices in the EU. Production within the B-quota would amount to subsidised sales on the EU internal market; producer levies would be introduced on these quantities to finance the subsidies. Finally, the C-quota would be exclusively for export. Producers would only be paid the world market price for milk delivered within the C-quota.

This latter reform option certainly is more easily to accept politically, however, several problems are attached to this alternative. First and foremost, for a more market-oriented CAP this alternative does not seem to be the proper solution, since more rather than less administration is required for implementing and controlling such a policy. In addition, competitiveness is certainly not strengthened through an ABC-scheme. Second, there are good reasons to believe that this option increases the burden on consumers (see Frenz, Mancgold and Salamon, 1997). Third, the compatibility with changes in other market regimes has to be questioned.

Structural Policies

The objectives of structural policies are to reduce the economic and social disparities existing between various regions in the EU, and to establish the external conditions for their similar growth. Differing economic and social developments at the regional level within the Union are considered to be detrimental to the overall economic and political integration of member states. Structural policies are designed to influence regional development, and properly implemented may reduce regional divergence.

For 1996, the appropriations for structural policies were almost ECU 30 billion of which 14 per cent belonged to the guidance part of the EAGGF, 45 per cent to the ERDF, 27 per cent to the ESF and 8 per cent to the cohesion fund. The remaining 6 per cent came from various sources. It has been estimated that an extension of structural policies as currently implemented in the CEAs will require additional budgetary outlays of roughly ECU 40 billion (Europäisches Parlament, 1996).[3] It is considered difficult to justify such an increase in spending at the EU level. Therefore, structural policies also have to be adjusted in order to reduce the financial strain on the EU budget.

The main adjustment to be expected is changing the criteria for classifying the various regions into certain 'objective regions'. As currently specified, the criteria used to define an objective-1 region, would classify the entire area of all CEAs as belonging to this group. Therefore, the criteria especially for this type of region (per capita income at least 25 per cent below EU average) will need to be changed in a way that provides for further sub-classification.

Objective 5a is to stimulate structural adjustment of agriculture. Financial support for this policy can be obtained only through the guidance part of the EAGGF. Objective 5b deals with the development of rural areas in general. The EU provides assistance through three funds; the guidance part of the EAGGF, the ESF and the ERDF. Especially, the latter might be adjusted to foster an integrated rural development rather than individual projects in regions which are especially exposed to structural problems.

Due to the integration process national borders may become less and less important and eventually completely obsolete. Whatever the outcome in this respect will be, the need for social cohesion is going to lead to the creation of new spatial entities, which might resemble the currently existing regions. Consequently, competition between regions is likely to substitute for that between member states in the future. The importance of rural areas in this competition is not certain. Urban agglomerations could in fact become the major players.

In structural policies, ecological aspects have gained in importance. Direct payments for the remuneration of special public services and positive external effects of agricultural production belong to this category. Especially, in the course of further liberalising agricultural markets and adjusting prices to world market levels, such measures can be expected to be used more often. However, these policies will only gain broad acceptance if the ecological and cultural benefits attributed to them are more precisely defined and accurately measured. Otherwise, they will be seen as a disguised form of income payments and thus as a potential source for trade disputes with third countries.

IMPACT ON CEAs

Which effects of transmitting the moderate or strongly transformed CAP to the CEAs can be expected? Which efficiency and distribution outcome for the CEAs can be expected? The following discussion is based on current exchange rates; an adjustment in the real exchange rate might change the picture provided.

Determinants

The impact of a CAP East Enlargement is mainly determined by the relative input and output prices as well as the relative level of technology in the CEAs as compared to the EU at the time of accession and their adjustment due to integration.

Prices

A comparison of farm-gate prices in the EU with those in the CEAs reveals that farmers in the EU are paid much better than their colleagues in the latter countries. In general, prices in the CEAs amount to only about 50 per cent of the corresponding EU prices, and often the ratio is even smaller. Also the price structure in the CEAs deviates quite considerably from that in the EU; for example the ratio of milk to wheat prices in Latvia is only one-fifth of that in the EU (Hartmann, 1995).

These price differentials with respect to level and structure are caused by three main factors. First, there is some reason to believe that differences in product quality and standards exist between the CEAs and the EU, for example quality assessment according to the classification system EUROP has not been introduced in many CEAs yet. Meat and dairy products manufactured in the CEAs are especially lacking in quality which might partly explain why farm prices are lower in the CEAs. Inefficiencies in the food industry and insufficient or lacking wholesale markets seem to be a second reason. Right now the food industry in most CEAs is suffering from severe over-capacities, increasing input costs, low labour productivity, outdated processing facilities and a lack of market orientation on the side of management. Besides these inefficiencies, market power still persists in the food industry and the distribution systems and can be regarded as an additional reason for relatively low farm prices in the CEAs.

Third, and of great importance as well, are pronounced differences in the protection rates between the CEAs and the EU. In Table 7.2, net producer subsidy equivalents are measured as a percentage of corresponding farm-gate prices prevailing in 1994 as reported for the EU and CEAs. On an average over all agricultural products, the EU protects agriculture to about 50 per cent, while the corresponding figures reach only about 20 per cent in Poland, Hungary and the Czech Republic. In Latvia agricultural protection is negligible (on average 1 per cent). In Lithuania and Estonia governmental intervention even induces a small discrimination of the agricultural sector. No comparable information was available for Slovenia, the Slovak Republic and the Balkan countries. However, there is some evidence that the latter discriminate their agricultural sector, while the former two countries are likely to protect their farmers to a similar extent as the other CEFTA countries.

It is not only the level but also the structure of protection that is similar among the transition countries considered in Table 7.2 but quite different between the CEAs and the EU. All CEAs protect their non-ruminant meat sector (pork, poultry and eggs) to a much larger extent than is the case in the EU. In Hungary, for example, egg producers receive a protection eight times higher than in the EU. Part of the high producer subsidy equivalents for non-ruminant meat products is due to discriminating feeding stuff (wheat and coarse grains), which implicitly favours those sectors that use these commodities as an input.

Table 7.2 Agricultural protection in the EU and selected CEAs in 1994[1] (measured as net producer subsidy equivalents)

	EU-12		Poland		Hungary		Czech Republic		Latvia		Lithuania		Estonia	
Wheat	57	(100)	7	(12)	−8	(−14)	4	(37)	−6	(−11)	−18	(−32)	7	(12)
Coarse grains	62	(100)	11	(18)	−6	(−10)	23	(4)	−5	(−8)	−7	(−11)	−5	(−8)
Oilseeds	57	(100)	3	(5)	−6	(−11)	2	(−5)	17	(30)	43	(75)	7	(12)
Sugar	59	(100)	9	(15)	35	(59)	−3	(17)	52	(88)	38	(64)	44	(75)
Crops	58	(100)	12	(21)	−4	(−7)	10	(54)	−34	(−59)	−3	(−5)	−20	(−34)
Milk	63	(100)	11	(17)	44	(70)	34	(42)	−2	(−3)	−65	(−103)	−6	(−10)
Beef and veal	60	(100)	−7	(−12)	17	(28)	25	(140)	−51	(−85)	−42	(−70)	−36	(−60)
Pork	10	(100)	36	(360)	29	(290)	14	(100)	71	(710)	50	(500)	36	(360)
Poultry	23	(100)	45	(196)	35	(152)	23	(27)	55	(239)	57	(248)	33	(143)
Sheep meat	59	(100)	34	(58)	43	(73)	16	–	34	(58)	9	(15)	−13	(−22)
Eggs	5	(100)	31	(620)	40	(800)	–	(52)	–	–	–	–	–	–
Livestock products	46	(100)	24	(52)	34	(74)	24	(40)	18	(39)	−10	(−22)	−2	(−4)
All products	50	(100)	21	(42)	20	(40)	20	–	1	(2)	−7	(−14)	−8	(−16)

Note: [1] Figures in parentheses are the ratios of the PSE-value for the product considered in the CEA to that in the EU.
Source: OECD (ed.), unpublished working papers.

Productivity

Also productivity is considerably lower in the CEAs as compared to the EU. In the Baltic states and Romania yields per hectare only reach 40 to 50 per cent of the respective output in the EU, while they amount to about 80 to 90 per cent in the Czech and Slovak Republics, Hungary as well as Slovenia. A potential for further growth in the long run seems to lie especially in countries with favourable natural conditions and very low productivity levels prior to the transition process (for example Balkan states).

Additional information with respect to productivity of the agricultural sector in the CEAs compared to the EU can be obtained by considering absolute and relative labour productivity. Absolute labour productivity in agriculture is lower in the CEAs compared to the EU; however, relative to that in all other sectors of the economy a different picture emerges. The relative labour productivity of agriculture is higher in all CEA countries except Poland and Bulgaria than in the EU,[4] which reveals a comparative advantage of this sector in most of the CEAs. Assuming that labour productivity in agriculture can keep pace with that of the rest of the economy, the numbers indicate that most CEAs should be able to become net exporters of agricultural products in an integrated and thus liberalised European market.

Transmission of the Present CAP

An eastern enlargement of the CAP would harmonise protection levels between the EU and the CEAs. If a market-oriented reform in the EU will not take place, this would induce a sharp rise in producer incentive prices for all commodities except non-ruminant meat products. Given this price increase, a considerable rise in agricultural production can be expected. The price effect and thus the production incentives would, however, be reduced if the CEAs do not succeed in increasing the quality of their agricultural products and in reducing the inefficiencies in their food industry and wholesale markets.

The efficiency effects of transmitting the present CAP, or an even stronger supply-managing policy, are detrimental for the CEAs. This is predominantly caused by the fact that the EU quota and set-aside schemes would have to be enforced in these countries. Since new production structures are just starting to develop in these countries, such measures would, however, prevent them from adjusting to their comparative advantage. In addition, losses would occur due to the considerable administrative costs of implementing and controlling the quantitative measures. In fact, it would be quite ironic to have countries who belonged to a centrally-planned system for so long, introduce a system of quantity measures in agriculture again.

The distribution impact of transmitting high EU producer prices to the CEAs is also problematic. High food prices especially affect the low-income population in the CEAs, who devote an average of 36 per cent of their total household expenditures to food. In some countries, such as Romania, and for the poorest part of the population these ratios are in fact much higher. In addition, high producer prices would provide an income boost to the farming population, which, compared to other sectors of the economy, cannot be justified.

Transmission of a More Market-oriented CAP

Thus, from the point of view of the transition country a more market-oriented EU agricultural policy reform would be desirable. If the EU succeeds in reforming its agricultural policy, the price gap between the CEAs and the EU would narrow. Nevertheless, in this case relative prices will also change in CEAs: initially output prices will rise relative to input prices, and prices of inputs traded freely on world markets will not adjust. However, those which are determined more or less by internal market forces may rise. To the latter belong, in particular, labour costs. The wage rate in the CEAs amounts to only about 20 per cent of that in the EU and is in many cases even relatively smaller. As time passes, labour costs are expected to increase since their current low level will adjust to that prevailing in the EU.[5] The explanation for this adjustment can be found in the Heckscher–Ohlin factor price equalisation theorem. If this change is going to happen, labour-intensive production techniques will gradually be replaced by those requiring a relatively low share of labour in total inputs. This will lead to an adjustment in production techniques to those prevailing in the EU.

It is difficult to assess what the relative change among prices of crops and livestock will be. This mainly depends on the adjustments in the EU agricultural policy prior to integration and prices in the different CEAs at the time of their accession. However, given the fact that protection for non-ruminant meat is at present already higher in some CEAs than in the EU, there is good reason to believe that prices for these products will decline rather than rise. In contrast, grain prices might even go up in the case of a reform, thus putting a second source of relative disadvantage on non-ruminant meat products. Higher grain prices will increase feeding costs which make up 45 per cent of total production costs of these commodities, although at the beginning a relatively large amount of starchy crops might be fed. With rising labour costs this is expected to become too costly and a gradual shift towards a larger share of feed grains, in the feeding ration can be expected.

Also, increasing prices of ruminant meats can be expected even if the EU is going to lower the price incentives for beef, milk and sheep meat. An increase in the production of these products in the CEAs is thus very likely. Given the soil and climatic conditions in many of the CEAs, production of ruminant meat is expected to have a comparative advantage; especially in the northern countries of the CEAs. These conditions provide an additional impetus for production growth.

Among prices of crops the adjustment is expected to differ between the various countries depending on the policies currently implemented. In some countries grain prices are seen to rise relatively to other crops. However, this need not be a strong shift, neither will it lead to a drastic increase in production since the climate conditions are often not for cultivating large shares of land with other crops than grains.

Extending the compensatory payments to the CEAs would be unnecessary if the payments are truly decoupled from production and thus distorting effects on competition are eliminated. In addition, a stepwise reduction and reorientation of these payments to the national level would be desirable (Tangermann, 1995, p. 282; Henrichsmeyer, 1996, p. 102).

Extending Structural Policies to the CEAs

Structural policies are expected to lead to different adjustment patterns. First of all, there is good reason to believe that while guarantee funds will decline, structural funds will gain in importance in the overall EU budget in the coming years (see pp. 180, 181). At the same time, the criteria and payments for Objective-1 regions, at present the largest structural spending programme, need to be changed in order to make an eastern enlargement politically acceptable and financially bearable (see the above discussion on structural policies). However, even in the case of a reform of structural policies in the EU it can be expected that the CEAs will receive considerable transfers from the structural funds of the EU, resources which can be used to aid the structural adjustment process in the CEAs. If properly used, these funds can contribute to the fundamental EU-objective 'cohesion' between different parts of the Union (Henrichsmeyer, 1996, p. 102).

Oversized farms, which exist especially with regard to animal husbandry, are expected to decline in magnitude. This will result in an increased competitiveness of these farms. Productivity growth in the agricultural sector also depends very much on utilising customised technical progress, and in this respect specific requirements of the CEAs have to be taken into account. Existing investment programmes, for example, are geared towards EU member states and thus might have to be adjusted to meet the needs of the CEAs more effectively. First and foremost, the structural policies will lead to a general improvement of competitiveness since rural development will be fostered by providing more and better infrastructure and supporting up- and downstream industries as well as wholesale markets.

By and large, the CEAs seem to be less in need of a high-level price and income support for their farmers than targeted assistance for restructuring, improving and diversifying their agricultural productive capacity as well as the downstream sector. Also, their rural infrastructure needs to be improved. For all these reasons, structural policies will be very important for these countries to develop their competitive potential within EU agriculture (European Commission, 1995).

SUMMARY

The EU eastern enlargement is motivated by a range of economic and political factors, some of which are rather strong. Hence, the enlargement is likely to happen. However, to ease the burden of the adjustment, changes in the CAP of the EU will have to occur, and several options are available. These alternatives lead to differences in the development of agriculture both in the EU and the CEAs. Although liberal agricultural policies in the future would lower the adjustment burden of the CEAs and increase the economic gains within the current EU, this scenario is rather unlikely. Political forces are more likely to lead to a further adjustment of the CAP rather than a complete liberalising. Nevertheless, this option would also be an improvement of the current CAP and keep the integration costs for the CEAs at a tolerable level.

Notes

1. The developing countries were granted a transitional period of 10 years and are required to meet only two-thirds of the tariff reductions. The least developed countries were given a complete dispensation (see United States Department of Agriculture, 1994).
2. Volume and price-related safeguard clauses permit the imposition of additional duties on products subject to tariffication.
3. See also Baldwin, 1994, pp. 169 and the references cited there.
4. The relatively low labour productivity of agriculture in Poland and Bulgaria is mainly caused by the high intensity of labour use in this sector.
5. Nevertheless, there is some evidence that factor prices (especially wages) will not adjust to the same extent as commodity prices. In the EU-15 there are still large differences in wages.

Bibliography

BALDWIN, R. E. *Towards an Integrated Europe*, London, 1994.
EUROPÄISCHES PARLAMENT *Entwurf eines Berichts über die Finanzierung der Erweiterung der Europäischen Union*, DOC-DE\PR\307917, Brussels, 1996.
EUROPEAN COMMISSION, DGVI *Agricultural Situation and Prospects in the Central and Eastern European Countries*, working document, Brussels, 1995.
FRENZ, K., MANEGOLD, D. and SALAMON, P. 'Zukunft des Milchquotensystems unter besonderer Berücksichtigung der GATT Vereinbarungen', in S. Bauer, R. Herrmann and F. Kuhlmann (eds), *Märkte der Agrar- und Ernährungswirtschaft – Analyse, einzelwirtschaftliche Strategien, staatliche Einflußnahme*, Münster-Hiltrup, 1997, pp. 179–91.
HARTMANN, M. 'Notwendigkeit und Chancen einer Reform der GAP vor dem Hintergrund einer Osterweiterung', in IWH (ed.), *Die Integration osteuropäischer Reformstaaten in die EU nach Essen und vor der Überprüfung des Maastricht-Vertrages 1996*, Sonderheft, Halle/Saale 1995, pp. 31–49.
HENRICHSMEYER, W. 'Problems and Perspectives of the EU: Agricultural Policy and Competition for Financial Resources', in K. Kaiser and M. Brünig (eds), *East-Central Europe and the EU: Problems of Integration*, Bonn, 1996, pp. 93–106.
MCCALLA, A. F. 'The Future Role of Markets, Prices and Policy in the World Food Economy', in S. Bauer, R. Herrmann and F. Kuhlmann (eds), *Märkte der Agrar- und Ernährungswirtschaft – Analyse, einzelwirtschaftliche Strategien, staatliche Einflußnahme*, Münster-Hiltrup, 1997, pp. 3–10.

SWANN, D. *European Economic Integration: The Common Market, European Union and Beyond*, Cheltenham, 1996.

TANGERMANN, S. 'Eastward Enlargement of the EU: Will Agricultural Policy be an Obstacle, *Intereconomics*, vol. 39, no. 6, 1995, pp. 277–84.

UNITED STATES DEPARTMENT OF AGRICULTURE *Agricultural Provisions of the Uruguay Round*, Washington D.C., 1994.

BUNDESMINISTERIUM FÜR ERNÄHRUNG, LANDWIRTSCHAFT UNDFORSTEN, Wissenschaftlicher Beirat beim Bundesministerium für Ernährung, Landwirtschaft und Forsten, *Zur Weiterentwicklung der EU-Agrarreform*, Schriftenreihe des Bundesministeriums für Ernährung, Landwirtschaft und Forsten. Reihe A: Angewandte Wissenschaft. vol. 459, Bonn, 1996.

8 Changes in Production Structures after Accession: Experiences from the Southern Enlargement of the EU and Prospects for Eastern Enlargement

Claudia Löhnig

INTRODUCTION[1]

Since the foundation of the European Union in 1958, its extension has served as a political measure to create and save peace in Europe after the Second World War. Nearly 40 years later, the hopes for economic advantages of an accession have become more and more important. In view of the applications for accession of 10 countries of Central and Eastern Europe, one of the questions most interesting is the one discussed in this chapter: which conditions promote the reduction of initially existing developmental lags between the richer European Union member states and a less-developed accession country? Having identified those conditions one can look for possibilities of making the integration easier and faster in order to reduce the costs of integration and to exploit the benefits at an earlier point in time. Looking at the economic theory there are a lot of starting points to analyse economic catching-up processes. Here, one argument is taken based upon the new real theory of international trade as well as on regional economics, and which is tested in the following with data from the former southern enlargement of the European Union:

> *Thesis*: A successful economic catching-up process goes along with an assimilation of industrial production structures of the accession candidate to those of the European Union as a whole. A divergent

structural development process renders the process of economic catching up more difficult.

To check this thesis, the traditional Heckscher–Ohlin idea and the inherent patterns of describing structural change are discussed in the following section. From there, a look at the empirical performance of the countries of the southern enlargement of the European Union in the 1980s offers a picture of 'success or failure' of the southern integration process. We then present the theoretical foundations of the thesis which is tested empirically with data from the manufacturing sectors of Greece, Portugal and Spain in the light of their economic developments in relation to the European Union. It will be shown that Spain is the most, Greece the least, successful country in this view. Finally we try to identify the special features of the industrial production patterns in the Central and Eastern European countries in comparison with the European Union, and the empirical results are discussed in view of the future eastern enlargement of the European Union.

STRUCTURAL CHANGE, THE TRADITIONAL THEORY OF INTEGRATION AND ECONOMIC DEVELOPMENT IN SOUTHERN EUROPE

The traditional theory of international trade shows that two countries or country groups gain from free trade, like the European member countries have, by specialising in the production of those goods which make use of the relatively abundant production factor relatively intensively. In realising the comparative advantages a process of structural change takes place in the two countries. The industrial sectors with comparative advantages will grow while those with comparative disadvantages will shrink in the course of time. The result from restructuring is an inter-industry trade pattern. This well-known static theory offers no information towards the question whether one country will gain more from free trade than the other. In a dynamic context the traditional hope for gains from free inter-industry trade is accomplished by the expectation of a convergent development process of the accession candidate to the European Union's development as a whole. Initial development lags are particularly hoped to be reduced after some time.

Changes in Production Structures after Accession

Looking to the southern enlargement of the European Union, Greece being accessed in 1981, Portugal and Spain in 1986, two facts can be observed:

1. Greece, just as Portugal, has mainly specialised in the production of labour-intensive goods along the traditional Heckscher–Ohlin model where the value added is not as great as for capital-intensive goods, for example. Labour is relatively abundant and therefore relatively cheap so there existed a comparative advantage at the time of accession. Spain, on the other hand, initially had a similar structure of comparative advantages but could change the relative factor endowment in the course of time in the direction of producing more capital-intensive goods.[2]
2. Looking at Figures 8.1 and 8.2 one can see that the GDP per capita of the three countries before their accession to the European Union was much smaller, and that the differences – in absolute and relative values – could not be abolished over time. During the whole time, Spain was ahead of Greece followed by Portugal. Progress can be seen to a moderate degree in absolute values of GDP per capita. Since accession, a trend towards the GDP per capita of the EU in relative values (Figure 8.2) can be seen for Spain and Portugal, but not for Greece. The value for Greece has rather fallen in relative terms.

Figure 8.1   GDP per capita: absolute value in constant prices and constant exchange rates (USD, basis year: 1990)

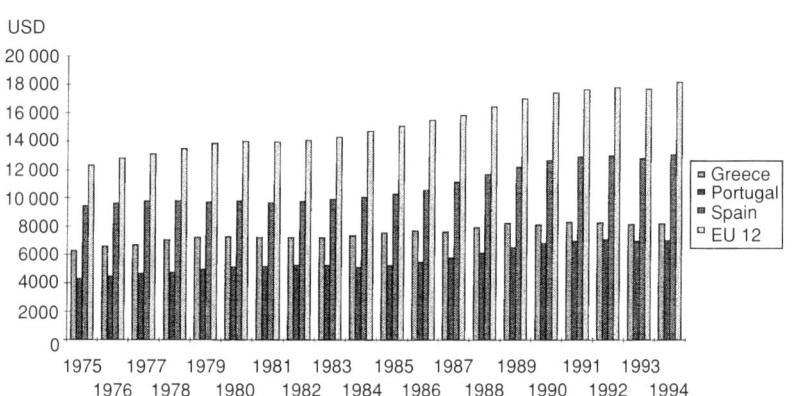

Source: OECD (1996), National Accounts Statistics I.

Figure 8.2 GDP per capita relative to EU12

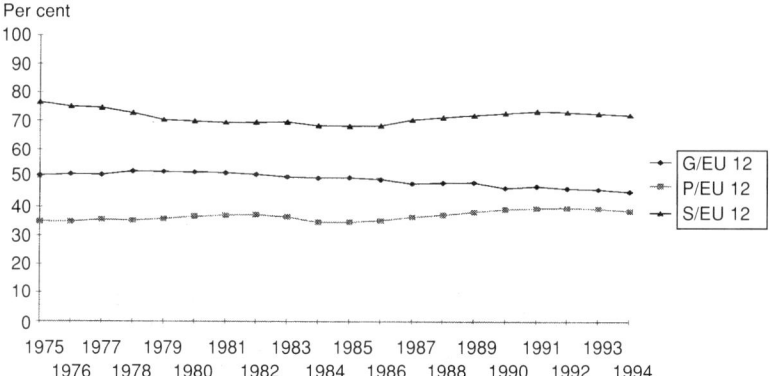

Source: Own calculations with data from OECD (1996), National Accounts Statistics I.

Altogether, Spain has had the best starting position and did not lose this advantage over time. In the light of convergence processes with the European Union, Spain and Portugal have been more successful than Greece which could not use its membership in the European Union for a further improvement in living standards measured by GDP per capita.[3] The hopes for economic convergence are not yet fulfilled.

Figure 8.3 shows the activities of foreign direct investors, and indicates that the market has obviously valued the accession positively. In the case of Greece even the application for accession in 1975 is followed by increased foreign investor activity, and the inflows of foreign direct investments (FDI) to the region as a whole have increased considerably since the three countries joined the European Union. With the beginning of the transformation process in Central and Eastern Europe the FDI inflows in Spain and Portugal began to decrease for the first time since their accession in absolute values. Figure 8.4 shows the relative importance of the three Southern European countries from the point of view of foreign investors. Greece lost its initial importance continually in favour of Spain, while Portugal gained importance after 1986 to Spain's debit.

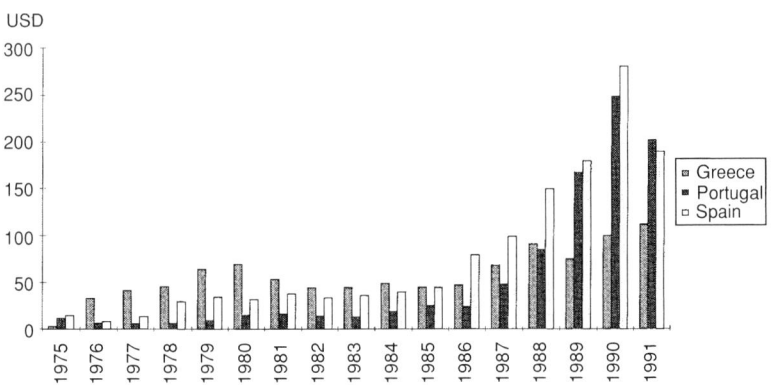

Figure 8.3 FDI inflows per capita

Source: IMF (1994), series 77bad.

THEORETICAL ASPECTS OF STRUCTURAL CHANGE

In looking for reasons why the Southern European countries have not been able to catch up yet, one may find interesting ideas from the modern theory of international trade.[4] The new approaches leave the world of fully-competitive market structures, of comparative advantages in the traditional sense of Heckscher–Ohlin, and therefore of inter-industry patterns of international trade. Trade theorists had to recognise that trade between countries of similar development status normally takes place in the same branches, especially the same product classes, a fact that cannot be explained by the traditional theory of comparative advantages. From a theoretical point of view it is necessary to introduce firms into the model which do not act like price-takers. Each of these firms produces one product which is similar to the products of the other firms in a special branch. The differences are small from the point of view of a representative household, so getting a monopoly rent is not possible for a longer time. Two kinds of product differentiation are observed – the horizontal and the vertical; the former refers to products which differ in some features other than quality, for example in colour, weight, appearance, while the latter differ in quality or in the degree of processing.[5] In both cases the household wants to buy all these 'variants' of a product – it is assumed to like diversity. To generate this kind of trade pattern in variants, on an aggregate level of industrial branches, the trading countries have to show similar industrial production structures. Inside

Figure 8.4 Relative distribution of FDI inflows per capita

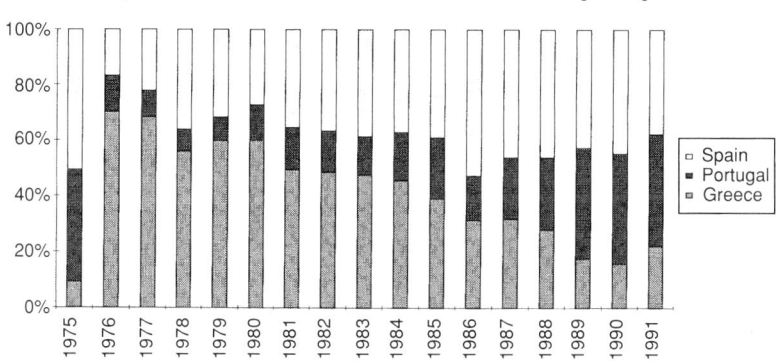

Source: Own calculations with data from IMF (1994), series 77bad.

a branch there have to be tendencies to specialise in the production of similar products. With respect to the enlargement of the European Union this means that convergence in industrial production structures of the new member states and the European Union as a whole goes along with economic catching up. On the other side, specialisation in products with (static) comparative advantages before unification would lead into an industrial pattern which renders the process of catching up more difficult.

Another theoretical approach originating from regional economics expedites a useful argument in explaining the so far unsuccessful process of economic catching up of the countries of the southern enlargement of the European Union, by explaining the observable disparate development structures of regions. Unlike the central European Union member states in Southern Europe, there are only a few local concentrations of industries belonging to the same industrial branch. The so-called *industrial cores*[6] bring a lot of positive externalities like spillover and synergy effects. In concentrating firms of the same industry at one location, a pool of work forces arises with firm-specific highly-skilled human capital; a firm can engage a worker without paying the otherwise high training costs. Moreover, such a local concentration will attract special firms offering goods and services as inputs and which can realise economies of scale in choosing locations near the industrial core. A third point can be made when considering the possibility of informal transfer of know-how between workers of different firms all working at one place. This transfer generates positive spillover effects supporting the research and development activities of the firms. All in all, industrial cores play a key role in the economic development and in the debate about industry location. In other words, the lacking of industrial cores makes it more difficult for a country to be successful in the context of international competition in comparison with countries which gain the profits of such industrial cores.[7]

Both theoretical arguments, the intra-industry trade patterns and the industrial core concept, support the idea that a successful assimilation in economic terms like GDP per capita goes along with an assimilation of industrial production structures. The following empirical analysis therefore looks at the changes in industrial production patterns in the context of the accession of the three Southern European countries to the European Union.

EMPIRICAL ASPECTS OF STRUCTURAL CHANGE IN SOUTHERN EUROPE

One central conclusion to be drawn from the theoretical reflections is that the industrial production structures of countries at comparable industrial development levels are very similar. Causes for failures in development can be found in restructuring processes leading, in exaggerated words, 'in the wrong direction', prolonging the assimilation process. In this section, therefore, the industrial data[8] of Greece, Portugal and Spain from 1975 until 1993 are analysed, looking for facts confirming such unfavourable restructuring processes; in other words the analysis looks for evidence of further specialisation processes in the Southern European countries compared with the European Union after their accession instead of further assimilation. Remembering the facts presented earlier (pp. 199ff), it is to be expected that Greece has suffered the most divergent process, Spain the most convergent.

Looking for structural changes on a high aggregate level it can be seen that the Southern European countries went through the same development as did other industrialised countries.[9] Table 8.1 shows the share of gross value added by kind of activity as a percentage of the total. In general, the primary and secondary sectors declined while the third sector grew over time. For the Greek economy in 1992, the primary sector (14.9 per cent) was still of great importance while the industrial sector (26.1 per cent) was smaller than that of the other

Table 8.1 Gross value added by kind of activity

	Agriculture, hunting, forestry and fisheries		Industry		Services	
	1970	1992	1970	1992	1970	1992
Greece	18.2	14.9	31.4	26.1	50.3	59.0
Portugal (1990)		5.8		38.3		55.9
Spain	11.3	3.5	39.9	34.4	48.8	62.1
For comparison:						
Germany (before unification)	3.4	1.2	51.7	39.6	44.9	59.2
Great Britain	2.8	1.7	42.5	31.7	54.6	66.6
France	6.9	2.9	41.5	29.7	51.6	67.4

Source: Institut der Deutschen Wirtschaft (1996).

two countries. Portugal had the largest industrial sector while Spain seems to have reached the western 'standard' with the service sector (62.1 per cent) as the most important sector.

Inside manufacturing the production patterns have changed, too. Here the three Southern European countries differ considerably. Using UNIDO data on a 3-digit level (ISIC 3), the Euklid measure of structural intensity was calculated (Figure 8.5).[10] Greece and Spain experienced several restructuring shocks while Portugal maintained a nearly constant 'medium sized' level of restructuring intensity over the whole period. While clearly a lot of external factors like the oil crisis have influenced the process of structural change, it is striking that high levels of intensity of structural change in manufacturing can be found in the years following the applications for accession (Greece, 1975; Portugal and Spain, 1977), and in the years after the accessions (Greece, 1981; Portugal and Spain, 1986). Interestingly, in Greece a high level of structural change is reached in the years of the accession of the other two Southern European countries to the European Union.

Looking behind these developments reveals a picture which is further differentiated. The cumulative output shares of the biggest three and biggest five industrial branches are presented in Table 8.2 in 1975, 1986 and 1993. The concentration in all three countries is higher than the European Union's average. The concentration grows over time in Spain but shrinks in Portugal.

Figure 8.5 The Euklid measure, I, of the intensity of structural change

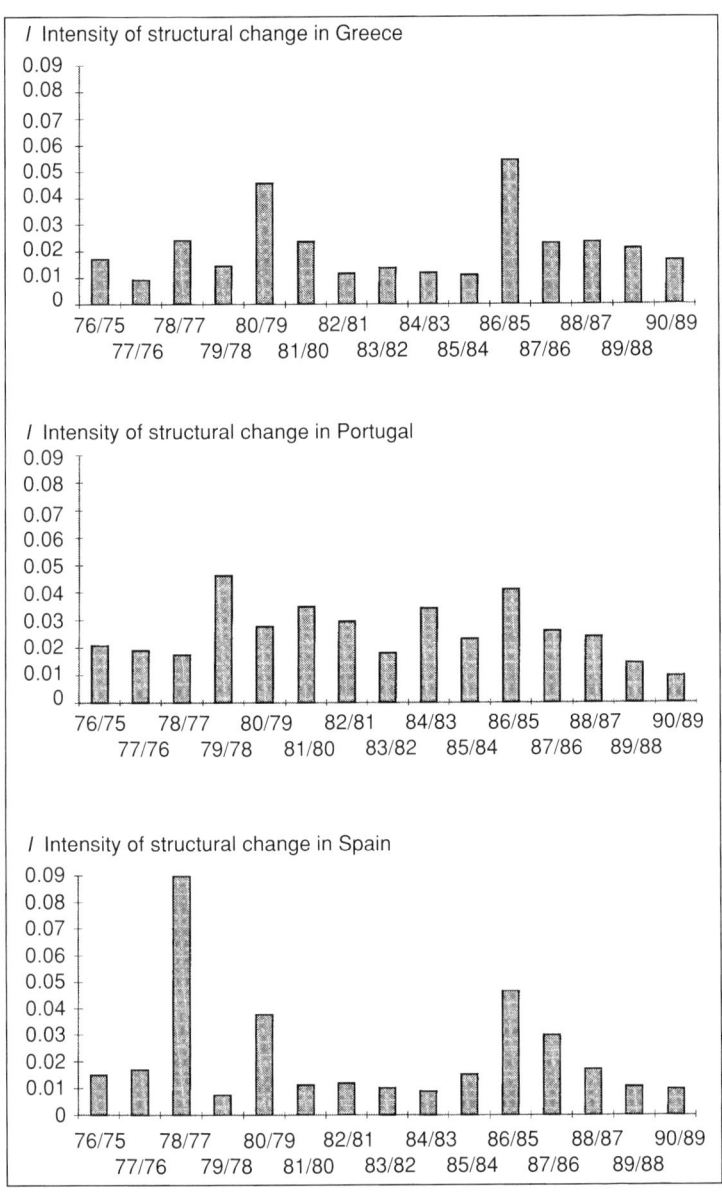

Source: Own calculations of the Euklid measure with data from UNIDO –, 1996; for further explanations see the text.

Table 8.2 Output of the biggest three and five industries in relation to output of total manufacturing

	Greece				Portugal		
Industries	1975	1986	1993	Industries	1975	1986	1993
3	0.40	0.41	0.38	3	0.43	0.41	0.33
5	0.51	0.53	0.50	5	0.53	0.53	0.45
	Spain				EU (12)		
Industries	1975	1986	1993	Industries	1975	1986	1993
3	0.35	0.35	0.39	3	0.32	0.35	0.32
5	0.48	0.46	0.50	5	0.48	0.49	0.47

Source: Own calculations with data from UNIDO, 1996.

Behind these three and five industries stand the main industrial branches shown in Table 8.3.

Food products (ISIC 311) is the most important industrial branch in all Southern European countries and the European Union (ranking position in brackets). Only in Spain, iron and steel (ISIC 371) were of greater importance in 1975. Meanwhile this branch has lost its importance completely – in 1993 it cannot be found under the largest five any more.[11] Altogether the production patterns of manufacturing have changed in the period considered in this analysis with the exception of Greece. Here nothing has changed over time concerning the ranking of the top three branches, and the output shares are nearly constant over time.

The degree of similarities in the production patterns of two countries or country groups can be recorded in calculating the correlation coefficients of the output shares in total output between two countries or country groups (again based on ISIC 3 digit).

Table 8.4 displays the results of estimates on a 3-digit level. On the whole it has to be held in mind that not only the Southern European countries were subjected to changes in industrial production structures, but likewise the European Union as the reference at the same time. There is a clear convergent process of industrial patterns of Spain and Portugal on the one hand, and a divergent process between

Table 8.3 Output shares of the biggest five industries in total manufacturing (ranking positions in brackets)

ISIC group		Greece			Spain			Portugal			EU (12)		
		1975	1986	1993	1975	1986	1993	1975	1986	1993	1975	1986	1993
Food products	311	(1) 0.20	(1) 0.20	(1) 0.20	(2) 0.13	(1) 0.18	(1) 0.18	(1) 0.23	(1) 0.18	(1) 0.16	(1) 0.14	(1) 0.14	(1) 0.16
Beverages	313												
Tobacco	314												
Textiles	321	(2) 0.13	(2) 0.12	(2) 0.09				(2) 0.14	(2) 0.13	(2) 0.09			
Wearing apparel, exc. footware	322		(4) 0.06							(4) 0.06			
Leather products	323												
Footwear, exc. rubber or plastic	324												
Wood products, exc. furniture	331												
Furniture, exc. metal	332												
Paper and products	341												
Printing and publishing	342												
Industrial chemicals	351				(5) 0.07	(4) 0.06		(4) 0.05	(4) 0.07				
Other chemicals	352			0.04 (4) 0.07					(5) 0.05				
Petroleum refineries	353	(3) 0.08	(3) 0.09	(3) 0.09		(5) 0.05	(3) 0.04	(5) 0.05	(3) 0.04				(4) 0.08
Misc. petroleum and coal products	354												
Rubber products	355												
Plastic products	356												
Pottery, china, earthenware	361												
Glass and products	362												
Other non-metallic mineral products	369												
Iron and steel	371	(5) 0.05			(1) 0.14	(3) 0.06					(4) 0.08		(5) 0.07
Non-ferrous metals	372												
Fabricated metal products	381	(4) 0.06	(5) 0.06		(4) 0.07		(5) 0.05					(5) 0.05	
Machinery, exc. electrical	382						(4) 0.05				(3) 0.09	(3) 0.09	(2) 0.08
Machinery electric	383			(5) 0.05						(5) 0.06	(5) 0.07	(4) 0.09	
Transport equipment	384				(3) 0.08	(2) 0.11	(2) 0.15	(3) 0.06		(3) 0.08	(2) 0.09	(2) 0.11	(3) 0.08
Professional and scientific equipment	385												
Other manufact. products	390												

Source: Own calculations with data from UNIDO, 1996.

Table 8.4 Correlation coefficients of output shares for Greece, Portugal and Spain, 1975, 1986 and 1993 (ISIC 3-digit)

	Portugal	Greece	EU-12
1975			
Spain	0.66	0.69	0.85
Portugal		0.95	0.72
Greece			0.70
1985			
Spain	0.79	0.77	0.91
Portugal		0.92	0.66
Greece			0.61
1993			
Spain	0.81	0.75	0.85
Portugal		0.78	0.71
Greece			0.81

Source: Own calculations based on data from UNIDO, 1996

Portugal and Greece on the other. Both developments lead in the same direction – Portugal is developing towards the Spanish production patterns and both developments are in the direction of the European Union countries' industrial production patterns. Especially in the case of Portugal may the benefits from assimilating EU production structures, expressed in a higher GDP per capita, be expected to be earned in the future.

Finally, a statistical measure is calculated which gives additional information on the degree of specialisation in industrial structures of each of the three southern European countries in comparison to the European Union. The idea is a very simple but instructive one: the output shares of the industrial manufacturing branches of a specific country are set in relation to those of the European Union as a whole.[12] The measure can take values between zero and infinity – values smaller than 0.5 indicate that a southern European country shows 'under'-specialisation in the given industrial branch compared with the European Union; values greater than 1.5 indicate specialisation.

210   *Changes in Production Structures after Accession*

Complete identity of the importance of a branch is indicated by a value of 1. The resulting specialisation patterns are presented in Table 8.5.

In the first three columns (specialisation), those branches indicated with an *x* show values greater than 1.5 in at least one of the three years under examination in the sample. The last three columns present the results for under-specialisation; values are smaller than 0.5. Only in Portugal has the number of branches with specialisation increased during the observed time period. Turning to under-specialisation another picture becomes visible; in Greece the number of branches is increasing while in Portugal it is decreasing.

Figure 8.6 illustrates graphically the results of specialisation. But are the branches considered those with high output shares? Table 8.3 shows that in Greece (ISIC 321, 352, 353) as well as in Portugal (ISIC 311, 321, 322) three branches belong to the group of the largest five branches in manufacturing. Specialisation in these two countries is therefore an important fact. Not so for Spain. Specialisation compared to the European Union is evident for 1993 in one industrial branch (ISIC 384) only, which belongs to the first three branches ranked by output shares. Summing the findings up and keeping the development of the European Union in view, the degree of specialisation in Spain in manufacturing is relatively low and the similarities in production structures are the highest compared with those of Portugal and Greece.

There is strong empirical evidence in the case of Spain that the process of catching up economically to the European Union has gone hand in hand with adjustments in industrial production patterns. In Portugal and Greece the visible tendencies are not uniform, and the relative success is smaller than in Spain.[13] These two countries have not yet reached a successful path in approaching the development of the richer northern European countries; instead they have specialised in the production of the so-called 'sensible' product classes (see Table 8.6), food products (ISIC 311) and textiles (ISIC 321), the later being highly labour-intensive,[14] which suffer from the high international competition pressure, and are counted as the most problematical industrial branches inside the European Union.

INHERITED AND EMERGING PRODUCTION STRUCTURES IN EASTERN EUROPE

Let us turn now to the eastern enlargement of the European Union. The ten countries which have applied for accession offer a heterogenous

Table 8.5 Specialisation patterns in manufacturing

ISIC group		Specialisation										Under-specialisation								
		Greece			Portugal			Spain			Greece			Portugal			Spain		
		1975	1986	1993	1975	1986	1993	1975	1986	1993	1975	1986	1993	1975	1986	1993	1975	1986	1993
Food products	311																		
Beverages	313		x	x															
Tobacco	314		x	x					x										
Textiles	321	x	x	x	x	x	x												
Wearing apparel, exc. footware	322	x	x	x		x	x												
Leather products	323	x	x			x													
Footwear, exc. rubber or plastic	324	x	x		x	x	x	x	x										
Wood products, exc. furniture	331	x			x	x	x	x	x										
Furniture, exc. metal	332												x						
Paper and products	341				x	x													
Printing and publishing	342									x									
Industrial chemicals	351												x						
Other chemicals	352						x			x									
Petroleum refineries	353		x			x	m											x	x
Misc. petroleum and coal products	354							x	x				x					x	x
Rubber products	355																		
Plastic products	356																		
Pottery, china, earthenware	361				x		x	x					x						x
Glass and products	362											x	x						

211

212

Table 8.5 (Cont'd)

ISIC group		Specialisation									Under-specialisation								
		Greece			Portugal			Spain			Greece			Portugal			Spain		
		1975	1986	1993	1975	1986	1993	1975	1986	1993	1975	1986	1993	1975	1986	1993	1975	1986	1993
Other non-metallic mineral products	369	x	x				x		x	x									
Iron and steel	371							x						x	x				
Non-ferrous metals	372							x					x	x	x				
Fabricated metal products	381																		
Machinery, exc. electrical	382										x	x	x	x	x	x	x		
Machinery electric	383										x	x	x	x					
Transport equipment	384			x			x				x	x	x	x	x	x	x		
Professional and scientific equipment	385													x	x	x	x	x	x
Other manufact. products	390													x	x	x	x		
Totals		7	8	5	6	7	9	6	5	4	4	4	5	8	7	5	3	1	5

Source: Own calculations with data from UNIDO, 1996. For further explanations see the text.

Figure 8.6 Specialisation patterns compared to the EU (12)

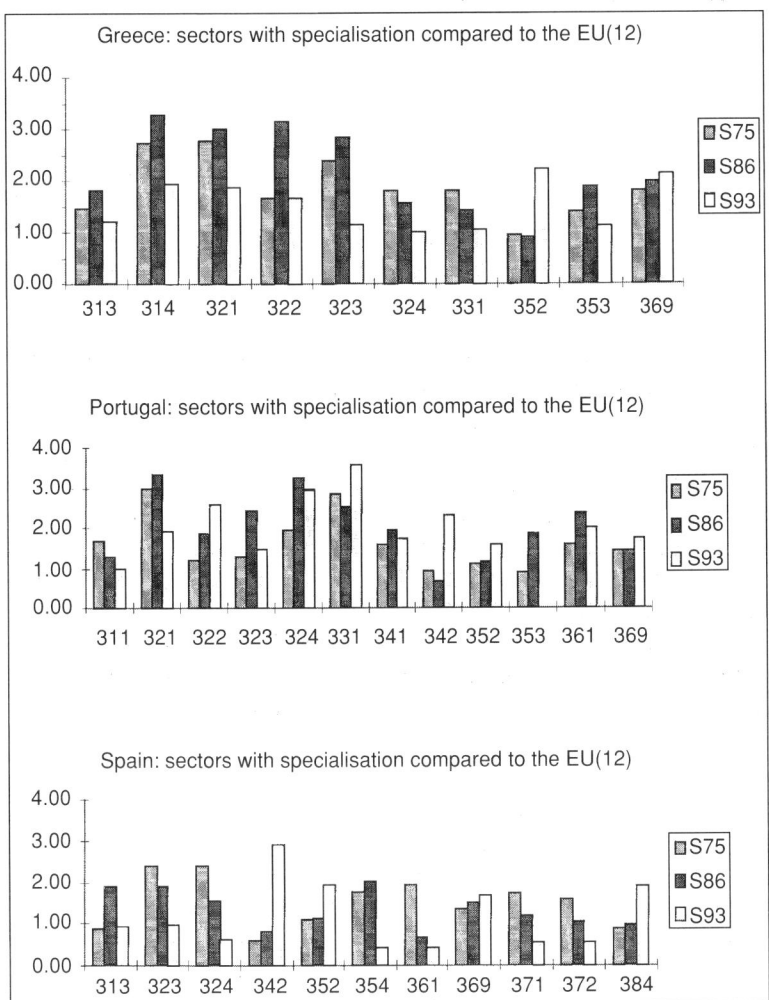

Source: Own calculations with data from UNIDO, 1996. For further explanations see the text.

picture. Remembering that all the countries considered except the Czech Republic were agrarian countries with a more or less developed industrial sector in the 1930s, the socialist development strategy created countries with rather large industries. The service-sector activities were

214   *Changes in Production Structures after Accession*

Table 8.6   Output shares of 'sensible' products in total manufacturing

		Greece			Portugal			Spain			EU (12)		
	ISIC group	1975	1986	1993	1975	1986	1993	1975	1986	1993	1975	1986	1993
Food products	311	0.20	0.20	0.20	0.23	0.18	0.16	0.13	0.18	0.18	0.14	0.14	0.16
Textiles	321	0.13	0.12	0.09	0.14	0.13	0.09	0.05	0.04	0.03	0.05	0.04	0.05
Iron and steel	371	0.05	0.04	0.03	0.03	0.02	0.02	0.14	0.06	0.04	0.08	0.05	0.07

Source: Own calculations with data from UNIDO, 1996.

underdeveloped and only few data were published officially. Looking at the reported data in this section one should hold in mind that in the year of consideration, 1993, the data are distorted: the transition shock and the necessary restructuring of the economies were not overcome at all, and the statistical methods of measurement were still under construction. Therefore, one must consider the results carefully. Nevertheless, we have an impression of the similarities and differences in the economic structure and the need of structural change in comparing Southern and Eastern Europe's experiences.

Table 8.7 shows that the Czech Republic, Hungary, Poland, Slovakia and Slovenia had a relatively small agricultural sector with shares of gross value-added less than 7 per cent. The Baltic States Latvia and

Table 8.7   Gross value-added by kind of activity, 1993

	Agriculture, hunting, forestry, fisheries	Industry construction	Trade, services
Bulgaria	9.4	30.0	60.7
Czech Republic	6.0	33.1	60.9
Estonia	9.3	23.0	67.7
Hungary	5.9	28.3	65.8
Latvia	11.7	27.3	61.0
Lithuania	11.0	38.2	50.8
Poland	6.6	38.6	54.8
Romania	22.0	43.6	34.4
Slovakia	6.8	43.4	49.8
Slovenia	4.8	39.3	55.9

Source: National statistics via IWH.

Lithuania with 11.7 and 11 per cent, and especially Romania with 22 per cent shares, on the contrary did not fully reach the first development stage along Chenery's structuralist model of economic development.[15] Although the inherited industrial sector of the formerly planned economies was oversized, the data from 1993 show a rather 'normal' picture for some countries like Bulgaria, the Czech Republic, Hungary and Latvia with share values of about 30 per cent. Romania and Slovakia depend heavily on industrial activities while the service sector plays a minor rule. Altogether, no fundamental country-specific differences in the starting positions of the Eastern European accession candidates can be determined in the early 1990s when comparing them with the Southern European countries in the 1970s. The main point is that the European Union itself has undergone an enormous development within these 20 years.

To what extent are the industrial production structures of the Central and Eastern European countries similar to the production structures of the European Union? A measure of similarity is provided by correlation coefficients of output shares using UNIDO data (ISIC 3) for 1993. All countries that have applied for accession were considered, except the Czech Republic and Estonia, for which the UNIDO did not provide data. The result of the analysis for eight countries is shown in Table 8.8. The first seven columns include the correlation coefficients that describe the similarity of output structures among the eight countries considered. The last column reports on the similarity of each country's production structure to that of the European Union. The figure in brackets shows the ranking

Table 8.8 Correlation coefficients of output shares for eight Central and East European countries, 1993 (ISIC 3-digit)

	Hungary	Latvia	Lithuania	Poland	Romania	Slovakia	Slovenia	EU-12 (Rank)
Bulgaria	0.76	0.88	0.83	0.77	0.73	0.80	0.58	0.78 (6)
Hungary		0.90	0.75	0.93	0.88	0.79	0.68	0.94 (3)
Latvia			0.91	0.81	0.85	0.69	0.73	0.85 (5)
Lithuania				0.65	0.67	0.55	0.57	0.69 (8)
Poland					0.91	0.86	0.59	0.97 (1)
Romania 1992						0.82	0.72	0.94 (2)
Slovakia							0.45	0.89 (4)
Slovenia								0.71 (7)

Source: Own calculation with data from UNIDO, 1996.

position. Poland, Romania, Hungary and Slovakia show a higher similarity degree with the EU than the other countries. They even show a higher coefficient value before accession than the EU member Spain (0.86) after approximately 10 years of membership. So far the starting conditions seem to be better for these four countries than for those of the southern enlargement. The two countries at the end of the ranking list – Lithuania and Slovenia – are small countries whose industries cannot differentiate like those of the larger countries.[16] Interestingly, similarity among former socialist countries is high only in few cases. The industrial production structures are very similiar in Latvia and Lithuania (0.91) and Latvia and Hungary (0.90).[17] A reason might be that in these three countries the share of food industry production (ISIC 311) in total manufacturing output is the highest among the eight countries considered (see Table 8.9). Slovenia's production structures are most different from all the other considered countries.

Table 8.9 presents the output shares and the degree of concentration of the largest three branches in manufacturing. The largest industry is throughout food processing (ISIC 311), albeit the absolute values of output shares differ considerably (between the countries).

Table 8.9 Output shares of the biggest three industries in total manufacturing, 1993 (ISIC 3-digit)

	Largest industry			2nd largest industry		3rd largest industry		Cumulated output sum of shares (rank)
	ISIC	Output share	Rank	ISIC	Output share	ISIC	Output share	
Bulgaria	311	0.17	6	354	0.10	390	0.07	0.34 (7)
Hungary	311	0.22	3	353	0.10	384	0.08	0.40 (3)
Latvia	311	0.34	1	384	0.08	321	0.07	0.49 (2)
Lithuania	311	0.31	2	383	0.12	321	0.11	0.54 (1)
Poland	311	0.17	5	353	0.10	384	0.08	0.35 (5)
Romania (1992)	311	0.18	4	382	0.10	371	0.08	0.35 (6)
Slovakia	311	0.15	7	371	0.14	353	0.09	0.38 (4)
Slovenia	311	0.13	8	384	0.10	382	0.09	0.32 (8)

Source: Own calculation based on data from UNIDO, 1996.

While Slovenia and Slovakia show an output share comparable to that of the European Union (14 per cent), this industry takes one-third of manufacturing output in Lithuania or Latvia. Hence, the degree of concentration, measured as the cumulated sum of the output shares, is very high in the case of two Baltic States. Both produce about half of their total industrial output in only three branches. Slovenia possesses the least concentrated production structure followed by Bulgaria, Romania and Poland.[18]

CONCLUSIONS

The theoretical arguments and the empirical results lead to two main conclusions:

- Firstly, one key factor of success for an accession candidate of the European Union lies in the assimilation of industrial production structures allowing an intra-industry trade pattern. This assimilation of production and trade patterns goes hand in hand with an assimilation of the relative factor endowments, that is the construction of a stock of modern physical and human capital. The experience of Greece and Portugal likewise shows that further specialisation in the production of labour-intensive goods along with comparative advantages based on history may entail industrial structures that have to be viewed critically. Either they will differ from those of the European Union as a whole, or they cannot survive in international competition without costly public protection for a long time. Existing problems inside the Union itself would be rather aggravated.

    The calculations show a heterogeneous picture of the industrial production structures of the Eastern accession candidates. Compared to the Southern European countries, the industrial production structures of Poland, Hungary, Romania and Slovakia seem to be more similar to those of the European Union. These countries except Romania show better suppositions than the other applicants for reaching assimilation and for closing the developing gap at an earlier point in time. (Romania is an exception insofar as it has a relatively small industrial sector only.)
- Secondly, the Eastern European accession candidates should regard the institutional framework as well as the present industrial production structures of the European Union as a *moving target*.

The institutional framework of the community is subject to change following the Maastricht treaty in a number of points that are of great importance with regard to the Eastern European accession countries. The financial reforms under construction are of particular importance: they determine the future of transfer payments from the common agricultural policy and the structural funds of the community. Uncertainty exists about the new orientation and the potential amount of these transfer payments, mainly of those aiming to support the development and restructuring of industrial production structures. The industrial production structures of the European member countries themselves will change because the European Union will face more competition pressure in global markets, and the pressure for adjustments in production will inevitably rise. This means that the now existing industrial production patterns in the European Union cannot be a fixed target for accession candidates who aim to assimilate their own industrial production structures.

Against this background of uncertainty, national governments should push the relative factor endowment at home into the right direction in order to generate an attractive framework for investments in physical and human capital. In this way necessary and already existing requirements for an economic catching up process in Eastern Europe will be improved.

Notes

1. I would like to thank Kimberly Crow, Thomas Meissner, Marianne Paasi and all the participants of the 'Workshop on Macroeconomic Aspects of an EU Enlargement to the East' for critical discussions and helpful comments.
2. This result can be found in Hohlfeld (1995) who analysed the development of the Spanish trade patterns.
3. Although of course nothing can be said about possible developments hadn't Greece joined the EU. Therefore, it could be valued as a success that the differences in GDP did not grow over time.
4. See Helpman and Krugman (1985 and also 1989).
5. An empirical study of Ballance and Forstner (1990) concludes that countries with different income levels show intensified trade patterns of vertical product differentiation.
6. See Krugman (1991). There the Silicon Valley is discussed as an example of an industrial core of the computer industry.

7. Parts of the Spanish automobile industry represent such industrial cores. See Langendijk (1995) for a fundamental analysis of their evolution and further literature.
8. The empirical analysis is based upon output data of the manufacturing sector from UNIDO, INDSTAT 3 at the 3-digit level.
9. Interesting surveys of the political and economic background developments in Southern Europe have been written by Pfeil (1993) and Fratzscher (1994).
10. The Euklid measure, I, is computed according to $I_{jt} = \sqrt{\sum_i (a_{ij,t} - a_{ij,t-1})^2}$

    with $a_{ij,t}$ as the output share of industry i in total manufacturing of country j at time t. See Meissner and Fassing (1989) for a detailed discussion.
11. See again Figure 8.5. The decrease (–51 per cent) of the output share of iron and steel (ISIC 384) in Spain dominated the first important structural change period in 1977/78. At the same time the relative importance of the food industry (ISIC 311) increased considerably (+27 per cent).
12. See Ballance and Forstner (1990). The formula reads $S_{ijw} = \dfrac{a_{ij}}{a_{iw}}$

    with $a_{ij}(a_{iw})$ as output share of industry i in total manufacturing of country j (country group w).
13. This result is supported by an analysis of the trade patterns of the three southern European countries with the European Union from CEPR (1992). Along with the first argument for assimilation of production structures discussed earlier (p. 217 ff) the fraction of intra-industry trade in total trade of each member country of the European Union in the years 1988–90 is calculated. While for Greece and Portugal the fraction of intra-industry trade with the Union is relatively small (Greece 29 per cent, Portugal 42 per cent), with 73 per cent Spain reaches the 'standard' level of other European Union member countries like West Germany (75 per cent), Belgium-Luxembourg (76 per cent), UK (77 per cent) and the Netherlands (77 per cent).
14. Ballance and Forstner (1990) rank the ISIC industries along their factor intensities. Textiles industry (ISIC 321) is very labour-intensive, rank 2 (4) at the average of the years 1970–77 (1978–85).
15. Chenery, H. et al. (1986).
16. Nevertheless, the results are not distorted by calculation because the method of correlation chooses only those pairs of data where both values are non-zero.
17. The correlation value for Lithuania and Hungary is not high because Lithuania is not present in all ISIC categories.
18. Interestingly, the level of intra-industry trade is very low compared with the Southern European Countries. Hoekman and Djankov (1996) have calculated the Grubel–Llloyd index for the years 1989 until 1994. The share of intra-industry trade in total trade with the European Union is

almost continuously growing over the years but still at relatively low levels, Bulgaria (25 per cent), Poland (27 per cent), Hungary (37 per cent) and Romania (18 per cent). Remember that Hungary, Poland and Romania are the countries with the highest values of correlation coefficients with the European Union, see Table 8.8.

Bibliography

BALLANCE, R. and FORSTNER, H. *Competing in a Global Economy – An Empirical Study on Specialization and Trade in Manufactures*, London, 1990.
CHENERY, H., ROBINSON, S. and SYRQUIN, M. *Industrialization and Growth. A Comparative Study*, Washington D.C., 1986.
CEPR, *Is Bigger Better? The Economics of EC Enlargement, Monitoring European Integration*, vol. 3, London, 1992.
FRATZSCHER, O. 'European Integration: Lessons from the South and Prospects for the East', in A. Schipke and A. M. Taylor (eds), *The Economics of Transformation – Theory and Practice in the New Market Economies*, Berlin, 1994.
HELPMAN, E. and KRUGMAN, P. *Trade Policy and Market Structure*, Brighton, 1989.
HELPMAN, E. and KRUGMAN, P. *Market Structure and Foreign Trade: Increasing Returns, Imperfect Competition and the International Economy*, Brighton, 1985.
HOEKMAN, B. and DJANKOV, S. *Intra Industry Trade, Foreign Direct Investment, and the Reorientation of Eastern European Exports*, Policy Research Working Paper no. 1652, the World Bank, Washington, D.C., September 1996.
HOHLFELD, P. 'Integration ungleich entwickelter Wirtschaftsräume – das Beispiel des EU-Beitritts Spaniens', *RWI-Mitteilungen*, vol. 46, 1995, pp. 237–55.
IMF, *International Financial Statistics Yearbook 1993*, Washington, 1994.
INSTITUT DER DEUTSCHEN WIRTSCHAFT, *International Economic Indicators 1995*, Köln, 1996.
IWH, *IWH database*, Institute for Economic Research, Halle.
KRUGMAN, P. *Geography and Trade*, Leuven, 1991.
LANGENDIJK, A. 'The Foreign Takeover of the Spanish Automobile Industry: A Growth Analysis of Internationalization', *Regional Studies*, vol. 29, no. 4, 1995, pp. 381–93.
MEIßNER, W. and FASSING, W. *Wirtschaftsstruktur und Wirtschaftspolitik*, München, 1989.
OECD, *Statistical Compendium*, Paris, 1996.
PFEIL S. *Die Konvergenz der wirtschaftlichen Entwicklung in den Staaten der Europäischen Gemeinschaft*, Erlangen, 1993.
UNIDO, *Industrial Statistics Database 1996 (INDSTAT 3), 3-Digit Level of ISIC Code*, Geneva, 1996.

Statistics

IMF, *International Financial Statistics Yearbook 1993*, Washington D.C., 1994.
INSTITUT DER DEUTSCHEN WIRTSCHAFT, *International Economic Indicators 1995*, Köln, 1996.
IWH, IWH database.
OECD, *Statistical Compendium*, Paris, 1996.
UNIDO, *Industrial Statistics Database 1996 (INDSTAT 3)*, 3-Digit level of ISIC Code, Geneva, 1996.

Name Index

Aizenman, Joshua 130, 148
Ardenia, P. G. 24

Backé, Peter 142, 145, 146, 148
Balassa, Bela 62, 92, 120, 121, 147, 148
Baldwin, Richard E. 3, 24, 99, 114, 115, 166, 172, 196
Ballance, R. 218
Barro, Robert J. 99, 114, 115
Bartolini, Leonardo 124, 134, 149
Bergstrand, J. 63, 92
Bhaduri, Amit 31, 60
Bhagwati, J. 62, 92
Bod, Péter 171
Brada, Josef C. 144, 149
Breuss, Fritz 23, 24

Calvo, Guillermo 120, 125, 131, 149
Chenery, H. 219
Claassen, E.-M. 40, 60
Clements, K. W. 75, 92, 93
Collier, I. 90, 93
Corden, W. M. 114, 115
Courchene, T. 98, 115

Dabrowski, Marek 148, 149
De Gregorio, J. 63, 92
Deaton, A. 90, 92
Diaz-Alejandro, Carlos 126, 146, 149
Diewert, W. E. 90, 92
Djankov, S. 219
Dornbusch, Rüdiger 62, 92
Drazen, Allan 124, 134, 149

Erdös, Tibor 152, 166, 172

Fassing, W. 219
Fiebig, D. 75
Finke, R. 90, 92
Folkerts-Landau, David 117, 119, 128, 131, 134, 148, 149

Forstner, H. 218
Franzmeyer, F. 24
Fratzscher, O. 219
Frensch, R. 22, 24
Frenz, K. 177, 196
Frohberg, Klaus xii, xxi

Gabrisch, Hubert xii, xix, 147
Giovannini, A. 63, 92
Girard, J. 112, 115
Goodwin, B. K. 24
Guidotti, Pablo 130, 148

Hartmann, Monika xii, xxi, 183, 189, 196
Hasse, R. H. 5, 25
Havlik, Peter 59, 60
Helpman, E. 218
Henrichsmeyer, W. 178, 194, 195, 196
Hoekman, B. 219
Hohlfeld, P. 218
Hölscher, Jens xii, xxi, 172
Houthakker, H. 75, 92
Hrncir, Miroslav 145, 149
Hunya, Gabor 59, 60
Hurst, C. 112, 115

Ito, Takatoshi 117, 119, 128, 131, 134, 148, 149

Josling, T. E. 23, 25

Kaser, Michael 166, 172
Kees, A. 5, 25
Kornai, Janos 151, 166, 170, 172, 173
Kravis, I. L. 62, 92
Krugman, P. 218
Kutan, Ali M. 144, 149

Landesmann, Michael 4, 25, 170, 173
Langendijk, A. 219

Name Index

Laski, Kazimierz xiii, xix, 31, 60
Lee, J.-W. 100, 115
Leiderman, Leonardo 131, 149
Lindner, Isabella 145, 148
Linne, Thomas 147
Lipsey, R. 62, 92
Lluch, C. 75
Löhnig, Claudia xiii, xxii

Manegold, D. 186, 187, 196
Mathieson, D. 39, 61, 117, 119, 127, 150
McCalla, A. F. 179, 196
Meissner, W. 219
Milesi-Ferretti, Gian Maria 126, 149
Muellbauer, J. 90, 92

Nessen, M. 24, 25
Nunnenkamp, Peter 98, 114, 115
Nuti, Domenico Mario 166, 173

Orlowski, Lucjan T. xiii, xx, 146, 148, 149
Orlowski, Witold M. xi, xx, 4, 25, 114, 115

Parsley, D. C. 24, 25
Pfeil, S. 219
Podkaminer, Leon xiv, xix, 38, 59, 60, 90, 92
Pollan, W. 15, 25
Pöschl, Josef 4, 25, 170, 173
Powell, A. A. 75, 92

Razin, Assaf 126, 149
Reinhard, Carmen M. 131, 149
Ricardo, David 62, 93
Rittenau, R. 20, 25
Rosati, Dariusz 40, 60

Sachs, Jeffrey D. 60, 111, 114, 124, 149
Sadka, Efraim 126, 149

Sahay, Ratna 120, 125, 149
Sala-i-Martin, X. 99, 114, 115
Salamon, P. 186, 187, 196
Salvatore, Dominick 149
Sampedro, J. L. 114, 115
Samuelson, Paul A. 62, 93, 120, 121, 147, 149
Schadler, Susan 117, 134, 135, 150
Schebeck, F. 23, 24
Schmieding, Holger 98, 114, 115
Seale, J. 75
Selvanathan, S. 77, 92
Sharma, Sunil 39, 61, 117, 119, 127, 150
Siebert, Horst 98, 114, 115
Stephan, Johannes xiv, xxi, 172
Suhm, F. E. 75, 93
Swann D. 181, 197
Szakadát, László 164, 173

Tangermann, S. 23, 25, 194, 197
Theil, H. 75–7, 90, 92, 93
Turner, P. 43, 44, 61

Ul Haque, Nadeem 39, 61, 117, 119, 127, 150

Vági, Márton 164, 173
Van't dach, J. 43, 44, 61
Végh, Carlos 120, 125,149
Vincze, Janos 171

Warner, A. M. 111, 114, 115
Wei, S.-J. 24, 25
Williams, R. A. 75, 92
Working, H. 90, 93
Wyplosz, Charles 147, 150

Yuen, Chi-Wa 126, 149

Subject Index

absorption 31
  and wealth real and financial 31–2
absorptive capacities 98, 113
accumulation 156–9
aggregate price level 4
agricultural market reform 184–5, 192
agricultural policy 177–80, 183–4, 193
agricultural products 21
agricultural protection 179–80, 190–1
agriculture 177–97
almost ideal demand system (AIDS) 64, 76–91
appreciation of the currency 4
  real 98, 101, 103, 105
arbitrage 6–10
  direct arbitrage effect 9
  see also price arbitrage
austerity programme, Hungarian 152

balance of payments (BOP) 4, 100
  'basic balance' of BOP 35
Brady bonds 140
budget deficit 27–8
  and domestic savings 33–4
  see also fiscal balance

capital account 126
capital formation 157, 167, 112
capital imports 100, 117–28, 152, 162–6, 170
  fiscal costs of sterilisation 129–136
  private 100–1, 103
catching-up process 198
Cobb–Douglas (C–D) utility function 64, 74–7, 86, 89–90
Common Agricultural Policy (CAP) 177–84, 187, 189–90, 192–3, 195
  reform of 178, 180, 184
  transmission of 192–4

comparative advantage 168, 192, 194, 199
competitiveness 33, 40–1, 161, 168, 170
consumption 105, 108, 111, 154, 157, 167, 171
  financing of 109
  government 105, 110
  private 111
convergence criteria 5, 168
  Maastricht criteria 167
convergence process 201
convertibility 154, 159
crawling peg 160, 163, 165
cross-country demand systems 74–7
crowding-out effects 101
currency substitution 127
currency swaps 134
currency union 7, 98
current account 104, 152–9, 161, 164–5, 170
  openness 126

debt
  foreign 151–3, 160–2
  public 110
demand for money (autonomous) 119
devaluation 6, 103, 159, 161–5
domestic demand 151–7
Dutch disease 4, 105
  generalised 105, 106, 109, 112

EU budget 178, 180–2, 187–8, 194
EU enlargement 182–4, 189, 194, 195
  eastern 3, 210
  southern 198
EU membership 151–2, 166–70
Euklid measure 205
Euro-commercial paper 136

225

Subject Index

Euro-medium-term notes 136
Europe Agreements 151, 167
European Monetary System (EMS) 11–13
European Monetary Union (EMU) 5–6
exchange rate deviation index (ERDI) 16, 42, 44–91
   in selected countries 40–2, 46
Exchange Rate Mechanism (ERM) 125, 147
exchange rate policy 5–6, 177, 184, 186–7, 192–3
   credibility of 158, 165
exchange rates 40–2, 46, 62–91, 100, 120–39
   exchange rate effect 10
   fixed 125
   nominal 4, 159
   real 4–7, 189
   real effective 136–8
export promotion 152, 163
export subsidies 163
export surplus 53, 54
exports 8–10
   gas 106
   manufacturing 105
   petroleum 105
extended linear expenditure system (ELES) 73–4, 89
extra-budgetary funds 155

financial repression 166
fiscal balance 110
   policy 6, 109
   stimulus 109
   see also budget deficit
Fisher-type index 74, 89
foreign direct investment (FDI) 15, 36–8, 100, 112
foreign exchange reserves 101, 164
foreign speculation 38–40
foreign trade 151–3, 160–2
   trade deficit 164
   see also exports, imports
full information maximum likelihood (FIML) 76–7

GATT *see* WTO
general exchange equilibrium 64, 70–4, 77–9
German unification 98

import multiplier 29–31
import tariffs 163
imports
   of capital goods 107
   elasticity of 105
   structure of 107
income 6–10
income multiplier 6–8
incremental capital–output ratio (ICOR) 112
industrial core 203
industrial production structures 198, 215
inflation 4, 152–3, 158–9, 161, 164–5, 170
   differential 11
   non-tradable 103–4
integration 183–4, 188–9, 193, 196
interest rate 103, 155, 161–2, 165, 169
   interest rate equalisation taxes 134
   international interest rate 115
inter-industry trade pattern 199
International Monetary Fund (IMF) 142
intra-industry trade pattern 204
investment 110, 112
   financing of 109
   infrastructure 113
   ratio 107–8
   risk 104
investment and savings 8–10, 27–35

Konüs index 90

labour 190, 192–4
   cost 100
   market 4, 22
law of one price (LOP) 4, 6, 8

Maastricht treaty 5, 6
market barriers 8

Subject Index

mark-up (rate) 21, 52, 87–8
  pricing 7
Marshall–Lerner condition 33
monetary policy 6, 109, 152, 161–2, 165, 171
monetisation 155, 161, 163
multiplier effects 4

non-substitution theorem 87
non-tradable goods 62–91
non-tradable services 21

open market operations 129
Organisation for Economic Co-operation and Development (OECD) 5, 16–20, 142

PASOK government 110–11
portfolio investment 100–11, 103
price arbitrage 6–7, 8, 21
  and macroeconomic consequences 51–6
  see also arbitrage
price convergence 5, 6
price differences 4
prices
  administered 156–9
  consumer 158
  domestic 7
  of non-tradables 114
  relative 193
  of services 104
  of tradables 114
primary balance 171
privatisation income 164
product differentiation 202
productivity 7, 178, 190, 192, 195
  capital 119
  labour 62, 87–91
profits 7
propensity to consume 109
public service sector 113

purchasing power parity (PPP) 16–20, 62–91
pure theory of international trade 68

restructuring process 204
Rotterdam model 76

savings
  domestic 108, 110
  foreign 100–1, 106, 108, 110, 113
  function 8, 53–59
Single European Market 6
social security funds, Hungarian 155, 168
social stability 111
social welfare 162
state budget 154–5, 161–2, 171
state-owned enterprises (SOE) 113
sterilisation 121–36
  fiscal costs of 129–36
  ratio 145
structural change 199–202
structural effects 3
structural funds 180–2, 194–5
structural policy 184, 186, 188, 194
  extension of 194

tradable goods 4, 6, 62–91
trade balance 4, 104
trade creation effect 104
transfers 98, 99, 100, 101, 103, 104, 112, 113, 195
  marginal utility of 98

wage infection 7, 9, 21
wages 158, 162, 165
  dumping 23
  money 7
  real and in USD terms 43
WTO 178, 179–80, 183–4, 185–6